# DROP YOUR SHOULDERS

How To Break Free From The Trauma Cycle

Understanding Childhood Trauma
Somatic Exercises For Inner Child Healing
and Emotional Safety

GERALDINE ZADKIEL

HEART CONNECTION PUBLISHING

ISBN 978-1-7646502-0-5

# Contents

# Preface

Trauma reaches far beyond the individual experience; it affects families, relationships, and future generations. This book is an exploration into the nature of trauma, moving beyond a purely clinical perspective to embrace the emotional, energetic, and lived experience of it. It's about identifying your own experience of trauma and simply having the will to choose to move through it and ultimately beyond it, creating lasting change.

While many books explore specific therapeutic techniques or personal stories, I have never come across one that truly resonated with me and sparked genuine change within. None of them gave a sense of personal freedom from the draining aftermath of trauma.

The **Drop Your Shoulders® Methods** carry the frequency of energy to remind you of who you are beneath the pain, beyond the stories, and before forgetting your true self. I am not here to instruct minds; I am here to awaken souls, speaking directly to your heart. Your life experience of trauma is acknowledged and given a voice. It is an invitation to know that every dark night, disappointment, deep pain in your heart, tears, and anger are your strength.

My aim is that by the end of this book, you will have received, understood, and embodied a practice — practical tools you can use each day to shift how you feel in the moment, empowering you to choose freedom from the past and move forward into your future. A practice that speaks directly to your heart.

**Trauma is an experience and a response; it does not define who you are.**

As we explore the energetic effects of trauma, we will explore the impact of trauma in all aspects of your life and how it affects you every day. Together, we will move beyond the experience of trauma and get down to exactly how I, and countless clients I have assisted over the years, have moved from trauma and survival responses to inner peace in a relatively short amount of time. You will meet trauma where it is activated in the subconscious mind and learn how to create lasting change.

You will explore the impact trauma has on your nervous system, emotions, relationships, and daily life, and how these patterns continue to shape your experience until they are brought into awareness.

This is not just another academic endeavour; this is a book to be felt, practised, and lived.

Its content is born from a deeply personal understanding of the physical, mental, and emotional impact of trauma. My own journey through childhood trauma and life's challenges led me to make it my life's work to understand and transform my emotional world.

Through that journey, I discovered an inner peace that had always existed within me. The practical tools shared in this book helped me find and maintain that peace and can be easily incorporated into daily life, as naturally as brushing your teeth.

Fueled by the desire to bridge the gap between understanding trauma and experiencing genuine transformation, I trust that you will dive into the following pages and commit to undertaking a new way of being. Learn how to work with your own subconscious, how to heal deep within your heart, and how to move beyond the layers of trauma that have you feeling trapped in a cycle of disempowerment.

Embrace these daily practices that empower you on every level. At the beginning of this book, my aim was to provide a practice — practical tools you can use each day to shift how you feel in the moment, empowering you to choose freedom from the past and move forward into your future. A practice that speaks directly to your heart.

Today a new life awaits you.

# Dedication

This book is dedicated to the resilient spirits who have navigated the treacherous landscapes of trauma, to those who have found the courage to seek healing, and to the unwavering support systems that have stood by them on their journeys. It speaks to the indomitable human capacity for growth, adaptation, and transformation in the face of adversity.

I also dedicate this book to my younger self, a child who longed for understanding and a safe space to process the pain and fear that shaped my early life. This work is the result of years of personal healing, study, and a deep commitment to cultivating a more compassionate and informed understanding of trauma.

May it inspire deeper awareness and offer solace, knowledge, and a pathway to a more integrated and wholehearted life. It stands as a testament to the strength found in vulnerability and celebrates the transformative power of self-empowerment and healing.

This journey hasn't been one of steady support or gentle landings. It was shaped by suffering, abandonment, betrayal, deep loneliness, and the constant feeling of being unseen. It shaped me. It stretched me. It nearly broke me.

But then came a pivotal moment, a shift in polarity — when I began to experience its opposite: inner peace, joy, and connection. It didn't arrive all at once, nor without effort. Inner peace first appeared in moments that stretched into days, weeks, and months, and when it did, it changed everything.

This book is born from that transformation. It honours the path of pain that became my foundation for healing. It is a tribute to the resilience of the human spirit and to the possibility that even in our darkest hours, there is light waiting to be remembered and felt.

To the special people who appeared in my life when I needed them most, thank you. To the earth angels who came to keep me alive, and to those who encouraged me to keep moving forward, I am forever grateful.

To anyone still suffering, hang in there.

And to the silent warriors, the ones who heal in the shadows, who keep walking even when no one notices, who break generational cycles without applause. This is for those of you who believe in something better, who know that love, real love, exists in this chaotic world and that there is a way forward.

This book is for YOU, and for those who, like me, came here to help shift the frequency of this planet and birth a new earth grounded in Love, Light, Truth and Freedom.

*Most importantly, I dedicate this book to my son so that he always has access to the tools, truths, and love I didn't grow up with. May these pages remind you that you are never alone, that your emotions matter, and that love and safety come from within. This book is a map back to yourself, a legacy of healing passed from my heart to yours. May it guide you when I can't be there, and may you always know how deeply you are loved.*

# PART I

## The Return to SELF: Embodiment Of Love And Safety

# Introduction To The Drop Your Shoulders® Method

Begin now, before you read any concepts. This book isn't about diving into trauma or reliving the past; it's about activating the real you, the part of yourself without trauma. It aims to empower you to change how you feel in any moment.

- The first step is to interrupt your physical stress response. Simply. Drop your shoulders.
- Now close your eyes and breathe in for 4, out for 4.
- Take a moment to feel into your body, scan your body for any areas of tension, tightness, or pain, and breathe into these areas, relaxing the muscles there.
- Notice instantly that something changes; notice the tension softens, the tightness releases, the pain dissipates, dissolves, or moves.
- Feel what it's like to be calm and present in your body, then open your eyes and look around. Notice that your vision feels wider, your thoughts clearer, and observe the difference.

- In just a few minutes, this process can create a somatic shift in how you feel in your body and interrupt your survival stress response.
- Repeat dropping your shoulders as often as you can today and every day.

## Why does this simple method work?

When you are triggered into your own stress response, which is your natural survival mechanism, an automatic physical and emotional process occurs in your subconscious. Your body floods with adrenaline and cortisol. Your system switches into survival mode, and your muscles immediately tighten, including your shoulders. For many people, this state has become normal, and you might find yourself in long-term adrenal stress without even realising it.

*Do you often feel stressed? Yes/No*

*Are your shoulders raised, and your jaw clenched? Yes/No*

*Are you feeling this tension in your body while driving to work, standing in the kitchen, or even sitting on the couch with the TV on? Yes/No*

*Has this tension in your body become normal? Yes/No*

*Do you remember what it feels like to be calm in your body and not on high alert? Yes/No*

Whether you have generational trauma, experienced childhood abuse, or faced specific traumatic events, you live in a chaotic world with constant notifications, headlines, opinions, and demands pressing from the outside, while memories, worries, and self-protection triggers are always being activated inside. You are being bombarded both externally and internally, and your nervous system is hardwired to be 'on alert'.

The **Drop Your Shoulders® Method** helps your body send a different message. It interrupts your stress response in real time, directly addressing your subconscious patterns and your body's reactions. When your shoulders start to relax and stay down, your body receives a clear signal: "I am safe." Your breath then follows in for 4, out for 4; your heart rate lowers to normal, and the chemical surge is regulated.

Words and talk therapy target the conscious mind; **Drop Your Shoulders® Method** engages the deeper layers of your being. When both your body and your conscious mind affirm "I am safe right now," your subconscious stress pattern weakens.

This is not just theory. Do it now and feel it. Let your shoulders drop by a centimetre, then another. Notice that initial sensation of something different. Your body begins to relax; your nervous system cannot sustain the constant fight-or-flight survival pattern. The physiology isn't aligned, and now you've disrupted the process.

This is why meditation, breathwork, and any practice that relaxes your physical body helps with stress and trauma, and I highly recommend these practices; however, your busy life does not always lend itself to having time for an extended practice. You will find that dropping your shoulders takes only a few minutes, and those minutes will change how you feel each day. You can begin this small action right now, in any place.

# My Own Experience From Trauma To Inner Peace

I grew up surrounded by chaos. I witnessed domestic violence, experienced long-term sexual abuse, and knew betrayal, rejection, and abandonment from a young age.

Dissociation became my way to survive when I felt unsafe; my nervous system stayed alert, always prepared for the next threat.

Although this is my story, it does not define who I am. I'm not sharing these scenes to evoke your own memories, but to show what is possible when you move beyond trauma and survival patterns. If at any point these words bring something up for you, stop, drop your shoulders — you are safe.

What matters is learning to shift from survival reactions to inner peace — to experience emotional and physical freedom.

As a young woman, I searched for answers and was constantly told what was wrong with me. "You have had childhood trauma; this is why you are like you are; you have fear of rejection, betrayal, abandonment," and so on. Over the years, no one ever showed me or taught me how to break the cycles and patterns, what to do in the moment when my nervous system was over-reactive, and I was overwhelmed with emotional pain, or when my anger erupted, or grief shattered my heart.

Repeatedly, these patterns played out in every part of my life, with my reactions and responses automatic. My neural pathways were hardwired for survival. I tried everything until the pain inside became insatiable, my breath shallow, and I felt I couldn't breathe. I wasn't truly living; I was stuck in a permanent state of surviving.

When I discovered kinesiology, something deep inside me shifted. I felt hope that it was possible to be free from the trauma that had followed me everywhere. I realised my past no longer controlled my future and that there was another way to break free from my survival patterns. I began to believe that changing my automatic reactions was possible, allowing me to create the life I had always imagined.

I embarked on a journey of learning and healing, pushing the boundaries of my emotional self, interrupting patterns, breaking down belief systems one by one, and creating a practice for truly living. Living each day no longer trapped in survival or my own reactions, but driven by inner peace. After completing my Diploma in Holistic Kinesiology, I walked 880km across Spain (Camino de Santiago) to test whether what I had learnt had permanently changed my nervous system — that I was no longer living in fear. It did, and those changes became permanent and integrated into my daily life.

I learned to tune into my body, to stay grounded in the physical, to DROP MY SHOULDERS, and to make different choices initially for myself, then for my son, and now for you.

This doesn't mean I don't get triggered or challenged; I am human, and my life is always changing. My survival patterns still exist, but now I have a choice. I know what to do when my survival reactions are triggered, and instead of letting them control me by playing out past trauma responses, I can choose to change how I feel in the moment.

I no longer remain in fear-based survival patterns for days, weeks, or months. I have practical tools to calm my nervous system, release emotional energy in less than 10 minutes each day, and then continue with my day in a calm, natural state.

As I practised the **Drop Your Shoulders® Methods,** my body didn't argue; it softened and relaxed. My subconscious created new reference points that embodied love and safety. My thoughts shifted from self-hatred to self-love.

My heart energy expanded, and I am living my life fully, grounded in my body.

Motherhood raised the stakes. I wanted my son to grow up in a home that felt safe; I did not want to repeat any of the generational patterns or trauma cycles I had experienced. I promised myself I would teach him what I did not learn as a child.

Although I had already been living and practising the **Drop Your Shoulders® Methods** for many years, and it had become a natural way of being, I was now inspired to simplify it so that it can be shared with my son and my clients as a straightforward method that is easy to practise with little effort and leads to lasting change. I wish I had been taught these tools when I was a child, a teenager, a young adult — I would not have suffered debilitating emotional trauma and pain for the better part of thirty years.

With over twenty years of experience working with clients and specialising in anxiety, depression, and trauma, I have shared these practices and concepts, witnessing countless clients experience instant transformations that can only be described as miracles in their lives. When you combine somatic and energetic practices, you bypass the story and enable deep healing to occur instantly in your subconscious, nervous system, and body, transforming every aspect of your life — how you feel, how you respond and empowering you from within.

When you use, explore, and adapt all of the methods in this book, you are not just dropping your shoulders; you are rewiring your nervous system, reprogramming your neural pathways, and creating new belief systems. As these practices expand into your daily life, you will learn how to release suppressed emotions, quiet subconscious overthinking, create healthier relationships, and respond to life's challenges with greater presence and emotional freedom. Together, these tools will support you in creating a life grounded in inner peace, joy, and connection. The **Drop Your Shoulders® Methods** have changed my life and the lives of many clients who have embraced these practices and transformed their lives. I expanded into retreats and circles where the positive effects on individuals extended into their relationships, families, and children.

I saw men who had spent years shut down and resistant, who became open to exploring their emotional landscape to finally feel their own strength without hardness. I saw women who had carried everything cry tears of relief.

I saw families change because one person chose to break the cycle and master their own nervous system instead of responding out of fear. I kept refining the practice until it was simple enough to do anywhere, anytime, and deep enough to hold the biggest feelings.

Today, I am an author, kinesiologist, retreat facilitator, mother, and a woman who has chosen her own path. These practices are a way of life; they become your new default pattern for your emotional growth. I still face days that demand everything from me. The difference now is that I know what to do the moment I feel triggered: I trust my body's alarm system, my intuition. I stop, drop my shoulders, and feel into my body. From there, I can meet anger with strength, grief with tenderness, and love with presence. I can set boundaries that protect what matters and deepen my relationships.

## Why You, Why Now, Why This Book?

You have chosen this book because you are ready; the **Drop Your Shoulders® Methods** are intentionally straightforward and easy to use in everyday life. You'll apply them in moments — while parenting, answering an email, sitting in traffic, opening a difficult message, or walking into a confrontation. The more you practise, the quicker your body responds. Over time, you'll notice less charge, clearer boundaries, steadier presence, and an increasing ability to choose your responses in any situation or event.

You will not be asked to become someone new. You are being invited to step into who you are when you are no longer living in constant physical and emotional survival.

This book is based on my personal lived experiences and professional work as a kinesiologist and retreat facilitator. If your history involves similar challenges and pain, you're not alone. Rest assured, you will not have to relive your trauma through these pages. You will learn to establish safety in real time and build a future your body can trust. Use this book as a living guide to be felt and experienced. The practices expand and adapt to suit your own living experience. It speaks to your conscious and subconscious minds simultaneously; it also speaks to your body.

It will encourage you to reconnect with the wisdom already residing in your body. Science matters, and so does your felt truth. These practices do not deny science; they complement what we already understand by including our emotions and spirit. They recognise the layers — emotional, energetic, and generational — that often go unseen and, as a result, unhealed. This is not about treatment versus intuition; it's about integration. The practices here walk alongside whatever healing journey you are already on, bringing presence and embodied choice into your daily life. They activate the essence of who you truly are, before the world told you who to be.

You won't be defined by labels. You will be seen as a whole person capable of breaking cycles and patterns to create something new.

Let this book unlock the key to your heart and free you from patterns that no longer serve you. Let the words reach your body as much as your mind. When the old pattern rises, STOP. Drop your Shoulders. Breathe. Choose. That is the practice. That is the path. And it begins now.

# How To Use This Book

Throughout each chapter, you will find daily or weekly **Drop Your Shoulders® Methods.**

Each Method is a practice that expands and grows with you as you move through the book, deepening your capacity to release, regulate, and return to yourself.

I invite you to trust the method and go through the practice before you read on. Stop now and follow the instructions. Take your time. Allow it to speak directly to your body and subconscious so the shifts happen at the deepest level first.

When you're ready, continue reading; the conscious mind can meet what the body already knows. This way, you're not just learning the **Drop Your Shoulders® Methods**; you're living it, integrating it, and transforming the way you experience your life from the inside out.

# The Drop Your Shoulders® Method

- Close your eyes, drop your shoulders.
- Feel into your body and notice areas of tension, tightness, contraction, or pain.
- Breathe in for 4 and out for 4, and concentrate on relaxing the muscles in these areas.
- Drop your shoulders as often as you can remember. Repeat at least five times per day.

Once you get used to dropping your shoulders, you can do it anywhere with intention in just a few seconds, and it will become an automatic practice. **From now on, when you see Drop Your Shoulders® Method, your body and subconscious will know what to do.**

# Chapter One

# Trauma Is Not A Buzzword

These days, the words "trauma" and "triggers" are splashed across social media feeds and conversations like passing trends, scattered without significance. Beneath the trend lies something deeper — YOU. You are beginning to ask the real question: *"What is trauma really, and how does it shape the way I live, love, and perceive the world?"*

Trauma isn't just a buzzword; it's a real and existing phenomenon. It appears not only in life's 'big events' but also in the subtle, unseen moments that shaped who you became when you were still too young to fully grasp what was happening.

This book is not here to teach you what trauma is or to give you another definition of trauma that makes you feel like there is something wrong with you. It is written to guide you to the places where healing is naturally activated. Not after months of talking and processing; right now, in this moment, as your body begins to remember what it means to feel safe, or if there is no memory of safety, to create and connect to new reference points.

The mind often tries to link trauma to an event that happened to you. But what if trauma isn't just about what occurred, but also about what didn't happen? The love that was never given, the truth that was never spoken, the safety that was never offered when it was most needed. Trauma isn't always an obvious wound. Sometimes it hides in your body as a contraction you've carried for years.

Trauma is not stored in your thoughts; it is stored in your body, especially in your nervous system. It resides in the parts of you that learned how to survive, even if that meant shutting down or dissociating — the parts of you overwhelmed by your thoughts, feelings, and emotions.

It reshapes the body, the nervous system, and the subconscious, not as ideas, but as lived reality. You will see how emotional overwhelm becomes stored, how the subconscious repeats familiar patterns to keep you safe, and how the nervous system adapts in ways that feel like anxiety, numbness, or disconnection. You will also understand how much of this is inherited and how much is environmental, and the roles you were forced to play. This is not about diagnosing or pathologising. It is about witnessing how trauma lives in your body and interrupting the cycle with presence, safety, and choice.

Understanding trauma means recognising how deeply it imprints on your system and influences how you trust, communicate, attach, and protect yourself. Whether your pain comes from a single event or years of feeling unsafe, unseen, or unloved, the impact is real. Healing begins when you learn to interrupt those patterns and create safety in real time. Not by fixing or denying your story or experience; your life experience is part of who you are, and you can begin creating a life where you feel safe and loved.

Healing does not occur in theory; it happens in those moments when you normally react, when you drop your shoulders, calm your nervous system, and choose a different response. When you show up fully for yourself, with your whole heart — embracing both the parts you've hidden and those you've already reclaimed. Bring your doubt, your fear and even your resistance, and let these words meet you where you are right now and accompany you wherever you go.

Healing modalities and self-help books that only address your conscious thinking do not access the areas where your trauma is stored. Healing from trauma is simple and doesn't need to take long.

## Reflection

*Have you seen practitioners and talked and talked about what happened from every different angle? Still no change in your reactions or how you feel? Yes/No*

*Have you been told why you have fear of abandonment, anxiety, depression or unresolved trauma? Yes/No*

*Has anyone ever explained what to do when your emotions get activated or triggered? Yes/No*

*Have you read self-help books, watched videos, followed experts, and done everything you were told would help? And yet, something inside you remains trapped in a cycle of emotional turmoil. Yes/No*

*Do you want to live your life with inner peace and understand how to change how you feel in any given moment? Yes/No*

*Are you ready for a new way forward and to experience real change? Yes*

Apply the **Drop Your Shoulders® Method** now.

This simple somatic practice of dropping your shoulders will become as natural as getting dressed in the morning, as it interrupts your survival response.

This is where it starts — not in the retelling of your story, but in the connection to your body, in the tension your body has been holding all along.

## Trauma Is Frequently Discussed In Categories

Acute trauma, complex trauma, and developmental trauma. These labels might provide a clinical framework, but they overlook who you truly are. You are more than just your trauma; you are a physical, mental, emotional, and spiritual being. Trauma triggers a survival response, but you are more than simply a survival response.

Pause for a moment and consider the possibility that many of the survival patterns you experience today began in childhood.

Trauma isn't just defined as abuse or neglect, although those experiences deeply imprint trauma patterns on your subconscious and nervous system. I invite you to consider that, to varying degrees, every person carries trauma that activates survival patterns.

I'm talking about the more subtle, invisible moments — like the first time you felt unsafe, unseen, unloved, or alone as a child. When you learnt that your physical, mental, or emotional needs wouldn't be met, or that your emotions were "too much", or that love must be earned, something inside begins to fragment.

There is a moment in each of us when shock is activated.

Shock isn't the event itself. It's your body's energetic rupture when something happens that you are unable to understand, process, or absorb. It's the instant the world no longer feels safe for you. This occurs in every child at a moment when the polarity is revealed.

**Shock is the first activation of trauma in your nervous system — The first fracturing of trust.**

Before trauma takes shape in your body, your subconscious, your neural pathways, before the beliefs, the behaviours, and reactions, there is *that* single moment.

**It is a *shock* to the system.**

## Shock Was Your First Experience Of Separation

When you were born, you entered the world in a state of wholeness. In life, we seek coherence, connection, and care, but at some point early in childhood or even before birth, this wholeness is disrupted.

It might be caused by a harsh tone that was used, your parents' emotional unavailability, a medical procedure, or sudden environmental changes. Your nervous system is developing, and your neural pathways are forming. Your survival responses are being triggered and conditioned either towards danger or safety.

Shock is the moment you, as a child, encountered polarity. Shock was your first experience of separation.

Shock was your first realisation that love can diminish, safety can vanish, and connection can be conditional.

It isn't logical. It's cellular. And it's immediate.

In that split second, your nervous system contracts, you hold your breath briefly, and your perception of reality shifts. If no one meets you in that moment with presence, holding, or truth, this experience becomes imprinted as danger. Your body stores it. Your energetic field retains it. And you learn to adapt to it.

From here, trauma takes hold in your subconscious, creating the neural pathways that activate your physical survival responses. However, it is shock that lays the groundwork. It is the frozen energy beneath the subconscious default patterns; it is the original point from which everything else spirals.

## Remembering The Original Shock

You might remember this moment; however, it's not uncommon if you don't recall your first moment of shock. It could have happened when you were in the womb or a small baby. You know it's there, you feel it, and you live your life reacting to it now.

When you start to unravel your childhood, you'll discover moments of shock.

You're not just revisiting memories; you're returning to the place where you first flinched, where you as a child initially felt shock and, in turn, formed a belief system. "I am not safe here."

Healing begins when you recognise and identify the initial moment of shock that lies hidden beneath your subconscious survival patterns and reactions. This is the instant your body triggered an immediate energetic response to an experience or event it could not process.

It's quick, silent, and often unseen, but it leaves a profound imprint on your nervous system. Shock pauses that moment in time. If no one helped you move through it or taught you how to return to safety, that energy remains stored in your body. This is the point where shock becomes stored trauma and solidifies within your body.

And from that point forward, your body remembers.

## Your Body Remembers

You don't need to recall this initial moment of shock consciously. Start by observing the patterns in your daily life now. Moments of shock and trauma do not hide from you; they repeat like a broken record. When you pay attention to the situations that trigger an emotional response in you, the people who unsettle you, or the emotions that rise out of proportion to the moment, you are tracing the thread back to its origin.

Your body is always trying to bring your attention to what remains unresolved. This is your invitation to go deeper and to know where to look. I am not asking you to detect this on a conscious level, trying to analyse or fix it. I am asking you to feel it in your body.

Notice the physical sensations, such as tightness in your chest, shallow breathing, clenched jaw, or the urge to run, fight, or freeze.

These signals indicate your body's survival response activating. Your subconscious is highlighting the moment when the initial shock happened, even if your conscious memory doesn't recall it. That's okay — you just need to understand that the answers can be found through how you feel in your body.

Begin to approach these sensations with compassion rather than judgment.

By practising the Drop Your Shoulders® Method, you learn how to soothe your nervous system and start to give yourself what was absent in that initial moment — presence, reassurance, and safety.

You do not need the memory; you only need the willingness to stay with the uncomfortable feeling in your body for a moment, witness it, and then allow it to be released.

As you practise the **Drop Your Shoulders® Method**, every time you find the tension and tightness in your body, relax the muscles to release it. This is how you rewrite the imprint ingrained in your nervous system by practising this as often as you can each day.

## Your Reactions And Responses Are Inherited

Your life experiences activate your subconscious survival patterns, as do traumatic events of abuse and neglect. How you react, respond, and process your emotions is a learned behaviour. You learn by watching those before you. If you were taught to numb, suppress, explode, or disconnect to process uncomfortable emotions, this becomes your default pattern. These patterns are passed through bloodlines, silently and powerfully.

*Did you learn to suppress your own anger or to project it outward?* How anger was expressed by your parents and caregivers at home influences how you express it now.

*Do you find yourself anxiously seeking love or completely dissociating?* The way your need for connection was responded to as a child shapes your attachment styles today. These are not personality traits; they are survival strategies your body developed to keep you safe.

The tragedy is that you can spend your whole life thinking your coping mechanisms represent who you are. You're not your emotions; they're simply your body's way of saying, "Hey, something's happened here."

As someone who has lived through it and come out the other side, I have created a pathway for healing that I can now share with you.

How I react and respond did not start with the specific events of abuse, the violence around me, or the vague memories of my early childhood years. It began with observing and learning how my parents reacted and responded, absorbing my environment — how they yelled, withdrew, escaped, and were emotionally unavailable. Ingrained in my DNA were ancestral trauma patterns and repeated survival responses playing out automatically.

**Truth.** Your parents and caregivers were also repeating generational patterns of shock and trauma, survival patterns on high alert. They were not capable of providing a safe environment for themselves before you were born, let alone after you were born.

Locked into automatic survival patterns and responses, I grew up feeling as if I did not belong — separate and disconnected. Rejection was stored in my body on high alert, and every relationship reflected this back to me. I experienced deep betrayals and carried intense emotional pain that I could neither understand nor explain.

The emotional suffering was relentless; I thought I was the problem, unworthy of love. I carried the energy of self-hatred and unworthiness.

It doesn't have to be this way. Just like you, my nervous system was hardwired to believe the world was physically and emotionally unsafe. It adapted to an environment where love was inconsistent, and danger was often present. This book isn't just a guide; it's a transmission from me to you. I have been where you are now and invite you to explore new perspectives, learn new skills, and take control of your nervous system and how you feel each day, where deep inner peace is your natural birthright.

When you practise the **Drop Your Shoulders® Method**, you will not only interrupt the stress response and alter your reactions, but also learn to listen to what your body is telling you and understand your energetic field. You will give your inner self the love and safety you may never have received and, on a broader scale, begin shifting generational patterns.

This is why healing shock and trauma isn't about categorisations and labels. True healing involves reconnecting with yourself, your body, your breath, and what it feels like to feel safe inside and out. You will release tension and establish new subconscious reference points of love and safety within.

Change doesn't need to take years of therapy. It can be immediate when energy is channelled the right way; it dissipates within a few minutes.

Begin with the **Drop Your Shoulders® Method** now.

Growth and evolution are your birthright.

When you're met with truth, presence, and energetic safety, and when you are given tools that genuinely work, your body begins to remember what is possible. The healing doesn't start in the story; it starts in your body, in the silence between your subconscious and your nervous system.

And this is where your personal journey really begins.

Trauma affects everyone, not just those with obvious wounds like childhood trauma, physical, emotional, or sexual abuse, parents' divorce, or bullying at school. Often, clients will say, *"I haven't had any trauma; I had a good childhood,"* yet within moments, the truth begins to surface — such as a bullying incident, overhearing parents fight, or being shut down or silenced. Trauma exists in the subtle as much as in the severe.

I have sat with men who swore they had no trauma. They weren't angry until we touched on the moment their father yelled at them or failed to acknowledge their achievements.

I have held space for women who carry the grief of their ancestors like an unwavering weight on their chest and have seen them let it go, recognising it is not their burden to carry.

As you begin to see trauma not just as memory but as an energetic imprint, you will notice that your body has been doing its best to protect you all along. When something overwhelming happened, and you had no way to process it, your muscles tensed, you caught your breath, and your energy froze. It was the intelligence of your own survival patterns being activated.

Over time, your body developed these patterns in response to the initial shocks and traumas. Your brain and neural pathways, shaped by your earliest environment, adapted to survive. If love felt unsafe, your nervous system adjusted. If your needs were not met, you learned to ignore them. Even without conscious memory, your energy field and biology remember, and these patterns become the default setting of your adult life.

The good news is that you can reprogram your subconscious neural pathways. You can calm your nervous system, interrupt the stress response, and learn to feel safe.

These default survival patterns don't define you, and it doesn't require years of discussion and analysis to change them. What you need is an open mind, the will to change, and a commitment to repetition. Offer yourself the compassion you may have never received. Gently interrupt the pattern repeatedly until a new pattern and response become your default, transforming the outcome.

Modern science is only now starting to recognise what your inner wisdom has always known: that trauma is physical, energetic, and relational.

Healing isn't about fixing the past; it's about learning to engage with it differently. What happened to you, whether subtle or severe, in one event or over many years, cannot be defined by labels. Trauma is not measured by how many times something happened but by how it was felt in your body. Your body did not count events; it remembered the feeling — the pain stored from each moment. It recalls that you were not held, protected, or understood. It remembers feeling separate when you were left alone, or the feelings of overwhelm and rejection. Those imprints etched themselves into your nervous system, into your energy field, and into the silent language of your subconscious. It remains stored there, not to punish you, but to be seen, heard, and released.

You have the ability to reprogram your subconscious emotional triggers and calm your nervous system with a few new skills and a daily routine. Using the **Drop Your Shoulders® Method** is a straightforward and simple practice that will assist you in gaining these benefits.

Healing doesn't require you to talk about or relive every wound or analyse every memory. It demands something much deeper; it asks for your willingness to feel safe enough with your nervous system to turn inward and simply be with what is present. To sit beside the younger versions of yourself who are still holding their breath, still waiting for someone to notice the weight they have carried in silence. Some pain shouts, some pain hides, but all of it deserves your presence and acknowledgement.

Trauma is just the areas inside you that require your love.

Apply the **Drop Your Shoulders® Method** now.

Today, in this moment, you decide to let love in. When you soften the walls you've built for survival and remember that your worth has never been in question. When you know that every part of you longs to be met with unconditional love and kindness, and this is now possible.

Your healing begins now.

# The Drop Your Shoulders® Method 2

## Calm Your Nervous System

- Right now, drop your shoulders.
- Feel into your body and notice areas of tension, tightness or pain.
- Breathe in for a count of 4.... and out for a count of 4.... focusing on relaxing the muscles in these areas.
- Now, say to yourself:

*"I am safe. Right now, I am just sitting here, reading. I am safe."*

- Practise this as often as you can, aiming for at least five times per day.

## Chapter Two

# Becoming A Master Of Your Nervous System

Now that you've begun to embody the **Drop Your Shoulders® Method,** you can release the need to overthink, relive experiences, and analyse from your conscious mind.

No more believing you are broken and need fixing. No more diving into memories and reliving them over and over. No more picking at the wound, re-traumatising yourself, or activating your subconscious survival patterns and nervous system.

The willingness to interrupt your survival response begins now, starting with practising and expanding the **Drop Your Shoulders® Method.** It involves learning how to reset your nervous system from a state of overreaction to one of feeling safe, both physically and emotionally.

You have spent enough time in fight, flight, and freeze states that your body no longer needs to hear another story about what caused these reactions. Instead, it needs to see what is different now — that you have the power to interrupt the stress response and soothe your nervous system. You are capable of changing how you feel right now, in this moment.

You will learn more about the subconscious mind and how to meet yourself in those moments when you get triggered, when you feel disempowered to change your reactions, when you feel that first feeling in your body. Not by suppressing what's happening to you or bypassing your emotional responses, but by choosing something new.

## The conscious mind, subconscious, and nervous system are yours to master.

To understand why you react the way you do, why your shoulders tense, your heart races, and your voice shakes in seemingly small or irrational moments, you need to understand how these three systems work together.

The conscious mind, subconscious, and your nervous system. This isn't just theory; it's the foundation of your lived experience.

Your **conscious mind,** the one reading these words, is analysing, planning, judging, and making sense of your external environment. It is powerful, but it only accounts for about 10% of how you operate. It's the part of you that thinks it's in control. However, in reality, it is **not** the part of your brain that drives your emotional reactions, behavioural patterns, or your deepest thoughts. It's not the part that activates your survival or stress responses.

Your **subconscious mind** is the quiet builder of your reality. It holds about 90% of your programming, depending on the research you look at. It stores every belief, emotional response, and every memory, especially those linked to pain, fear, and survival. It does not measure time. It cannot tell the difference between what's happening now and what happened decades ago. It doesn't ask whether a threat is emotional, mental, or physical. It just reacts. Your subconscious mind is always working behind the scenes, scanning for what feels familiar and whether it's physically, mentally, or emotionally safe, based on your entire life experiences so far.

It's like a database that searches for an appropriate reaction. It doesn't intend to hurt you; it simply identifies and applies a suitable physical, mental, and emotional response to any situation or event.

If a memory is activated and perceived as positive, it will trigger a positive response; if it's perceived as negative, it will trigger a negative response. Even before conscious thought occurs, the subconscious reaction has already begun.

Now, enter your **nervous system,** your body's rapid response team. It is tightly intertwined with your subconscious. When your subconscious perceives a threat, a tone of voice, a facial expression, or a feeling of abandonment — it sends a signal to your nervous system. That signal bypasses logic and the conscious mind and instantly triggers your automatic survival response: fight, flight, or freeze.

Once activated, it can take up to an hour for your body to return to a calm and balanced state. Unless you know how to interrupt this survival response — which most people do not — it automatically takes over. If you're being activated or triggered four to five times a day, as is common with trauma imprints, which I believe we all have to some degree, you are likely living in a constant state of adrenal stress. This adrenal stress becomes your new normal, making you wired, reactive, exhausted, and numb all at once. Most people are so used to this state that they no longer remember what it feels like to be calm, centred, and happy.

**Truth.** This is your body, your nervous system. You are not at the mercy of your nervous system or your automatic subconscious reactions; you have the power to interrupt the process and to change the outcome. You can change how you feel in any given moment. You can teach your body, over time, that it is safe now. That it is not in danger, and learn to choose your responses.

This next part of the book will show you exactly how to do this, not with ideas or concepts, but with practical steps to calm your nervous system in real time. Use the **Drop Your Shoulders Methods** daily. This is not just about healing; this is about reclaiming your authority over your body.

Change begins in the body, not in the mind.

A nervous system that knows how to return to safety forms the basis for all healing you will ever undertake. The **Drop Your Shoulders® Method** is a daily practice that will become automatic, a part of your life, just like driving a car becomes automatic.

Your subconscious is always on the lookout for familiarity. It doesn't interpret time the way your conscious mind does. It doesn't distinguish between past and present; instead, it responds to the tone, energy, and emotional charge in each moment. When a current situation mirrors something unresolved from your past, your system reacts as if it's happening right now.

It stores what you've been through not as stories, but as sensory imprints and patterns. When these imprints are connected to fear, rejection, or pain, even a neutral situation can trigger a full-body response. Your shoulders tense up. Your heart races. Your breath becomes shallow. You might feel tension, numbness, or the urge to fight, run, or freeze. This isn't logical; it's an automatic reaction.

In contrast, when what is familiar is calm and safe, your body reacts with gentleness, deeper breaths, and openness. When you experience real love and safety within, you are then free to explore responses of joy, laughter, and happiness.

The difference is in your life experience, your subconscious programmed responses, and neural pathway default patterns developed during childhood.

This is also the space where change becomes possible. Not by forcing a new way of being, but by becoming aware of what is happening now and offering your subconscious a new **reference point connected to a new reaction.** One that brings you back into the present, to feeling safe and a response you can now choose.

I want you to know I'm here with you in this. I've been in the same place you are now, learning about the conscious and subconscious mind from a different point of view, realising just how much my own subconscious programming was shaping my reactions, responses, and experiences. Sometimes, it felt completely beyond my control. My body would react before I even understood what was happening, responding from a place of shock and trauma. It was my subconscious doing what it had always done — scanning for the smallest signs of rejection, betrayal, or abandonment, looking for physical, mental, and emotional danger and activating survival patterns before I had a chance to choose anything else. I had to learn what it meant to feel physically and emotionally safe.

Learning to feel safe means understanding the difference between physical safety and emotional safety.

## Unlocking Pathways To Emotional Safety

When we talk about safety, do you consider it in physical terms? A locked door, a secure home, staying out of harm's way. Physical safety is crucial; it's a basic human right and a non-negotiable foundation, especially for those living in or recovering from environments marked by violence, coercion, or threats. Domestic violence, whether overt or subtle, continues to weaken this foundation for too many. If this has been your experience, remember that prioritising your physical safety is not only valid but essential, and you must heed your survival instincts and move to a safe environment.

However, even long after the body is no longer in immediate physical danger, the nervous system stays alert. Not because of what is happening now, but because of what happened before and how it still lives inside your subconscious, your neural pathways, and your nervous system.

### This is where emotional safety comes into play.

Your subconscious does not only react to physical danger. When you are physically safe, it is now constantly scanning for emotional risks. *"Am I loved? Is it safe to be seen? Is it okay to feel the way I do? Do I matter? Am I too much? Will I be abandoned if I express this truth? Will I be rejected?"*

The fear of not feeling emotionally safe runs deep into your being, and often, it's not the situation that overwhelms you, but the emotion itself. Anger that was never allowed to be expressed. Grief that was never held. Vulnerability that was once shamed. I know this territory well; I carry the fear of anger, both in expressing it and in receiving it. The fear of grief and deep sadness that has no conscious memory, only a felt memory — not just because it hurts, but because the pain of it feels endless, unmanageable, too big, too much.

That fear, the fear of experiencing big emotions or suppressed feelings like anger and grief, is enough to trigger your survival responses of fight, flight, or freeze constantly because your system has learned that these emotions are dangerous and will not be met with love.

Without a new experience or reference point for your subconscious, your body still thinks emotions are unsafe and reacts accordingly. This affects how you behave in your adult relationships with family, friends, and colleagues. That's why the same situations and people keep triggering you. Your subconscious isn't punishing you; it's protecting you. It just hasn't been shown that things are different now or given new reference points to respond to.

Even just thinking about feeling anger or grief can trigger your subconscious survival and fear responses. Or thinking about upsetting someone else and seeing their anger, grief, and disappointment. The very idea of big emotions coming up makes your shoulders tense, your jaw clench, your stomach feel queasy, and your heart races. This isn't an overreaction; it's an automatic pattern that combines memory and response.

Today, as you read through these pages, you start the process of showing it something different and establishing new reference points for your subconscious to respond to.

Not by suppressing or forcing yourself through with willpower and strength, but by creating enough safety within your body and nervous system to gently face what you have been avoiding and fearing. Each time you apply the **Drop Your Shoulders® Method,** interrupt the stress response, or calm your nervous system, you are healing the past.

This is where you begin to connect with yourself in a way you have never experienced before. This is where you start to feel emotionally safe.

When you practise the **Drop Your Shoulders® Method,** you create a new reference point in your subconscious to calm your nervous system. Each time you intentionally drop your shoulders or even just say the words, your subconscious responds, and you feel it in your body. You're giving your subconscious new evidence that it is safe to feel. It is safe to be yourself, to feel emotions, and to be in control.

Practise. Practise. Perfect the dropping of your shoulders every time you notice your shoulders tense.

Now, expand on the **Drop Your Shoulders® Method** with the following affirmation: *"I am safe. Right now, I'm just sitting here, reading. And I am safe."*

The nervous system doesn't respond to thinking or ideas. It reacts to physical practice, and your nervous system responds to feeling safe. If you've spent years in a tense body, you won't find peace just by thinking. The action of dropping your shoulders is your way back to yourself.

One of my clients came to me during a period when anxiety overshadowed every moment of her day. From the moment she opened her eyes in the morning until she finally went to bed at night, her body and mind were in an ongoing state of tension. She worked in a call centre, handling call after call from unhappy customers, many of whom were angry, with some outright abusive. Her nervous system had no chance to rest; each conversation kept her on high alert, reinforcing the belief that she was under attack.

I introduced her to the **Drop Your Shoulders® Method.** She committed to practising it five times a day. She didn't wait until she was overwhelmed; instead, she wove it into her daily life, using it both during her breaks and at moments when she felt the tension starting to rise in her stomach. She put reminders and alarms in her phone. Within just over two weeks, she returned with a lightness I could see before she even spoke. Her anxiety had reduced by around 80%.

She told me she could breathe again, think clearly, and walk into her day without the same dread that had been weighing her down for years.

With that new stability, we expanded her practice into deeper layers of the method and healing techniques that address past trauma, which had kept her subconscious on high alert for rejection and criticism. She learnt new communication skills to build healthy boundaries, so she could navigate her work and personal life without losing herself. The key was that she first learned how to calm her nervous system in the moment. From there, she could begin to rewire the patterns that had been running her life for decades.

Notice when your shoulders are already tense — whether you're driving to work, thinking about someone who has upset you, or watching an action movie. Use the tension in your shoulders as a reference point to acknowledge that your nervous system has been activated, triggering your survival responses. These moments provide an opportunity to interrupt the stress response and calm your nervous system.

## Reflection

*Where in your daily life do you notice your body automatically tensing from fear of conflict, rejection, or criticism? At home or at work?*

*Do you notice your jaw tightening? Yes/No*

*Are your shoulders tense? Yes/No*

*Do you feel uncomfortable when you try to relax your body or meditate? YesNo*

*Are you snapping at the people around you? Yes/No*

*Do you feel the anger rising from the pit of your stomach? Yes/No*

*Do you feel grief sitting in your chest or a lump in your throat? Yes/No*

*Are you forgetting to eat or are you over-eating? Yes/No*

*Do you put your own self-care at the bottom of your list? Yes/No*

*Are you always on the move? Yes/No*

*Are your thoughts racing out of control? Yes/No*

If you answered 'yes' to any of these questions, choose one of these moments today to activate the **Drop Your Shoulders® Method**.

The time to practise is now, not when you have reached your breaking point. As soon as you feel that first sign of tension in your shoulders, stomach, or anywhere else in your body, drop your shoulders.

Notice what's different in your body. Notice you automatically feel calmer, the tension leaving, your stomach relaxing, and your breathing starts to slow down.

These questions aim to reveal how your stress pattern appears in your life. They are all interconnected symptoms of long-term stress, with your nervous system sounding the alarm. When your nervous system repeatedly enters a fight, flight, or freeze response — whether due to childhood trauma, daily overwhelm, or emotional suppression — you are experiencing chronic adrenal stress. Your body begins to adapt and responds from a heightened state of awareness that feels normal. There's more going on than just your external reactions; your body overcompensates every day. Understanding what happens when you are triggered into these survival responses helps clarify your reactions.

- Your digestive system isn't processing food properly.

- Your body reroutes blood away from your core organs.

- Your heart rate rises, putting stress on your heart.

- Your breathing becomes shallow.

- Your bloodstream becomes flooded with hormones and cortisol.

- Your muscles overcompensate, leading to neck pain, shoulder pain, and back pain.

These are just a few examples. Over a long period in this state, you start to forget what it feels like to be calm and happy. Your physical survival patterns become your default and can be all you have ever known. If left unchecked, over time, your survival responses can manifest or amplify physical illness and disease.

Unexpressed emotions or suppressed feelings do not simply vanish. They find a place in your body. Anger resides in the liver, fear settles in the kidneys, and grief lingers in the lungs. Over time, this accumulates as silent, dense, and unprocessed energy. If the survival response isn't interrupted, or if your emotional energy isn't allowed to be expressed, it begins to harden into the tissue. This is how emotional pain turns into physical pain.

Shock, in particular, is one of the most overlooked forms of frozen energy stored in the body. It is a moment when the body says 'too much', and the system shuts down to protect you. It only takes a second for the energy to solidify as protection, and this protection has been blocking you from moving forward for years. Shock creates a freeze point, an energetic stop sign, and unless it's addressed, you will find yourself repeating the same patterns over and over again.

This is why you might feel like you're self-sabotaging or 'stuck.' It's energy that's still frozen in time and keeps cycling over and over.

The physical and emotional pain are real. Yes, you will explore a medical diagnosis or a response from Dr Google to find that what you are feeling does not really fit the diagnosis, and the medication has had an impact on some of the symptoms or provides short-term relief, but now more symptoms are popping up, activating more physical or emotional pain.

These symptoms serve as a message for you to look deeper and understand that you are not just a physical body, and that all physical illnesses are connected to your emotional and energetic fields. These symptoms are your body's way of telling you that your emotions need your attention, and that your stress levels and survival responses are now affecting your physical experience. This isn't an invitation to overanalyse or try to fix your physical body with your conscious mind; it's simply an opportunity to listen to your body, which signals that there is more happening than just physical symptoms. It's an invitation to incorporate all the **Drop Your Shoulders® Methods** into your daily activities by embracing holistic healing.

Every time you interrupt the stress response, every time you practice these methods and connect with your body to calm your nervous system, you create a shift. You're establishing new reference points — not just for your mind, but for your cells, fascia, and energetic field. In these quiet moments, physical, mental, and emotional healing occur. Integration happens subtly and gently when you're not even aware of it.

I see it every day with my clients and on retreats, where immediate changes occur in their physical bodies; chronic back pain that has persisted for years often disappears. One client came in with a swollen hand; she was a writer, and through clearing past trauma patterns, her hand returned to normal right before my eyes.

From our Alchemy of Men Retreats, I observed physical changes in participants. One man, who arrived hunched over from years of stress, was standing tall and straight after just three days. Another man, who had long-term nerve pain, reported that the pain was gone after the retreat.

I have seen absolute transformations occur physically and emotionally in people through practising the **Drop Your Shoulders® Methods.**

# Drop Your Shoulders® Method 3

## Releasing Tension And Pain

- Begin now by dropping your shoulders.
- Tune into your body and notice areas of tension, tightness, or pain. Notice where you feel the pain or physical discomfort in your body. Is it in your stomach, chest, throat, or head?
- Breathe into the location of the tension or pain in your body and focus on relaxing the muscles in this area.
- Say to yourself or out loud.

*"I give my body permission to release what it no longer needs.*
*I am safe, right now I am..."* (Insert whatever you are doing at the time of practice, eg, sitting on a chair, driving to work, etc.)

Feel how much the moment shifts when you slow down enough to connect with your body and release stored energy. Notice the energy flowing out as you imagine letting it leave from every cell in your body. As your entire body begins to relax.

# Chapter Three

# Creating Emotional Safety From The Inside Out

When you start to create emotional safety in your body by interrupting your survival patterns, releasing frozen energy, and telling your nervous system it is safe to feel emotions, you realise this practice is not as confrontational as you might think.

*Have you ever been told you have anxiety? Yes/No*
*Or was it called something else?*

Panic Attacks, Social Anxiety, Generalised Worry

Beneath all the labels, the truth is straightforward: anxiety, fear, and survival responses are all the same thing. It's your nervous system doing exactly what it was trained to do — protect you.

There is only one response your body has when it perceives danger: FEAR. This is your survival response; what has been labelled as anxiety is also described as your automated Fear/Survival Response. Muscles tense, heart rate increases, digestive system shuts down, tunnel vision occurs, and hormones are released into your body. The physical experience is the same.

We have already looked at that initial moment of shock or trauma -the moment your body couldn't understand what was happening when you were a child or in the womb, when safety was shattered, and something deep inside you froze. That's the imprint your nervous system still reacts to today as an adult. This is why you can't just think your way out of anxiety or trauma. Because it didn't start in your thoughts; it started in your body the moment you felt overwhelmed, and there was no one there to help you feel safe again.

Right now, right here, this is your body, and you have the power to interrupt your fear or survival process, to change the outcome, and to choose how you want to respond now. Healing isn't about overriding fear; it's about creating safety within yourself by consistently practising the **Drop Your Shoulders® Method** until it becomes an automatic response.

Each time you relax your shoulders, you change the pattern, creating new reference points of feeling safe in different situations — giving you choice.

Let me show you what this looks like. Note: if you identify with even a small part of this, please remember these are normal reactions to trauma, and you're not alone. This is not how you will always feel.

My nervous system was stuck in a heightened state of fear for over thirty years. I wasn't just alert; I was hyper-vigilant. Constantly scanning and on edge, my body was always on the lookout for danger, even when nothing obvious was happening.

My emotional pain was deeply buried within my cells, and although I managed to function with a mask of confidence, when I couldn't hold it in any longer and something triggered my core wounds of rejection, betrayal, and abandonment, this energy and these emotions flooded out and spiralled out of control. It hit like tidal waves — unbearable and overwhelming. For me, emotional pain felt worse than physical pain; the negative thoughts were uncontrollable.

There were days when I wanted to disappear just so no one would see the emotional pain I was carrying inside. I learned to minimise it, hide it, and push it back beneath the surface, and when that didn't work, I would withdraw for days and avoid interacting with the world. The emotional pain did not go away; it was like black ink flowing through my veins, invisible to others but all-consuming inside.

If my emotional body had been visible like a physical wound, I'd have had cuts all over and would be in intensive care. No one could see it, and I wouldn't let them; what they saw was someone who, in their eyes, was always happy.

There were times I didn't want to be here. Suicidal thoughts arose not because I wanted to die, but because I wanted the pain to cease. I drank not to silence, numb, or escape; alcohol for me did something different — it became a bypass of the survival response, where I felt alive, free, in control, connected to spirit, grounded, and highly aware. I was free to access joy, laughter, and spontaneity.

I was so aware. I remembered everything — every conversation, every experience — even though I might have consumed enough to pass out, I was still aware, alive, awake. These times gave me brief escapes from the constant inner turmoil. I often vanished, retreating to a safe place where the pain would explode in tears and screams of its rawness. I didn't realise then that this was my body's way of trying to protect me. I only knew that it was intense and all-consuming.

I didn't start healing my past trauma patterns by talking about them or revisiting every traumatic memory. Instead, I began by learning how to calm the physical stress response through my body and nervous system. I created the **Drop Your Shoulders® Methods** not as a 'coping skill' but as a way of living for deep, lasting healing. I reclaimed my ability to feel safe in my own body. My goal is and always will be inner peace.

I began with one day at a time, one moment at a time, followed by the next. I started to drop my shoulders and breathe into my body. It was hard at first, as I had been shallow-breathing for so long. I couldn't breathe properly. My chest would tighten with pressure. My stomach was nauseous. There was a lump in my throat, a painful knot blocking my breath. I couldn't breathe any deeper than the top of my lungs. Sometimes it physically hurt to breathe deeper. I practised it by dropping my shoulders, one breath at a time.

From here, I expanded the **Drop Your Shoulders® Method** to establish reference points of safety deeper within my nervous system. Trauma patterns are layered so gently that once I mastered dropping my shoulders, I was able to expand the practice. I first incorporated one affirmation into the process: "I am safe right now, right now I am..."

I did this as often as I could, and I started to notice a change. I began to experience moments of inner peace and calmness, where there was no emotional pain or internal struggle. It was as if the heaviness in my chest had lifted.

I didn't aim for perfection, nor did I need to. I only needed to practise every day. For me, it marked the start of my healing journey and growing hope that it was possible to be free and feel calm inside. My body had received a different message, a new message that healing is possible. I was creating new reference points in my subconscious, and my nervous system was responding.

This was my experience, and although mine stemmed from my own unique circumstances, you don't need to have experienced such trauma for this process to work. I believe that as we grow as human beings, we all expand our emotional body, which involves healing generational trauma stored in our DNA and learning new tools to evolve. It's not complicated and doesn't take years. Complementing existing therapy programs, this process is now well refined, allowing you to feel the changes immediately. Within a few months, you'll start to notice physical changes in your body, your thoughts, your emotional reactions, and your relationships.

If I can do it, so can you. Not perfectly, and not all at once. Start with the intention that it is possible.

Now drop your shoulders, breathe into your stomach and say *"I am safe, right now I am..."*

You have just started to activate either the memory of what safety feels like, or, if you don't have that memory, you are creating a new pathway: feeling calm in your body equals safety. Not as a thought but as a lived experience. As a physical sensation in your body.

Every time you drop your shoulders, you're not just shutting down the stress response; you're rewiring the very foundation of your nervous system.

By interrupting old patterns of fear and telling your body you are safe now, you are creating new subconscious reference points linked to your nervous system and a calmer response.

You'll notice the changes straight away; however, for lasting, permanent results, this isn't a quick fix. It's an ongoing practice that reprograms your subconscious automatic survival responses.

Start today, drop your shoulders as often as you can throughout the day, and watch the difference. Make it a daily habit — a tool that will rewire your nervous system until it becomes an automatic part of your life, just like getting dressed in the morning.

You're demonstrating to your body what no one taught you as a child: how to regulate your nervous system.

How to self-soothe and come home to your body instead of leaving your body and disconnecting or dissociating.

You are taking back control of your nervous system and, with it, your life.

## Emotional Safety As A Default Pattern

*Are you starting to notice the difference in your body when you feel calm versus when you feel tense? Yes/No*

Every time you practice the **Drop Your Shoulders® Method**, you connect with your nervous system and begin to change how you feel.

There is a sabotaging pattern that is hidden in the background: negative thoughts and beliefs. When you calm your nervous system and the thoughts emerge, the negative thoughts that creep in become louder when things go quiet. The first ones that surface are conscious and protective.

*What if it doesn't last?*

*What if something goes wrong again?*

*What if I still do not feel safe?*

This is not sabotage; it is your conscious mind trying to understand what is happening for you. Unfortunately, this kind of overthinking traps you in an endless loop of questions with no answers. The conscious mind focuses on short-term thinking, analysis, and planning, and cannot access the subconscious database of your entire life experience to find the answers.

This kind of overthinking involves a never-ending cycle of questions with no solutions.

The answers come when you bridge the gap between the conscious and subconscious minds so they are aligned. So that what you verbally express consciously matches what your body feels and responds to from your subconscious and your nervous system.

You can consciously repeat "I am safe", but if your shoulders are tense, your breath is shallow, and your nervous system is on high alert, the words will just be words. Alternatively, positive affirmations, when not anchored, can have the opposite effect and fully activate your survival response. Not because your intention or the affirmation is wrong, but because your subconscious is activated into scanning for survival and recognises every moment you were not physically or emotionally safe.

Your subconscious isn't rejecting the affirmation. It's just indicating areas where safety was never fully felt or experienced in your body.

This is where you start to see yourself differently through feeling and conscious awareness. By practising listening to what your body is holding beneath the noise of overthinking, you can reach the depths of subconscious patterns that hold you back. This is the internal war between conscious and subconscious thoughts.

This is where I want to introduce you to a broader version of affirmations.

Active Affirmations go beyond simply speaking affirmations consciously. They are not just words; they involve recalibrating your nervous system. It's a merging of language with feeling, sensation, and presence.

Linking your conscious and subconscious mind by combining physical action (**Drop Your Shoulders® Method**) with an emotional anchor (*"I am safe"*).

# Drop Your Shoulders® Method 4

## Active Affirmations

- Now, drop your shoulders.
- Feel into your body and notice areas of tension, tightness, or pain.
- Breathe in for 4, and out for 4, focusing on relaxing the muscles in these areas.
- Now, choose your affirmation

*"I am safe. Right now, I'm just sitting here, reading. And I am safe."*
*"I am enough; I've always been enough."*
*"I take back my power."*

- Create your own affirmation.
- Practice this as often as you can remember, aiming for at least five times a day, while adding your own affirmation.

## Chapter Four

# What Does It Mean To Feel Safe?

Using the **Drop Your Shoulders® Method** as a physical anchor while deliberately saying the affirmation creates a strong reference point for change.

One of the most important affirmations is *"I am safe."* As you drop your shoulders. Breathe into your stomach. And gently repeat: *"I am safe."*

Let the words soften your nervous system just a little more than before.

*What do the words "I am safe" mean to you?* We started by referring to physical safety

*"Right now I am sitting on this chair; I am physically safe"*

Now we're going to delve deeper into emotional safety.

*Do you know what it means to feel emotionally safe? Yes/No*

You might not yet know what it genuinely feels like to be emotionally safe.

*Did you grow up with childhood trauma or even the subtle, persistent undercurrents that made you feel it was unsafe to express yourself? Yes/No*

Emotional safety can seem like an intangible concept rather than a real experience.

*Did you learn early on to guard your feelings, measure your words, or stay small to avoid provoking anger, rejection, or withdrawal from those around you? Yes/No*

*Alternatively, did you become the peacekeeper, the performer, or the invisible one, always scanning the room for signs of danger before daring to speak your truth? Yes/No*

Over time, these patterns are connected with these belief systems, becoming the only 'normal' your nervous system recognises.

When emotional safety was never modelled or reinforced, your body equated survival with control. You quickly learn to manage your external environment, responses, reactions, finances, and relationships.

For me, physical safety became connected with financial security because that financial security gave me some control over my environment, and that, in turn, was how I tried to protect my emotional safety.

Emotional safety equals inner peace. It happens when your nervous system is in harmony with your external world, and you feel safe to express your emotions as they come up. It's the freedom to be yourself completely and honestly, without fear of emotional punishment or love and safety being withdrawn. If you've never truly experienced emotional safety, your subconscious and overactive nervous system will try to protect you from what it believes might harm you, especially the unknown or what it's wired to think is impossible. This can mean keeping love, opportunities, or genuine emotional safety out of reach.

As a child, I saw physical and emotional safety as connected. It meant having choices and not being in unsafe environments.

Over time, my emotional safety became inseparable from my physical safety.

When I asked myself what *"I am safe emotionally means to me,"* the answer was instant — money. Not excess money, not greed. But the kind of money that gives me the choice to protect myself physically, which, in my mind, prevents any situation that could be traumatic or trigger shock and trauma.

From a young age, I was left to look after myself. The adults in my home left before 6 am and didn't return until late at night. I caught the train to school and remember walking home alone in the dark. Realising that this memory had linked money with safety was both confronting and life-changing.

I began to examine my emotional triggers more carefully. *"What triggered my stress response? How did I react? Why did I feel unsafe so quickly?"* I realised that as I got older, money gave me freedom — the freedom to catch a taxi home when it was dark, to avoid situations that activated the constant rush of fear in my body. So I asked myself, *"How much money do I actually need to feel safe?"*

Looking back now, I laugh at how this had subconsciously played out in my life. I hoarded money, hiding it in different places, keeping it *"just in case."* Just in case I was in danger. Just in case I needed to buy my way out of danger.

I would find money stashed in places I no longer remembered putting it. The amount was never enough, and I was still in fear every day. By exploring this process as a concept, I realised that my nervous system was constantly triggered into overdrive.

No amount of affirmations could override the deep, embodied memory that a *"lack of money equalled no safety."* Later, in relationships and with the introduction of joint accounts, when my bank balance dropped below my subconscious 'safety threshold,' the pain was instant, my reactions were excessive, and my sense of control vanished. Fear would switch on automatically, and I wouldn't even understand why.

After some honest reflection, I put a few thousand dollars in a bank account that I would never touch, and then felt my nervous system drop into a state of emotional safety I had never experienced before.

Since that moment over 20 years ago, I haven't needed to access this account, and now my spoken words align with my subconscious reality. I feel physically and emotionally safe when I say *"I am safe."* This was just one example of a safety reference point; most people will have three or four key reference points.

Your definition of emotional safety will be different, and that is exactly the point. This is just the start of the process.

You don't need to pinpoint every moment you feel unsafe.

Instead, focus on one thing you can start working on today — one belief you formed as a child. This is the belief that is hardwired into your subconscious patterns, your nervous system and triggers your survival response automatically.

Your emotional safety is non-negotiable. Once identified, you can work towards creating safety in this area of your life.

One of my clients shared something so familiar when she explored what 'I am safe' means to her.

She knew her relationship was unhealthy, even abusive. When we explored the deeper truth of what her core physical and emotional safety pattern was built around — fear of being alone — she realised that being alone felt more dangerous than being mistreated.

She remained in abusive relationships, as the stress and fear she experienced there paled in comparison to her fundamental fear of being alone, which was automatically activated within her. Not because she lacked the desire for freedom and safety — she did — but because she was unaware of this subconscious fear. This fear had been quietly controlling her nervous system for decades, tying physical safety and emotional safety into the same knot. Being alone had always felt like danger, abandonment, and vulnerability.

When we slowed down the process and really examined it, a different truth came to light. We could see through the pattern to understand the real truth. Being alone also meant no abuse — no one to control her or hurt her, and no one to withdraw love as punishment. The absence of an abusive relationship could actually represent physical and emotional safety. There were some decisions she needed to make for this to happen, but now it was possible, no longer sabotaged by her subconscious fears and nervous system.

There are many examples, and another one I can share where 'I am safe' is as simple as knowing the doors are locked at night.

My client realised that every evening she felt fear and anxiety. Her shoulders tensed, and her breath became shallow. When we explored it, she remembered growing up in a house where the doors were often left unlocked, and that there had been a break-in when she was a child. That memory had stayed in her nervous system ever since.

Her solution was not complicated. She purchased a video alarm system. She would work with the **Drop Your Shoulders® Method** and say, *"I am safe and protected in my home,"* and feel her body soften just a little more each day.

Over the weeks, her nervous system learned a new reference point for safety, not a conscious idea, but a sensation she felt in her body.

It didn't take years of effort or major life changes. Just one small action, done with awareness, was enough to start rewiring the fear response.

This is the work of an Active Affirmation. It's not about saying what you wish you believed; it's about creating an embodied reference point where you feel physically and emotionally safe. Don't rush this process. Take a moment to ask yourself softly.

*"What do I need to feel physically and emotionally safe?"*

Drop your shoulders, now feel into your body — *where in your body does it feel uncomfortable?* Focus on relaxing the muscles in this area of your body.

*What are the thoughts that come up when you ask this question? What are the opposing thoughts?*

These opposing thoughts are consistent; they do not change over time. When you listen, you will realise there are one or two core beliefs and thought processes that automatically trigger your stress or fear response regarding physical and emotional safety.

At first, you might jot down everything that's not working in your life at the moment. But in stillness, when you genuinely ask, one fear will remain constant throughout.

Once you identify what that is, you then have the power within to find a solution, seek more clarity, and continue working with your nervous system.

**This is where emotional safety truly becomes real within you.**

In these quiet moments of realisation, where the affirmation is not just spoken but now felt in your body, something shifts. A deep sense of safety and inner peace that lives within you is ready to be felt.

Take your time to understand what this means for you.

*What does your nervous system need to believe the words you are consciously saying?*

*What does physical and emotional safety look like, feel like, and require from you in real, practical terms?*

You don't have to solve it all now.

Even if you cannot act on the solution yet, just identifying it and dropping your shoulders will create a calmer response. Having a plan or goal to work towards brings clarity and inner peace. A tangible sign of safety tells your body, "I'm listening now, and I am safe."

And then something beautiful unfolds. Now, when you say *"I am safe,"* combined with dropping your shoulders, you genuinely feel it every time — not just as a concept or words spoken, but as a lived experience. A deep sense of inner peace arises each time you drop your shoulders, and this inner peace becomes automatically activated. You are now in control of your own nervous system and creating a new reference point for inner safety.

Take a moment here to acknowledge the times you've felt calm in your body, the times you've felt safe since starting this book.

Notice that your body is already automatically activating the **Drop Your Shoulders® Method.**

Overthinking is a normal part of life. However, what you may or may not know is that there are two types of overthinking. Conscious overthinking involves replaying a conversation from earlier in your day or week, wondering if you said the wrong thing. Or you might overthink as you remember something you forgot to do, starting a list of everything you need to take care of tomorrow. You also overthink the safety of someone you love, which we call worry.

It's surface-level chatter. It involves planning, analysing, and repeating tasks or conversations. It keeps you busy and sometimes masks something deeper. Mostly, it is a barrage of questions with no answers. *"What if?", "How come:, "Why?"* — these are continuous questions on repeat.

There is another type of overthinking, called 'subconscious overthinking'. The constant voice in the background. Not the voice of reason, but the voice of your subconscious overthinking.

This is where your core beliefs are activated, running the same narrative you've heard for so long, you're no longer aware of them. They exist in the background like static, quietly influencing how you feel and what you do each day.

These are reference points of pain and self-punishment that you carry like a deep dark secret.

Thoughts that drag you down into a spiral of darkness and emotional pain. They come disguised as truth and pierce your heart like a dagger.

You hear them from within: *"I'm not enough,"* or *"No one loves me,"* or *"Something must be wrong with me."*

They arrive in moments of silence, sadness, or uncertainty. You not only hear them in your mind but also feel them in your body. These are the ones that break through your survival patterns of avoidance and masking. They trigger the lump in your throat, the pain in your heart, and the dread in your stomach.

Most people have two or three core beliefs that quietly repeat in different ways in their minds across various situations, always in the background. Saying them out loud can trigger a strong fear response or emotional overwhelm.

These statements are not random. They are core imprints, beliefs formed in childhood. They are the thoughts that make you cry, even when no one else sees or hears them. These are the thoughts that break your own heart.

**Truth.** They are not even complete thoughts; they are fractured, unfinished statements.

Take the belief: *"I am not enough."* It's a broken statement; it's incomplete. In its current form, it doesn't mean anything. *"Not enough for whom? Not enough for what?"*

Your subconscious halts the sentence prematurely, and your nervous system fills in the rest with fear.

These statements now turn into expanded assumptions — a broader belief:

*"I'm not enough for anyone. Ever"*

*"I feel like I don't deserve to be successful."*

You now subconsciously think, *"I am not enough"* in every situation.

When you were a child, usually not long after your first 'shock' moment — a specific event or gradually over a long period you began to feel "not enough" for one person: your father, your mother, a teacher? At some point, this statement was formed. It's similar to shock being a frozen energy that crystallises and settles in your body. This belief became anchored in your cellular structure and subconscious, and it impacts your sense of self.

The emotional pain you felt was real in that moment. From the perspective of a child — a two-year-old, a five-year-old, a ten-year-old — I want to acknowledge that a child's brain, at any age, is not yet developed enough to see the bigger picture. Your entire world and sense of safety are dependent on a parent, guardian, or caregiver. This person was your whole world. As a child, you couldn't survive without them, so these feelings of rejection and abandonment were real at that time. As a child, you believed you were not enough; in your world at that moment, that seemed true. Your entire universe revolved around one or two caregivers; at that time, they were your entire world. The statement at that time was true.

The real emotional pain was triggered when this statement wasn't updated as you grew older or given a new context; instead, it remained buried deep in your subconscious as an unfinished and fractured statement.

As your world grew and you became an adult, your circle expanded, with more people and connections. This core belief and fractured statement, once related to one person in your childhood, now applies to everyone you meet in your broader world. It translates into *"I am not enough for anyone."*

It's time to transform the fractured statement into a clear and accurate one that can be rephrased and rewritten. This powerful process and realisation can immediately break the cycle of self-harm that has been repeating itself in your life.

For example: Using the fractured statement *"I am not enough,"* and asking the question, *"I am not enough, for whom?"*

Expanding the fractured statement to *"I am not enough for my dad"* helps clarify that this is just one person on the planet, not all people, events, or situations — just one person. Once you reframe the statement to be *"I am not enough for my dad,"* often the pain that has troubled you for years begins to fade and dissolve. Your heart can handle feeling like you're not enough for one person on the planet; it cannot cope with believing this is true for everyone, in every situation.

In addition to it relating to one person, it may or may not have been true, considering it was created from a child's inability to grasp the bigger picture, your father's emotional landscape, and the generational patterns behind him. Was your grandfather hard on your dad? *"Does he also carry the burden of the belief 'I'm not enough'?"*

We will explore this later in the book with understanding and compassion, depending on the person you are referring to. *Did they do their best with the information available to them?.*

For now, it's important to understand that the statement *"I am not enough for anyone, for everyone, for all people"* is not entirely true.

Let's examine the fragmented statements and why turning them into absolute declarations has caused you so much emotional pain. If I heard you say, *"I am not enough,"* I would respond by telling you that your statement made no sense to me. *"You're not enough for whom?"* Be specific. If you said, *"No one loves me."* I'd respond with, *"I don't understand who no one is — who are you really talking about here?"*

Imagine hearing the same statement from someone else, and it doesn't make sense. *"Who are you talking about? Who made you think that? Who said that to you?"* In my experience with clients, it's usually a parent, caregiver, teacher, family friend, uncle, aunty, brother or sister — someone close to you from childhood.

Asking these questions can help identify its origin.

*I'm not enough for whom?*
*Who did I feel didn't love me?*
*I have to be better for who?*
*Who told me I cannot achieve my goals?*

This marks the start of reprogramming your subconscious from within, not by battling your inner thoughts, but by listening to them with compassion and choosing truth.

Now it's time to reframe the statement.

*"I am enough for myself, for my friends, for my partner, and for my children"* Insert whoever you need to and reframe it to suit your life. Be specific and make it true.

For example, one of my fractured statements was, *"No one loves me."* I carried it like a truth carved into my bones. Every argument, rejection, and silence all confirmed that belief. *"No one loves me."* Reinforcing that belief over and over. This fractured statement caused me so much emotional pain, breaking my own heart day after day. It shaped how I viewed relationships and how I showed up in all situations. I felt unsafe to open up, trust, or be seen.

The truth about my belief is that I didn't feel loved by my mother. This deep wound, rooted in the belief that *"no one loves me,"* has affected me for as long as I can remember. It has shown up in various ways, from *"no one loves me"* to *"I am not lovable."*

When this statement was expanded to *"My mum didn't love me."* This refers to one person on the planet — my primary caregiver — and does not apply to all others in my life, such as my adult relationships, friendships, colleagues, etc.

My heart can handle one person on the planet not loving me, even if she was my primary caregiver. But my heart cannot cope with no one loving me.

When I reconsidered it, I realised the fractured statement wasn't entirely accurate from the beginning. I now believe my mum did love me in the best way she knew, considering her own emotional pain and generational trauma.

I rewrote and expanded this statement to say, *"I love myself, my son loves me, my friends love me, and I would use specific names, ...loves me."* The list then becomes a long list of positive truths, and I accept that *"I am loved."*

Now you can turn the fractured statement into *"I am enough for myself, for my friends, for...."* (Specifically name the people in your life who love you.)

Your core fractured statements are not your fault; they come from the perceptions of your inner child's mind.

They were shaped by moments when you needed something vital that wasn't there. Those moments left an imprint—fractured statements that quietly run in the background as absolute truths, constantly activating your subconscious survival patterns and responses. Today you can change them.

# Drop Your Shoulders® Method 5

## Transform Subconscious Overthinking

It's time now to upgrade your personal fractured statements and their context, and to broaden your perception.

- Begin to drop your shoulders.

- *What are your core fractured statements?* Write them down. They are the ones that keep recurring in your subconscious; they are not creative; they are repetitive.

- Choose one fractured statement to work through using his method. (Later, go back and work through the others).

- *Do you use absolute words like Always, Everyone, No one, Forever, Can't? Yes/No.* Cross out these words to rewrite the statement.

- Now ask the question: *Who is this statement referring to — a parent, caregiver, teacher, an adult of influence in your life when you were a child?*

- Expand the statement into a complete sentence with the name or names of the person this fractured statement relates to. For example, *"I am not enough for my Dad,"* or *"My mum didn't love me,"* or *"I am not worthy of success".*

- Rewrite the statement. *"I am enough for myself", "I am enough for my partner, my friend, in my job."* These are your new affirmations.

- Say your new affirmation as an Active Affirmation, as you drop your shoulders. You now have a new reference point in your subconscious. Your nervous system will recalibrate to this new affirmation. You are rewiring your nervous system from emotional pain to inner peace and truth.

- Breathe deeply into the centre of your body, scan for any tightness or tension where you're holding onto the pain of this fractured statement, relax the muscles, and let go of the tension. Feel what it feels like to feel calm in your body.

- Now say your new Active Affirmation to yourself or out loud.

*"I am enough for myself, I am enough for..."*

- Allow the new affirmation to become your truth. Drop your shoulders and allow your subconscious to establish a new reference point, one that is true and safe.

- Notice over the next couple of weeks, whenever you start to think of your original fractured statement, automatically expand it or change it to your new active affirmation.

- Notice that the emotional charge you once felt from your heart breaking is now different, less, or gone entirely. If you do feel the emotional charge arising, you can correct it by automatically recalling this process and the truth. *"That statement is not the truth; it relates to one person, i.e., my mum or my dad; it does not apply now."*

- Each day, your nervous system will become calmer and more centred. Physically and emotionally safe.

## Chapter Five

# Breaking The Cycle Of Trauma

You were born into a world already shaped by inherited emotional patterns and unspoken dynamics passed silently through generations. These include generational trauma and unresolved emotional pain. A lineage of voices that never truly knew how to express love, grief, anger, or joy without distortion. These patterns were passed to you not just through words and fractured statements, but also through energy, tone, silence, gaze, and absence.

As a baby, your emotional world was wide open. You felt everything — joy, sadness, hunger, delight. You didn't question your feelings or filter your needs. You cried when you needed something and reached out for love and connection. You lived in full expression. It was natural to cry, scream, laugh, or jump up and down in excitement to release the built-up energy of emotion; your body was designed to release emotion this way. You had only one truth: love and connection are life itself.

You were born into a body still developing and a nervous system still unfolding, into an energy field not yet separate from the surrounding world. From birth to around age seven or eight, your brain and nervous system constantly absorb everything.

You exist in the most open frequency possible, like a sponge, soaking up your external environment — you feel the lightness or tension, the silence or loud voices, and the emotional atmosphere of your environment.

At this stage of your growth, your energy is open and porous, absorbing the world without resistance. You have no need to guard or defend yourself; you simply receive. Every tone, glance, and unspoken feeling moves through you, imprinting without question.

You learn through the rhythm of others' voices, the warmth or absence in their touch, and how their presence settles or unsettles your own. You absorb not because you choose to, but because you are human; your DNA is wired for connection and, in turn, survival. You are learning through the physical and emotional intelligence of your parents and primary caregivers how to survive in the world you are now in.

You watched how they behaved, you mimicked their emotions, and you mimicked their reactions.

You sensed when love was there and when it disappeared. You observed the shifts in their mood, the change in their voice, the sudden coldness or alteration in their posture. You instinctively started to adjust your own nervous system responses, your needs, and your voice as a model for how to behave and respond. This isn't a conscious decision; it's part of growing up.

The developing brain, in its wisdom, forms neural pathways to create safety — not just physical safety, but emotional safety.

When you cried, and no one came, a pathway was formed; likewise, if you cried and were nurtured, a pathway was formed. A reference point is established, indicating whether you feel loved and supported or abandoned and rejected.

Whether you laughed or felt discomfort, these pathways were created. When you were praised for being 'good' or scolded for being 'too much', reference points were etched into your subconscious and into your developing nervous system.

This is where trauma patterns are born, not just through major traumatic events, even though our definition of trauma considers an event or experience. Big events like divorce, death in the family, and physical and emotional abuse create deep, hardwired neural pathways. However, other trauma patterns form through long-term repetition — such as the daily unmet needs, unacknowledged cries, and the silent conditioning that taught you love must be earned, emotions must be managed, and authenticity must be suppressed.

Your subconscious and neural pathways were adapting to your environment. You just did what every child does: you shaped beliefs, reactions and emotions around what would keep you connected to love and safety.

If the environment around you is safe, it enables you to self-regulate, self-soothe, and feel secure in the world. When your environment is unstable, disconnected, unsafe, or emotionally shut down, your body responds with intelligence.

You learn to freeze, dissociate, and become quiet, invisible, helpful, or pleasing — not because it is your nature, but because you are automatically adapting to the only way to protect your physical and emotional safety and a sense of belonging.

At this stage, you do not yet understand the concepts of *right* or *wrong*. You were not making moral judgments or assessing your family dynamics. You simply reflected what was happening around you and took it as *normal*.

I now realise that as a child growing up in abuse and neglect, I wasn't consciously aware I was being abused. It was just how life was.

You absorb, observe, and grow, and your neural pathways develop to determine,

*"This is what love looks like, and this is what I must do to be safe."*

This is how the subconscious mind was formed. Not through logic, but through physical and emotional patterns and by observing and feeling your environment. It is not logical; it is relational.

As you start to grow, your brain matures, and your energy body begins to individuate; this occurs around age 9/10 and older, and now the comparisons begin.

You start to notice that other families and how they behave are different from your own. You see parents who laugh with their children. Homes where touch is warm, not tense. You begin looking at TV and movies and notice different pictures of family environments and the schoolyard, and realise that not every family is the same. Your friends tell a different story.

And now, you're old enough to notice the cracks but still too young to fully understand them. This is when confusion begins.

You start to think.

*"Why do I feel this way? Why does my family act differently? Why does my mum yell or my dad drink? Why is my mum crying? Is this my fault? Why do I feel like I don't belong now?"*

To some extent, this happens to all of us; there is always comparison and confusion, especially during puberty. This is when emotional pain becomes internalised, and the confusion of childhood hardens into a belief system.

You feel different; somehow, the world no longer feels safe or normal. You begin to create your own ideas of right and wrong. You start to feel separate or alone, and your memories become distorted — what you once thought was love now feels painful.

*Could that have been abuse, or is this love?* During your teenage years, you begin to set boundaries and push back. You want to be heard, and you feel the emotional pain in your body. You are forging your own identity based on the information you gathered in your early years.

You start to believe it was your fault, and those core beliefs are triggered. You start to feel this way because you believe the fractured statements;

*"I am not lovable."*

*"No one loves me."*

*"I am not good enough."*

*"I am not enough."*

You think you caused the love to vanish, or was it never there in the first place, creating internal chaos.

This is not the truth; however, it did become your reality.

Your inner voice, the one that tells you you're not worthy, not safe, or not enough, didn't appear out of nowhere.

It was shaped by the emotional world of your parents and caregivers, who, in turn, were influenced by the generation before them in the same way.

Your parents and caregivers are not deliberately trying to hurt you. They are people with emotional trauma passed down through generations without access to the tools or understanding to heal.

No matter what your subconscious negative belief was, such as *"I am not enough"* or *"no one loves me"*. The story that was repeated, or whatever it was that you identified as your fractured statements earlier. It often mirrored how they felt, too.

Not just once or occasionally. It was embedded deep within them, in their subconscious, buried emotions from childhood trauma patterns. They lacked the tools to fully understand the impact of their emotional outbursts on you; they didn't know how to change the outcome or how to soothe their own nervous systems, emotional triggers, and reactions. They were unable to teach you to heal what they had not yet healed within themselves.

You are here, moving forward and changing the outcome for yourself, your children, and future generations. And in this moment, as you read these words, *you are safe*. You can drop your shoulders, breathe more deeply, and only listen to what resonates with you.

Your parents or caregivers and the past generations did their best with the information they had at any given time. They didn't have access to knowledge on how to heal deep subconscious trauma patterns. Their ability to heal and the methods to do so were not readily available to them.

You may have heard your father say.

*"My dad hit me, but I never hit you," or "It wasn't like this in my day; boys and men don't cry, simple as that".*

And in his mind, he broke the cycle. He moved forward, believing he was better than his father in how he managed his emotions. Or he blindly repeated the patterns with no awareness of their impact on you because the real pain within him is too great to acknowledge. He shut down and never spoke about it.

Hardwired into his neural pathways from childhood is how to survive physically and emotionally, which means shutting down emotions and avoiding them at all costs until they burst out unexpectedly in his reactions to you and those around him. Alternatively, he might have used coping strategies to dodge uncomfortable thoughts and feelings — like withdrawing completely and escaping into work so much that he was absent the entire time, or turning to alcohol to numb the feelings.

No matter what he did, it would result in an angry outburst, a clenched fist, silence, disconnection, or him avoiding eye contact when you cried.

Each generation responds by either repeating the pattern or trying to change it.

Or was it your mother, who yells when she feels unheard or goes quiet and pretends everything is okay, was once the child whose voice was dismissed, who felt disempowered or criticised. She was told to be quiet, to be good, and not to make a fuss.

She screams not to hurt you but because her pain is spilling over, finally demanding to be heard. She didn't know how to say,

*"I'm hurting"*, or "*What happened to me was not ok,*" so she said, *"Why can't you just listen to me!?"*

The louder the voice, the deeper the wound or the longer the silence, the deeper the wound. She was never taught how to be heard with softness and presence, so she learned to fight for love and connection the only way she knew how, through learnt behaviour and survival-based imprints.

This is not about justifying their behaviour. This is about witnessing the truth with open eyes and a kind heart. They carried unhealed emotional wounds just like you, without the tools to understand or heal them. They were also running the hardwired neural pathways and subconscious responses developed between birth and age 8.

This is how generational trauma repeats and is passed down through physical and emotional survival strategies, like family heirlooms.

And yet, you're here now, doing what they didn't know how to do.

Dropping your shoulders, breaking the pattern, breathing into your body, feeling the uncomfortable feelings, releasing them, and changing the outcome.

You are healing generational patterns by gaining awareness and breaking cycles that have repeated through your family lineage.

You might be the first in your family to speak the truth aloud.

To say, *"That hurts."*

To ask, *"What do I need now?"*

To choose a different voice — one of love, clarity, or personal power.

You're choosing not to carry or pass on what was never yours. It was never your fault or your responsibility to carry the emotional pain from generations gone by.

You are no longer a child repeating your parents' emotional trauma. Now you see the truth and can let it go once and for all.

You are the one who can honestly say *"This story ends with me."*

# Drop Your Shoulders® Method 6

## Connecting With Your Inner Child

- Always start with dropping your shoulders.
- Think of a childhood memory that causes you disharmony or an emotion or event that has been triggered in the present time. Write it down.
- Identify the emotion: is it anger, shame, guilt, grief?
- Feel into your body and observe areas of tension, tightness, or pain. Notice where the emotion is stored in your body. *Is it in your stomach, your chest, your throat, or your head?*
- Breathe into that area and focus on relaxing the muscles there.
- Now imagine yourself as a young child of any age that comes to mind.

- Visualise that little girl or boy standing in front of you. Imagine he/she is expressing this emotion, having a tantrum, screaming, yelling, or crying.

- Now tell this part of you, your inner child.

*"You are safe. You are not alone. It is not your fault. It is not your energy to carry."*

- Repeat the words if you need to; drop your shoulders even more and allow your body to relax.

- Now imagine this part of you, your inner child, calming down. Offering even more reassurance, tell him/her.

*"You are safe. I love you."*

- Focus on your physical body; notice your body is relaxing and softening even more.

- Imagine taking the image of your inner child into your heart centre, merging together as one, feeling calm in your body.

- Scan your body again and notice the areas of tension that have now dissolved, dissipated, or moved. This is not a one-time realisation but a practice, a recalibration.

You have now released suppressed emotional energy you have been carrying from your childhood, from your parents and caregivers. Emotions of anger, grief, shame, and guilt.

Notice in the coming weeks that you begin to speak to yourself in a new way, reclaiming the parts of you that were pushed away — not because they were wrong, but because the generations before you didn't know how to heal the past.

You are breaking generational cycles and patterns, and it begins here with you taking back your power.

## Reflection

Ask yourself now, "*Where in my body are these old patterns being stored?*

*What generational patterns am I repeating?*

Identify the patterns that are repetitive, the ones you automatically repeat. Write down the patterns you find yourself repeating now. Perhaps you people-please, overgive, seek approval, avoid conflict, suppress your emotions, fear rejection or abandonment, struggle to set boundaries, overthink every decision, or carry responsibility for everyone around you.

This isn't about blaming your parents and ancestors for their behaviour; it's about reclaiming your own nervous system.

**Truth.** The voice inside you was shaped by the experiences of your parents and caregivers. You now have the power to reframe and change these patterns, making your own choices. Speak to yourself with a new voice and choose love, compassion, and truth even when the fractured statements speak loudly in the background.

Your parents did the best they could with what they were taught. Their emotional tools were limited by what was passed down to them. This doesn't excuse the behaviour; however, it offers a new perspective on what you've been through.

When they told you to *"stop crying"*, it wasn't because your tears were wrong; it was because they didn't know how to sit with what your sadness stirred in them — memories of being told the same thing.

When they told you to *"be quiet,"* it wasn't because your voice was too loud; it was because your aliveness touched a part of them they had long silenced.

They didn't know how to handle your raw, genuine emotions because no one had taught them how to manage their own feelings.

They felt your emotions in their body — your sadness, anger, and frustration — and it awakened something unresolved within them. It was like a mirror, reflecting their own experiences, shaped by voices that weren't theirs, passing down generational patterns.

They were also shut down when they cried, punished for being angry, told to *"suck it up," "stop being a baby," or "just get over it".*

So when they saw those same emotions coming up in you, their own body tensed, trauma responses kicked in, and survival patterns and emotional triggers played out unconsciously. Their nervous system reacted instantly, not to you, but to their own emotional pain that had been buried long ago.

They were not intentionally rejecting you or your emotions; they were protecting themselves from feelings they didn't know how to handle, and this is how generational patterns keep going.

Unfelt pain doesn't disappear; unspoken fear doesn't vanish; it reverberates.

What isn't healed passes down through your DNA, nervous system, and pattern repetition. Sometimes, you don't recognise it as a generational pattern until you're the one repeating it.

I remember when my son was four. He used to make this groaning noise, a deep, guttural sound that would rise out of nowhere. And I found myself getting so uncomfortable. I didn't understand it at first. My whole body reacted, and I just wanted it to stop. I wanted to shut him down to make the noise go away.

Then I stopped. I dropped my shoulders and felt the uncomfortable sensation in my body as I interrupted my own survival response.

I asked myself, *why is this bothering me so much?* The answer came loud and clear: I had never been allowed to make that noise. I had never been allowed to express those deeper sounds, the ones that carry emotion when you don't have words for what you feel. Those parts of me had been silenced. Now they were being heard through him, and my body didn't know how to process it.

The groaning wasn't the problem; after all, it's just a sound. It was the emotion inside me that triggered deep sadness, anger, and frustration. One day, we were driving in the car, and he started the groaning — that unmistakable noise. This time, instead of feeling fear and discomfort and wanting to stop it, I joined in. I copied the noise.

At first, he looked at me and said, "Mum, stop!" Then he started laughing, and I started laughing too.

The groaning ceased; he never made that noise again, not because I silenced him but because I gave it a voice so it could be heard. I realised then that if I ever heard it again it wouldn't trigger me; I would hear it as just a sound, a groan. Something deep had shifted within me.

That moment revealed something very powerful. Unresolved trauma often feels uncomfortable in our bodies when our children express what we were never allowed to. Unresolved trauma triggers survival responses and the automatic instinct to shut it down, to correct it, to make it wrong, to make it go away, not because it's wrong, but because we carry unresolved pain from our own childhood.

So when you see or hear your children, or even other people's children, expressing emotions you were not permitted to feel, it brings unresolved trauma to the surface and triggers your own survival responses. Have you ever heard someone say in a restaurant, shopping centre, or public place, "*I wish they would just stop that child from crying*"? Often, it is not the child's emotions that are uncomfortable; it is the unresolved feelings those emotions awaken within us. A child's sadness, anger, fear, or distress can mirror the parts of ourselves that were silenced, dismissed, or told to stop feeling. In that moment, it is not just the child being triggered — your own nervous system is responding as well.

This is how the cycle and reactions of shutting down what is normal continue until you choose something different. Now you are empowered to decide what you will do in these moments.

Today, you begin the sacred act of choosing your own emotional truth and breaking the cycle of generational patterns.

Every time you stop and drop your shoulders, you change the frequency of your entire lineage. Now the voice inside you becomes your own. You then reframe and rewrite the fractured statements of your subconscious overthinking, creating new reference points and a new experience.

The journey doesn't end here. This is where you delve deeper into healing the past.

The voice in your head is only part of the process. Beneath the words, there is a backlog of emotions that your body has been storing, sometimes for years, sometimes for generations. You will now learn how to let this energy move, changing the fractured statements that have become your inner voice.

Practice the **Drop Your Shoulders® Method Overthinking** to identify and clear fractured statements still influencing you.

You will now explore how to release suppressed emotions. You will see emotion as energy, not as 'negative' or 'positive,' but as the energy of pain your body is holding.

**Emotion is Energy** that wants to leave the body; there is nothing to fear.

You can do this; it only requires a few minutes of practice each day.

# Drop Your Shoulders® Method 7

## Scribbling

Releasing physical, mental, and emotional pain, the Scribbling Method is designed to somatically release physical, mental, and emotional pain. It expands on theb **Drop Your Shoulders® Method**, which you will use most often.

- Find a blank sheet of paper and a pen or pencil that flows easily.

- Drop your shoulders, breathe into areas of tension or discomfort in your body, focusing on relaxing the muscles. Now start moving your hand on the paper, letting the pen scribble freely — without thinking, controlling, or judging.

- Visualise the discomfort in your body and imagine the pen giving it a voice through its movement from your arm, through your hand and fingers, onto the pape

- Let the lines be wild, chaotic, messy, circular, straight, long, or short. Allow the pen to move faster as the energy builds and slower when it softens.

- This is not a drawing, nor is it intended to make sense. Do this for about 2-5 minutes, until you feel calm in your body. As you relax those areas in your body while scribbling, notice how the tension, discomfort, or pain shifts, dissipates, or dissolves.
- When finished, you can safely burn the paper or rip it up and dispose of it, symbolising the permanent release of energy that has been stored in your body.

I recommend doing this daily initially, and more often if you feel triggered into physical, mental, or emotional pain and survival responses. Continue this practice whenever you are emotionally triggered and feel overwhelmed.

# What Is Scribbling?

Scribbling is a way to let your subconscious communicate without words. Scribbling is a practice, a practical tool you can use regularly to release physical, mental, or emotional pain and discomfort somatically through your body, giving your subconscious patterns a voice to release stored energy and reference points. Scribbling helps release physical, mental, or emotional pain from the body.

It is a direct pathway through the layers of stored energy, bypassing the rational and logical mind and reaching the deeper, wordless parts of your being. Your subconscious mind does not understand words; it understands patterns, symbols, and sensations. It holds the memories and emotions that your conscious mind has long forgotten. It stores the unspoken truths, buried grief, and unexpressed rage.

Every scribble is unique because you are unique, and your life experiences stored in your subconscious are unique to you. There is no right or wrong way to scribble. You are not creating art or trying to make sense of the marks on the page. You are allowing your body to express what it has been holding onto without judgement, analysis, or the need to explain it. The page simply becomes a safe place for your subconscious to release what no longer needs to be carried.

Scribbling lets you give these emotions a voice without reliving the story, creating a link between your body and mind so trapped energy can be released freely. It is a direct expression in the language of your subconscious mind.

## Why Scribbling Works

When you scribble, you are forming a physical, energetic, and neurological pathway that breaks the continuous patterns keeping you stuck.

You are giving your subconscious mind a way to express what it has been held in your body. You are allowing the energy to complete its cycle and find a way out.

You might notice that as you scribble, the tightness in your chest starts to loosen, the lump in your throat begins to soften or dissolve, and the ache in your stomach begins to change and fade. You may even find that the memory linked to the emotion starts to surface, or that an old belief or a fractured statement comes into your awareness. Notice that sometimes the energy just dissolves, dissipates, or moves, and that is enough.

## A Note On Resistance

You might feel a bit silly the first time you try this. Your mind might tell you it's a waste of time, that you're just doodling, or that it can't possibly make a difference.

That is the resistance of the conscious mind. It doesn't understand this process because it is not meant for the conscious mind. This is for the part of you that exists beneath language, beneath logic, beneath the polished surface of everyday life.

So when your feel the resistance rising in your body, breathe through it. Drop your shoulders, let your hand keep moving. Trust the process.

You are not only releasing your own energy but also clearing generations of unspoken pain, inherited fear, and unresolved grief. You are giving your body permission to complete what it was never allowed to finish. You are reclaiming your power that was frozen in time.

## After You Scribble

When you feel the energy shift, when your body feels lighter, and your breath deepens, stop. Look at the page covered in ink. Notice the lines, the patterns, and the movement. Observe if the feeling in your body has changed.

Notice when your shoulders have completely relaxed, when your jaw has unclenched, and when your heart feels a bit more open. Recognise that when you look at the scribble, your subconscious knows what has been spoken here and released.

Ground yourself. Imagine your feet are on the earth with roots extending from them, grounding you in your body and in the earth. You have just released something profound. You have just taken a step closer to personal freedom. As you burn your scribble pages safely, take a deep breath in and exhale, letting the energy leave from every cell in your body.

## When To Scribble.

Initially, set aside a few minutes each day to breathe into your body. Find areas of pain, tightness, or tension, and scribble until they dissipate, dissolve, or move. You don't need to activate a stress or trauma response to do this work. It is more important to make it a regular practice so that when something big happens, moving the energy out becomes a natural response.

All you need is a starting point. You can concentrate on a physical pain and scribble.

Or you might be overthinking, and your thoughts could be overwhelming. Drop your shoulders, connect with your thoughts and somatically feel into your body, and scribble. Or you might already be feeling an emotion; notice it in your body where it feels uncomfortable — an ache in your heart, a tightness in your throat, or heaviness on your shoulders. Ask yourself what the emotion is and scribble.

**This process takes up to 5 minutes or less each day.**

After a few weeks, you can continue daily, but you'll naturally start to recognise when it is helpful for you. I have integrated this process into my daily routines so that it remains accessible whenever I need it.

I often have a clipboard with paper and a pen by my bed and scribble on it at night if I wake up overthinking.

Some of my clients have adapted this process by downloading a whiteboard app on their phone. That way, you can scribble anytime you get triggered into a stress response. You can set reminders on your phone to practice this technique. You can also just imagine scribbling into thin air; however, having something tangible to burn and symbolise the energy that has been released and cleared works exceptionally well.

You will discover the method that suits you best.

## When It Doesn't Work

**Drop Your Shoulders® Method Scribbling and Woodchopping** (next chapter) does not work when your aim is simply to make the pain go away, especially when your aim is to reject, avoid, or run away from it.

This is a somatic process of feeling into the body, experiencing the uncomfortable feelings, and scribbling or woodchopping until the energy moves or dissipates.

Your focus is to somatically release the energy, tension, and tightness stored in your body, cells, and DNA.

Resistance is the cause of all suffering. If you find the process isn't working; Surrender**. Drop your shoulders,** letting go of the need to make the uncomfortable feeling go away. Focus on giving the energy a voice without judgment. Let the energy leave with acceptance. Be open to receiving the messages your body is giving you.

# Intention and Release

## Examples

Your scribbles will be different each time it reflects different emotions, memories, and energetic imprints within your body. Some scribbles may appear chaotic, dense, repetitive, circular, light, or flowing. The purpose is not to analyse or interpret the image but to allow the subconscious mind to express itself freely. These examples demonstrate how stored emotional energy can be expressed through patterns and movement on the page. Your scribble does not need to make sense to your conscious mind for the process to be effective. Trust in the process.

*Scribbling Creates Balance Within*

# Chapter Six

# Emotion Is Energy — I Take Back My Power!

As a whole, humanity is only just starting to develop emotionally. For centuries, our ancestors were functioning in physical survival. Their main focus was physical safety, shelter, food, and basic survival. The emotional body, the subtle layers of feeling and intuition, were not priorities. Life was tough, and emotions were often a liability, a distraction, a vulnerability.

Think of a hunter-gatherer trying to survive in the wild. Emotions like fear and anger were vital for immediate survival; they triggered the fight-or-flight response, sharpened the senses, and prepared the body for battle or escape. The same applied as we faced wars and the depression.

There was no time to sit and process grief, to talk about feelings, or to unpack childhood wounds. The focus was on physical survival, survival of the fittest.

Even as societies changed, emotional repression stayed the norm.

The stoic warriors. The tough settlers. The industrial workers. The soldiers of war. The men who were raised to be strong, silent, and providers. The women who were taught to nurture others while putting their own needs aside.

Is it any wonder we can now see generations of unprocessed emotion? Generations of shock and frozen energy. Generations of unspoken grief, rage, fear and pain.

And now, here you are — the one finally feeling it all.

The one breaking the cycle and reclaiming your right to feel.

This isn't just about working on yourself; you're healing ancestral pain. You may be the first in your family line to say, "*I will not pass this on; it ends here with me.*" You are the one thawing the frozen emotions of your ancestors and reawakening what it means to emotionally evolve.

Yes, it's intense. Yes, it can feel overwhelming. Yes, it can seem like too much.

Why? Because you're not just feeling and healing your own pain; you're also carrying the weight of generations and moving energy that has been stuck for decades, even centuries. You are transmuting trauma, not just for yourself, but for those who came before you and those who will come after you.

You live in a world that teaches you to fear your emotions and to reject anything that makes you or others feel uncomfortable. You were taught to aim only for the positive, to "*think happy thoughts,*" "*act in an acceptable way,*" and "*be your best at all times*".

From a young age, you were conditioned to view emotions through a distorted view of right and wrong. Anger was considered bad. Sadness was suppressed and shamed. Joy is acceptable but only in controlled amounts. You were taught to adapt, suppress, and override the waves of emotion.

Are you telling yourself — "*No. I don't want to be the one to heal their pain, especially when there's so much pain in my family and previous generations. It's not my responsibility, and I don't feel strong enough to do it.*"

*Are you feeling the resistance of how big that might seem? Yes/ No*

It is important to know that you do not need to feel all the emotions or relive past trauma to heal it. You just need to want to heal yourself, and the generational patterns will automatically resolve.

So if you find yourself overwhelmed by a wave of emotions, remember that the majority of the emotion you carry is not yours and is therefore easy to release. That emotion is energy that wants to leave the body, and if given the right opportunity to do so without attachment or resistance, it will exit gracefully.

You are reading this book because you are ready to break the cycle and patterns, ready to learn how to move forward and be empowered to live the life you have always wanted. A life where you find inner peace, both within and around you. You are already doing it, right now, as you read these pages, as you interrupt the stress response and expand on the **Drop Your Shoulders® Method.**

Imagine emotion as an energy wave, a frequency of energy that contains polarity — the rise and fall of vibrational frequency. The low (what we call 'negative') and the high (what we call 'positive') are part of the same vibrational frequency.

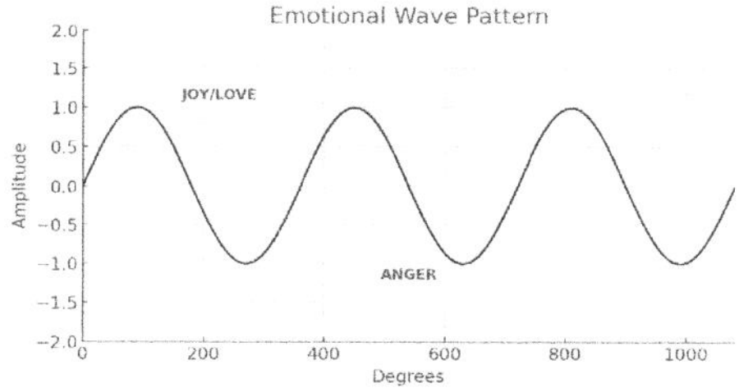


You can see in the wave above, at the highest point, 'love and joy', and at the lowest point of the wave, 'anger'.

When you reject a negative emotion, you eliminate the entire vibrational frequency, and as a result, you prevent yourself from experiencing the positive emotion.

You cut yourself off from the full experience of being alive, of being human, of evolving your emotional body. You cannot feel love and joy fully if you refuse to feel anger and grief. You cannot embody peace if you haven't met your rage.

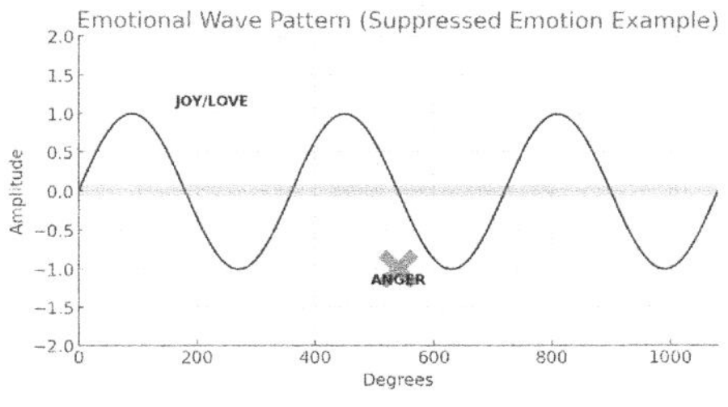

Now, you're striving for positive experiences and feelings without letting go of the negative ones. These negative emotions won't just vanish; **they need to be given a voice.** They are valid feelings that must be heard and expressed. Not in the way you think — that you have to relive all the pain — no, this is about giving the energy a chance to leave your body.

To reclaim your wholeness, you can now allow the energy of emotion to move freely. You can use the **Drop Your Shoulders® Method Scribbling** as a way to give your emotions a voice. All emotions are valid, including anger. When you release the energy of anger, you don't need to go into every specific experience or memory of anger and release each one separately; instead, you can release all of it at once with the intention to let go of the anger stored in your body.

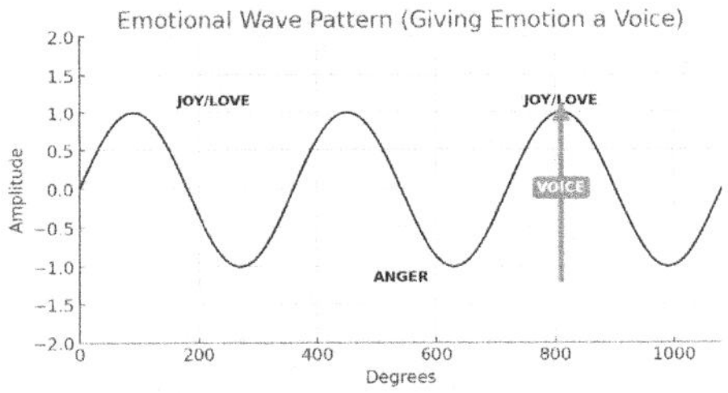


Emotion is a form of vibrational energy; it resides within your cells. When this energy is resisted — held back, denied, or repressed — it doesn't simply vanish. Instead, it contracts and solidifies, storing itself in your cells, tissues, and muscles. This contraction is what feels uncomfortable and activates fear and survival patterns.

## This is not just an emotional truth; it is a physical reality.

When you are empowered to release emotional energy physically, by feeling it in your body and allowing it to rise, move, and exit without resistance or attachment, you reclaim your personal power. Emotion is no longer outside of your control, and you are empowered to express and release all your feelings. Releasing the energy of emotion physically opens the energy pathways for physical, mental, and emotional healing.

# Drop Your Shoulders® Method 8

## Recognising Emotions And Releasing Blocked Energy

- Start with the **Drop Your Shoulders® Method Scribbling.**
- Drop into your body and notice areas of tension, tightness, contraction, or pain — *where is the emotion being held in your body? Is it in your stomach, your chest, your throat, or your head? Where is it being stored?*
- Drop your shoulders, breathe into your body, and focus on relaxing the muscles there.
- Now identify the emotion: *is it anger, grief, shame, or guilt?* Name it.
- Drop your shoulders even more, focus on relaxing the muscles.
- Now say,

*"I allow my body to let go of what I no longer need. I am safe."*

- Surrender and feel how different the moment becomes when you slow down enough to meet the emotion.

- Notice when you soften your body — *do you feel the tears come?* Don't block them; let them flow. If you start to feel overwhelmed, continue scribbling to give them a voice.

- Do this for approximately 2-5 minutes until you feel calm within your body.

- When you're finished, you can safely burn the piece of paper or rip it up and put it in the bin—letting go of the stored energy permanently, physically, mentally, and emotionally.

You are creating a pathway for vibrational energy of blocked and stored emotions to leave.

## Releasing, Expressing and Recalibrating Energy

Every emotion you feel is simply energy trying to leave your body. It's your body's way of releasing, expressing, and recalibrating. This natural flow of life moves through you, inviting you to feel, release, and transform. Your body is built to let go of energy — crying and shedding tears release energy, yelling and using your voice to release the energy, and so does movement.

Now, you are given another way to release this energy from your body through the **Drop Your Shoulders® Method: Recognising Emotion and Blocked Energy.**

You were not taught that emotions are energy, that tears are not weakness but a release valve, or that anger is not dangerous; it is the projection and voice of an unmet expectation or a crossed boundary. That grief is not depression; it's the space between what you longed for and what actually happened.

As a child, you knew this instinctively: you cried when you were hurt, screamed when you were scared. Your body trembled with fear and moved when you wanted to be heard. This wasn't just a "tantrum" or an "outburst" — it was your nervous system releasing energy and your body doing exactly what it was built to do.

Over time, you were taught to suppress this natural response. To hold it back and block it.

You learnt to suppress your natural energy flow and push it down, and, worse, you learnt not to feel. You began to believe that there are good and bad emotions, and that some emotions are unacceptable to express. This is when you started to apologise for crying or to hold your tongue and not speak your truth, not get angry. Then came the guilt, the guilt for feeling happier than those around you.

Amid all the chaos, you detached from the most powerful, natural, and instinctive way your body has to heal itself.

**Truth.** Emotion is not your enemy; it is the life force within you, calling for expression and showing how your body communicates, clears, and renews itself.

When you learn to listen, stop fearing, fighting, or resisting the energy of emotion, and instead start moving it and giving it a voice, everything begins to change.

Keep practising releasing emotion from your body using the **Drop Your Shoulders® Method Scribbling.**

The resistance you can sense at this point is fear.

Fear that if you open the floodgates, you will be overwhelmed, or if you let the anger out, it might consume you or lash out and hurt someone.

This fear is real. It's wired into your nervous system and woven into the very fabric of your being — it's a survival instinct.

Why? Because at some point in your life, allowing others to witness your emotions became dangerous, activating your fear of judgement, being shut down, or total abandonment.

Emotions are not dangerous; they are energy. It is the fear of emotion that is dangerous. Your survival responses are there for you to survive at all costs; when you are in fear, you will do whatever you need to do to survive. This means projecting outward onto others, often through controlling and manipulating behaviours.

## Reflection Point

*When you were a child, were you ever hit or punished for crying? Yes/No*

*Were you ever made to feel ashamed for being too sensitive? Yes/No*

*Were you ignored when you expressed your emotions? Yes/No*

*Did you learn that anger leads to violence, chaos, things being broken, or people leaving? Yes/No*

*Did you absorb the blows of anger, hiding in the corners, fearing that anger would become danger? Yes/No*

No matter your experience, your nervous system has made a decision. "*It's not safe for me to feel this.*" You learnt to suppress your emotions, thinking that your needs and your expression of emotion caused disharmony. You believed that if you could just be calmer, quieter, and smaller, you would be safe, so you shut down your emotions.

**Emotions are not the issue; suppressing your emotions causes blockages in your body's energy flow. This energy becomes trapped in your body.**

Energy that is pushed down does not vanish. It gathers. It tightens. It hardens. It becomes the persistent stress you carry, the tightness in your chest, the fire in your stomach, the knot in your throat.

It manifests as panic attacks, sleepless nights, unexplained back pain, emotional outbursts that feel larger than the moment, and a long list of disharmony affecting your life today. Physically, it shows up as migraines, a tight jaw, chronic fatigue, neck pain, shoulder pain, and the dull ache in your chest that you can't quite identify.

Emotions are not dangerous; you have simply never been shown how to release them safely.

Emotions aren't bigger than you; they are energy in your body that seeks to be released.

**Truth.** You were created to express emotion; before learning to hold back, you would cry, scream, and move to let it out. As a baby, you didn't hold back — you let the energy flow through your tiny body without hesitation, returning to a calm and peaceful state.

Your nervous system resets, energy clears, and the body relaxes. This is what your body was designed to do.

Through generational trauma patterns, you were taught to stop, hold your emotions in, ignore your body, and suppress the energy.

It was during these moments that the energy became heavy.

The human body isn't designed to store emotional energy; it has natural processes to release it.

Your muscles, fascia, and nervous system are built to move, shake, and release. To enable energy to flow freely through you, rather than stagnate.

When you suppress the natural process of releasing emotional energy, you're not avoiding the emotion; you're trapping it in your body. You're freezing it in time, creating a pressure cooker that will eventually explode, whether through physical illness, emotional breakdown, or psychological and emotional overwhelm.

**Truth.** You don't need to fear this process or be afraid of your own energy.

I invite you to let go of the story that your emotions are too much or too overwhelming. Release the belief that you need to control, suppress, or silence the waves of emotions rising within you, and remember that your body is designed to release energy.

Your body knows how to do this naturally. When you cry (tears release energy), yell (sound releases energy), and move (movement releases energy). Fear is your survival response, and this response can be interrupted.

Now, Activate the **Drop Your Shoulders® Method.**

The most powerful part is that you are now working somatically with your body and your subconscious to release suppressed emotions without having to relive the emotional pain repeatedly.

You already have the practical tool to release deep emotions from the body. You possess the power within you now to let go of emotions through the **Drop Your Shoulders® Method Scribbling** (to release physical, mental, and emotional pain).

This is the *most powerful* process I have practised to date for releasing deeply suppressed emotional trauma, generational patterns, and suppressed emotions. It can instantly change how you feel and free you from physical, mental, and emotional pain both somatically and subconsciously.

Scribbling is your new best friend, the one habit that can transform your life. I encourage you to make this a part of your daily routine.

Anger is one of the most dreaded emotions, so we'll start with anger first.

Anger is always the difference between your expectation versus your reality.

# Chapter Seven

# Expectation vs Reality = Your Anger

This is one of the most powerful truths you'll ever learn: Let me reiterate, anger is **always** the difference between your expectations and your reality. It's the moment that what you expected or believed should happen didn't occur or match your reality.

Think of the last time you felt angry; you first noticed an uncomfortable feeling in your stomach, tingling in your arms and legs, and tightness in your chest as this energy rose in your body.

Anger happens instantly within milliseconds — before you even have the chance to consciously count to 10, it's already taken hold. The sharp words spilling out of your mouth, your raised voice, a look of judgment, a criticism or complete withdrawal.

*Are you aware of what is happening in your body when you get angry? Yes/No*

*What are your expectations in that moment?*

*And what was your actual experience?*

The straightforward formula of Expectation versus Reality.

We live in a world full of *unrealistic* expectations.

Here are some real-life examples of this.

You expect your partner to understand you've had a tough day, but instead they talk over you or ask what's for dinner.

You expect your child to listen calmly when you ask, but instead, they yell or push back.

You expect your friend to support you, but they vanish when you need them most.

The anger builds in you, not just because of what they did or didn't do, or how they behaved. It happens because you needed or wanted something, but you didn't get it. The anger arises inside you because you created an expectation of what you wanted to happen, yet your reality didn't match that expectation.

It also stems from what you hoped for that was denied, what you believed 'should' have happened, but never came to fruition.

Apply the **Drop Your Shoulders® Method** now.

Feel the difference between your expectations and your reality.

It is impossible not to have expectations; however, it is possible to adjust your unrealistic expectations to realistic ones. Where your expectations align with your reality. We will now explore whether your expectations are realistic or not.

# Drop Your Shoulders® Method 9

## Identify Your Realistic And Unrealistic Expectations

- Drop your shoulders and start by asking yourself the following questions.

*What are my expectations?* Write down what makes you feel angry.

*Am I or are they capable of meeting this expectation physically, mentally and emotionally in the moment? Yes/No*

This is a new approach to understanding realistic abilities. Often, a person might be physically capable but not emotionally or mentally capable, or vice versa. They might be emotionally capable but not physically capable.

*Are you or are they able to manage their own emotions and take responsibility for them? Yes/No.*

For example, if the person is triggered into a stress or survival response, or feels fatigued in that moment, they are not capable of meeting your expectations. However, at other times, when they feel on top of the world and empowered, they are capable of meeting the same expectations. In this case, the answer is 'no'; they are not able to meet the expectation all the time, so it is an unrealistic expectation.

*Has the person ever behaved differently? Yes/No*

This is a really important question I ask my clients when they are angry and upset with their partner or child. Most of the time, the answer is NO; they've always been like that.

*"Where did I get the expectation that they would behave differently or that they are capable of behaving differently?"*

*Where did this expectation originate? Was it from your parents, movies, teachers, or religion?*

*Do you think 'movies or TV shows' contributed to creating your expectations for healthy relationships? Yes/No*

*Did you build an image based on 'hope' that one day you will wake up and the other person will behave differently? Yes/No*

*Have you ever clearly communicated your expectations to whoever you have placed them on? Yes/No*

*Do you just assume they know what your expectations are? Yes/No.*

This is another important question: often, you can feel angry towards someone who has no idea you're expecting something from them.

When you start this process honestly, if you receive just one 'no' when answering these questions, then you have identified an unrealistic expectation.

Begin to drop your shoulders to calm your nervous system

When you feel calm, rewrite the expectation to a realistic one. Write your realistic expectations now.

*My realistic expectations are...*

Now you have identified a realistic expectation. Notice how you feel when you think of the original unrealistic expectation.

*Do you feel lighter, calmer? Yes/ No*

*Do you feel less emotional charge in your body? Yes/No.*

Do this process as often as you can, especially when you start to feel the uncomfortable sensation in your body — before your survival responses are activated and you find yourself yelling or withdrawing. When you notice the sensation in your body, it usually starts with an uncomfortable feeling in your stomach. This is the first sign that you are feeling angry, frustrated, or annoyed. Ask yourself,

*"What is my expectation? Is this a realistic expectation?"*

Once you have identified if the expectation is realistic or unrealistic, you can release the energy of anger from your body, and when you are ready, you can create a new expectation.

## Now start the Drop Your Shoulders® Method Scribbling

Scribbling releases suppressed energy of anger, bypasses the story, and allows the energy to leave the body. Scribbling is a process that gives anger a voice; it's not just scribbling on a piece of paper, but a subconscious pattern. The subconscious does not use words; your anger and pain are held in patterns. Scribbling traces the pathway of anger back to its original point, allowing it to be seen and heard in ways that the conscious mind cannot comprehend or understand.

It may feel odd at first to scribble, but stay with it — the process works and is by far the best tool you will ever learn to release emotional energy from the body instantly. Every time you scribble, you are releasing the pain of past anger, grief, frustration, sadness, guilt, and shame from your body — physically, mentally, and emotionally — without having to revisit or relive all the previous pain and trauma. Scribbling only takes about 5-10 minutes to clear.

It's like when a child screams for five minutes, letting out all their anger and rage, and then feels free to laugh for the next five minutes. It's a process of giving your emotions a voice without delving into the story or the emotional pain. Sometimes tears and memories may surface while you're scribbling; aim to notice them with curiosity (that must be what this is about) and let them go.

Sometimes scribbling just isn't enough to clear the intense feelings of anger in your body.

This is when the anger, rage, or deep grief won't be softened through conscious understanding or the **Drop Your Shoulders® Method Scribbling** alone.

Even after scribbling and acknowledging the unrealistic expectations, you still feel it in your body — the sense of injustice deep within your cells. No matter what you do, you're still angry. You can't find the neural pathway to acceptance or understanding that these expectations are unrealistic. This is where movement is needed to release blocked energy through the **Drop Your Shoulders® Method Woodchopping** to relieve long-term or intense anger.

# Drop Your Shoulders® Method 10

## Woodchopping For Anger Release

This practice is used when there is injustice or unfairness, or when your anger originates from being abused either in childhood or as an adult. This powerful technique releases years and lifetimes of anger, aiming to free all anger from the body.

- Begin to drop your shoulders to calm your nervous system.

- With intention, focus on releasing the frequency of the energy of anger. You do not need to identify or analyse the 1000 experiences of anger or rage; you only need the intention to release the frequency of anger from your body.

- Find a spot in nature where you can move freely, ideally somewhere you won't feel self-conscious or restricted. If you don't have access to nature or an open space, you can do this in your backyard or garage. Just ensure you are physically safe and have enough room to move.

- Stand with your feet slightly apart and firmly grounded on the earth. Visualise roots like tree roots extending from your feet into the ground, anchoring you. Take a moment to connect with your surroundings. Feel the earth beneath your feet. Breathe deeply into your stomach. Drop your shoulders. Remind yourself that you are safe and present in this moment.

- Set Your Intention – Think of something that has made you feel angry.

- Place both hands on your stomach and say:

*"I take back my power. I release all anger from my body. This is my free will and choice."*

- **Do this three times in a row.** Take a deep breath in, and as you breathe in, bring the energy up from your stomach while raising your arms high above your head.

- On the exhale, release all the energy with a primal, guttural sound (scream, growl, roar) as you bring your arms down forcefully in front of you towards the ground, as if chopping wood, to release the stored anger in your body. Use your whole body and let the sound come from your stomach. If you let the sound come from your throat, you might hurt your throat; the energy must come from your stomach. You will feel energy start to move through your arms, legs, feet, lips, and the top of your head. You will notice this energy moving and leaving your body as tingling sensations.

- Tingling is experienced in the hands, feet, mouth, top of your head, and all the pathways where energy flows. Don't be scared of the tingling; it won't hurt you. It's just the energy leaving. When you feel it for the first time, it's a new sensation and can seem a bit scary, out of control or overwhelming.

- Drop your shoulders, calm your nervous system, and let the energy leave.

- You can place your hands on the ground or earth; this will help this energy leave your body. If there have been a lot of suppressed emotions, the first time might feel intense, with tingling all over the body. If this happens, you can lie on the earth or have a shower and let the water wash it away, allowing it to leave the body.

- As the energy of anger leaves and the tingling subsides, you might feel the need to cry; allow the tears to flow. As you allow the energy to leave without trying to block, control, or analyse it, it will.

- Don't let this stop you from exploring the 'woodchopping' exercise. Most people will not need to cry; the movement itself allows the energy of grief to leave the body.

- If there is grief present, I suggest you 'cry' in the shower. This helps release the energy and creates a sense of safety and privacy. Limit it to 5–10 minutes before getting out, with the intention of saying:

*"I allow the energy of grief to leave my body."*

- Again, drop your shoulders and focus on calming your nervous system. Say aloud:

*"I am safe. I am free. I am no longer carrying what is not mine."*

- Breathe deeply, shake out your arms and legs, and feel the lightness within you.

This is not a one-time practice; it's something you can return to again and again whenever you feel the weight of anger rising within you. You don't need to feel angry to do this; you just need to recognise that anger is in your body and set the intention for it to leave.

This is when woodchopping becomes part of your practice.

When you have had a bad day at work or feel anger and rage rising while driving home, and someone cuts in front of you, take a moment to find a park, or you can do a version of this in the car before you get home. This is the time you are empowered to express your anger without taking it home or projecting it onto your loved ones. This is when you are in control of your anger and can choose to release it safely. Anger is no longer something that happens to you; it's something you give a voice to and allow the energy to be released.

You are not just releasing this for yourself; you are clearing the path for those who come after you, for your children. You are clearing the way to be yourself and enjoy the rest of your day. Use the **Drop Your Shoulders® Method Woodchopping** to release anger as a daily or weekly practice.

# Drop Your Shoulders® Method II

## How To Release Anger In The Car

- Start dropping your shoulders to calm your nervous system.
- Pull over to the side of the road. As you sit in the driver's seat, take a deep breath and notice the weight of the seat beneath you, the steering wheel in your hands, and the solidity of the car around you. This is your space. You are safe here. You are supported. No one is watching, and you can take this moment for yourself.
- With intention, focus on releasing the frequency of the energy of anger. You do not need to identify or analyse the 1000 experiences of anger or rage; you only need the intention to release the frequency of anger from your body.
- Set Your Intention – Think of something that has made you feel angry.

- Place both hands on your stomach and say:

*"I take back my power. I release all anger from my body. This is my free will and choice."*

- Grip the steering wheel tightly. Feel the tension in your hands, forearms, and shoulders. Imagine all the anger and suppressed energy from your day rising up from your stomach into your chest, into your throat, and into your arms. Pull your hands back and flick them forward, releasing that energy with a deep, guttural roar or scream. If you're worried about someone hearing you, turn up the music and let the sound blend in — don't hold back. Let the sound come from your stomach, not just your throat. You are releasing the anger from your body.

- Tingling is experienced in the hands, feet, mouth, top of your head, and all the pathways where energy flows. Don't be scared of the tingling; it won't hurt you. It's just the energy leaving. When you feel it for the first time, it's a new sensation and can seem a bit scary and out of control.

- Drop your shoulders, calm your nervous system, and let the energy leave.

- Say aloud:

*"I am safe. I am free. I am no longer carrying what is not mine."*

- When you feel calm, start driving again, roll down the windows, and let the wind carry away the last remnants of energy. Feel what it's like to calm your body and drop your shoulders.

Beneath anger lies grief over what the expectation means to you.

We have explored the energy of anger and the importance of creating realistic expectations. Anger protects grief. Grief is what that expectation means to you. It is the sadness that arises when you realise something you hoped for, needed, or believed would happen did not. The grief may be about a relationship, a loss, a childhood experience, a dream that never came to fruition, or the realisation that someone was unable to give you what you needed. Grief begins when you accept what is, rather than holding on to what you wished could have been.

Your anger has been shielding this grief all these years. The deep sadness of realising the person you gave everything to could never meet you halfway or give you what you needed.

The emotional pain of recognising that you held on to the potential of a relationship longer than the reality.

In this moment, something sacred is taking place.

You get to rewrite the expectation, accept the truth you've always known, and in this moment, reclaim your power.

Feel into your body now and say;

*"This was my expectation...(name it)."*

Then state, "*It was an unrealistic expectation.*"

This is the moment when the cycle of anger begins to soften. And anger that once consumed you or the anger that was sitting beneath the surface starts to fade.

This is a very powerful process, and it's important to understand that this same process applies to the expectations you place on yourself.

Personally, I expected to work all day, see five clients, pick up my son from school, take him to after-school activities, cook dinner, get him to bed, and not feel fatigued or angry by the end of the day.

It was unrealistic to think I wouldn't be exhausted despite having no time for myself, and wouldn't feel guilty about rushing my son to bed to squeeze in half an hour for myself.

A kinder, more realistic approach is to see three clients, take some time for a walk or a 20-minute meditation, pick up my son from school, be present with him, give him the energy and love he deserves, cook dinner together, and share the best part of our day at bedtime.

This is where your freedom begins when you understand you can let go of the unrealistic expectations you've created. Dissolve the hidden contracts and silent agreements you never consented to. You can let go of survival patterns that kept you trapped in the cycle of anger. You start to release others from roles they were never capable of fulfilling and, more importantly, you begin to release yourself from unrealistic expectations that are never achievable and only set you up to fail.

Creating realistic expectations and a different outcome.

Here are some more examples;

You expect your partner to do the gardening.

*Where does this expectation come from? Gender roles imposed on you from society structures? The roles your parents played, TV, Movies, etc?*

*Have you asked any questions or just told him/her to do it? If you have not communicated clearly, you can now ask;*

*Do you enjoy...ie. gardening? Yes/No*

*Would you like to accept this responsibility? Yes/No*

Keeping in mind this is your expectation, not theirs.

*What meaning have you attached to the expectation? What does it mean to you when your partner takes care of the gardening?* For example, *"when my partner does the gardening, I feel supported, loved, and cared for."*

Deciding whether your expectations are realistic or not is one of the most empowering things you can do for yourself. Changing how you create your expectations can help you set expectations that align with your reality.

Often, what we call expectations are actually assumptions. Instead of assuming, ask a question:

*"How are you feeling? Are you able to take care of the garden this week?"*

The answer could be,

*"No, I am not feeling well"* or *"I have a lot of work to do."*

You can then ask additional questions, such as;
*"Can you clarify when you will be able to complete this task?"* to expand your communication and gain clarity.

## When Your Expectation Is Linked To A Core Wound Of Grief And Deep Sadness.

In my experience, I expected my parents to keep me safe, emotionally and physically, but my reality was that I was not safe.

For years, I carried a lot of anger towards my parents. I was afraid of my own anger because it shielded the deep grief within me that became layered, ranging from not feeling safe to feeling unloved or like I didn't belong.

This anger then deepens with feelings of injustice and unfairness. So, it's not just anger; it now intertwines with profound grief and sadness rooted in my core belief system, fractured statements from childhood that *"no one loves me, I am not loved."* These subconscious fractured statements would break my heart every day. This alone caused me great suffering and ongoing emotional pain.

Simply recognising that my parents were trapped in a constant state of survival and emotional chaos, and that they couldn't offer a safe environment because they didn't feel safe within themselves, wasn't enough to achieve a new understanding that would allow me to heal. I had to truly believe they were unable to provide a safe environment before I was born, let alone after I was born.

There was already domestic violence before I was born. As the youngest of five children, I needed to understand the physical, mental, and emotional pressures they carried without the tools to manage their survival responses, which were hardwired through generational patterns of childhood trauma. I began to accept that they did the best they could. Accepting this was challenging because it unlocked the deep grief that my internal anger had been protecting — the deep sadness of not feeling safe and loved as a child.

So, through embodied experience and the need to release anger, the **Drop Your Shoulders® Method Woodchopping** to release anger was developed. This technique helped me let go of years of stored anger that had been suppressed and held in my body. It was used alongside other techniques, including the **Drop Your Shoulders® Methods of Scribbling, Active Affirmations,** and **Overthinking processes.**

I practised these methods daily or weekly, working somatically and energetically with my body. Each time I released, I felt lighter, clearer, and more present. Over time, I started to notice that the changes became permanent. I was able to calm my nervous system in just a few minutes, and negative beliefs and self-talk vanished, replaced with positive, active affirmations that changed my neural pathways. My ability to feel calm in my body increased, with longer periods where I was now naturally responding differently.

The **Drop Your Shoulders® Method** became an automatic response at the first sign of being triggered into a survival response or old patterns. I was able to change how I felt within minutes and return to internal balance. I wasn't bypassing my emotional pain; I was changing the outcome and how I felt each moment throughout the day. I was discovering my own truth, rewiring my nervous system, and shifting my neural pathways from survival responses to responding from a place of inner peace.

As you can see, there are both large and small expectations; however, the first step is to identify them.

At the first physical sign of feeling annoyed, frustrated, or angry. Ask yourself,

*"Is this a realistic expectation?"*

Work through the questions of the **Drop Your Shoulders® Method: Identify Your Realistic and Unrealistic Expectations.**

When your answer is no to any of the questions, it is an unrealistic expectation. Take the time to create realistic expectations for yourself and others. Take responsibility for your own expectations and anger and release the energy of anger from your body. Remember that anger protects grief; making room for grief is an important part of the process. Grief is what the expectation meant to you. We will explore grief in future chapters.

If this feels overwhelming, rest assured, this is a simple practice, and this feeling leaves quickly.

I believe that if I can do this, so can you.

Through these simple daily practices, the **Drop Your Shoulders® Methods** will enhance your life. They address the generational patterns of anger and emotional trauma passed down to you, as well as unmet needs for love and safety.

## Chapter Eight

# The Imprint Of Generational Anger

We will now explore where anger originates, not only in you but also through your generational patterns.

Anger isn't just an emotion; it's a generational imprint, a force inherited through bloodlines, encoded in your very cells. It's the clenched jaw of a father who never felt seen, the sharp tone of a mother who felt trapped, the explosive rage of a grandfather who returned from war. It's the unspoken, the unprocessed, the unresolved energy that represents all their unrealistic expectations and grief transferred onto you.

In the past, your family's anger wasn't just felt; it was wielded as a tool of control. It served to establish power within families.

*Did your father raise his voice or become violent to silence the household? Yes/No*

*Did your father use silence to build unspoken tension that was felt deep inside? Yes/No*

*Did your mother withhold affection to regain control when she felt overwhelmed? Yes/No.*

*Did your grandfather's strict discipline create a tight knot in the stories, "You would never get away with that in my day"? Yes/No*

No matter how it was expressed for generations, physical punishment was seen as normal, even essential. Hitting children was regarded as a way to teach discipline, to 'keep them in line,' and to prepare them for the harsh world they would soon face.

Unknowingly, it was this mindset and their way of projecting their anger that made the world harsh. It's not something you need to prepare for; you are already living it through your parents, grandparents, and caregivers.

*Do you remember your grandparents or parents talking about being hit with a ruler at school as a form of punishment? Yes/ No*

Punishment was justified as love, as care, as the only way to raise strong, resilient children. But in reality, it was control. It was an attempt to impose order on chaos, to silence the unpredictable nature of a child's emotions, and to mute the mirrors that reflected their own unresolved rage and anger.

What was often handed down wasn't just acts of violence but the underlying belief systems that viewed control as essential for survival. That power must be preserved at all costs. That a child's spirit had to be broken to mould an obedient, 'respectful' adult. Confusion happens when you, as a child, grew up in an environment where love is mingled with abuse or violence. The same parent or caregiver who provides food and shelter is also the one who causes pain. The message becomes unclear, and you can begin to associate love with control, abuse, and violence. As a way of showing affection or feeling loved.

*Have you heard the story of a boy being mean to a girl he really likes, or vice versa? Yes/No*

*Can you identify the distortion in this pattern? Yes/No*

*Have you formed distorted beliefs about love and safety in your own life? Yes/No*

**Truth.** Love is not control, abuse, or violence. Love is kind, gentle, and nurturing. Confusion happens because these distorted beliefs become our main ways of loving. The nervous system learns to link love with fear, care with pain, and connection with control. Growing up, you never know when the next outburst or prolonged silent treatment will come, so you're always on edge, constantly hyper-vigilant, ready to brace for impact. You're wired into patterns of physical and emotional survival. This leads to a split in your identity: one part that seeks love and connection, and another that fights to protect itself.

This connects to the origin of emotional survival patterns: the shock in the nervous system that we discussed in the first chapter — the moment you, as a child, felt physically or emotionally unsafe, unworthy, or unseen. This frozen energy blocks the flow of energy, and your default and emotional survival patterns are formed in your subconscious.

Anger is often the first response after a shock. It functions as the body's way of saying, *"This is not okay. This is a violation. This is dangerous."* When anger is met with punishment, shame, or further abuse or violence, it doesn't simply fade away; it becomes trapped. It transforms into a cycle — an emotional survival pattern that repeats itself, triggered by anything that vaguely recalls the original wound.

Imagine your nervous system learnt that showing anger resulted in punishment. As a result, you might have learnt to suppress it and push it down, which can later turn into depression, resentment, or passive-aggressive behaviours. Alternatively, you may have learnt to explode with rage, mirroring the very behaviours you vowed never to repeat, feeling the same shame your parents felt but never spoke about. This forms an emotional survival pattern — feeling trapped, disempowered to change it, always reacting, always on edge.

Anger is a powerful force for change; its opposite is passion. It is the fire that can burn away what no longer serves you, the energy that rises when a boundary has been crossed, or the wake-up call that sparks transformation. It is the fire that highlights injustice and becomes a force for change. It is an essential part of being human.

I grew up witnessing this firsthand. I have memories of my father's violent outbursts towards my mother, how he would erupt in an instant, with rage spilling out uncontrollably, the fear it invoked in my young body, and the shock that froze my nervous system. These moments of violence shaped my earliest understanding of anger and influenced how I saw the world — whether it was a safe or unsafe place. I remember the intensity and the tension in the air; I felt it in my body, frozen in fear.

As a child, I lacked the words to describe the fear I felt in every cell of my body. I didn't understand that my father's anger wasn't about me or even my mother. It was an inherited storm, a generational force passed down through his bloodline. A rage he probably never understood himself, having left home at fourteen to escape whatever cycles he was already caught up in, only to repeat them in his own family.

This is where I hear my clients say, *"I'm not like my dad; he used to beat me, and I do not hit my children, but he still hit his wife, not his children,"* or the next evolution, *"I'm not like my dad; I don't hit my children or my wife."* However, the anger and rage are still expressed in silence, avoidance, judgments, looks, and criticisms that seem to come from nowhere. The anger remains, represented in more controlled and socially acceptable ways, but it is still beneath the surface.

I now see that my father was a free spirit, a man trapped in a world with little freedom, burdened with the responsibilities of five children, working from his early teens to provide for a family he was not emotionally or mentally ready for. He bore the weight of expectations, financial stress, and a life that must have sometimes felt like a cage. His rage wasn't a personality trait; it was a survival response, a desperate attempt to regain control in a life that felt out of control.

None of this justifies his violence, but it provides context. It uncovers the layers beneath his anger, the places where his spirit was fractured, and where he felt trapped and restricted. I don't know the details of his upbringing or the emotional wounds he carried, but I can feel the cycles of it in my own body — my fiery nature, the protection of injustice, the suppressed grief, the unspoken fear, and the disempowerment.

Then there was my mother, who carried her own responses for survival. When she left him, being the youngest, I was separated from all my family members, and it was just me and her. The anger didn't simply disappear; it transformed. Now expressed through her, it became sharper, more withdrawn, and often aimed at me in ways that felt unfair and unpredictable.

Her survival mechanisms, shaped by her own trauma, meant she also couldn't hold me or keep me completely safe. She had her own wounds, fears, and struggles with low self-esteem and insecurities, unable to manage her emotional survival patterns.

I sensed her anger in the way she would snap at small things, the sharpness in her tone, and the way her body would stiffen when I needed comfort. The substance abuse and her inability to look after herself or make decisions to protect me from harm. It was as though her nervous system had become so wired for survival that there was no space left for tenderness, softness, or the nurturing and protection I so deeply craved and needed.

This captures the deep confusion of growing up in a chaotic emotional environment. You don't just learn to fear others' anger; you internalise it. You absorb it, making it part of your nervous system, cellular memory, and subconscious patterns. It becomes uncontrollable emotional survival responses that trap you, causing you to repeat the same reactions you once feared, turning into the very thing you promised yourself you'd never become.

It took me years to realise that my own anger wasn't entirely my own. It was the unspoken fury of generations, built up from years of violence and abuse — physical, mental, emotional, and sexual. I carried these patterns and reacted accordingly.

These patterns are deeply rooted in my bloodline, so they don't end there. My reaction to anger and how I express it are ingrained in my DNA and cells. Although I can now manage and release the energy of anger using the **Drop Your Shoulders® Methods, Scribbling and Woodchopping,** these patterns still activate from time to time. I learnt to express myself in safe, conscious ways, and I began to find inner peace.

My default patterns still activate when I'm pushed too hard. This is part of being human and isn't something that warrants punishment.

These are the moments when simply dropping my shoulders can interrupt my emotional survival response; this is when I need love and compassion the most. At those times, I remind myself that love is kind, gentle, and nurturing.

I remember hosting a men's retreat and being asked, *'When my partner yells at me, is she seeking to punish and control me?'* The answer is no. It is actually the opposite. Your partner feels so disempowered in these moments, backed into a corner, which triggers their emotional survival patterns. If he/she does not yell, they will withdraw, which is an equally violent response. I have clients say to me that silence is so painful, they feel like they are being stabbed with anger.

I explained to the group that when this happens, instead of seeing the person you love yelling at you and responding defensively or matching their anger, see that the person before you is in pain and feels disempowered. Meet them with love and kindness. In this moment, you can interrupt the emotional survival response and help them create a new reference point. Having compassion for yourself and others in these moments and offering love and kindness is the path to healing the past.

**Truth.** Beneath the projection of anger, there exists disempowerment — disempowerment to alter the outcome, disempowerment to feel physically or emotionally safe within or without.

## The Deeper Truth About Anger.

Anger is not inherently destructive. It is a response to a boundary that has been crossed, a need that has been ignored, or a truth that has been silenced. When expressed with awareness, it can be a powerful force for healing, transformation, and the ability to choose a different response.

Anger is one of the most misunderstood and suppressed emotions in the human experience. In your experience;

*Do you believe anger is dangerous? Yes/No*

*Does it damage relationships? Yes/No*

*Does anger lead to violence and chaos? Yes/No*

*Do you feel deep anger within yourself that has no origin? Yes/ No*

*Has anger become a forbidden emotion? Yes/No.*

*Have you been taught to fear it, to suppress it, to push it down into the depths of your body where it waits to be expressed? Yes/No*

Often people say they are not angry, do not get angry. There is not a human being that does not have unmet expectations. Hiding anger and pretending it's not there, that it will somehow go away. Anger cannot be suppressed; it leaks out and is projected outward onto others. Anger cannot be contained. You now have two powerful methods for releasing anger without projecting or causing harm to another person or yourself.

The **Drop Your Shoulders® Methods, Scribbling and Woodchopping,** are powerful techniques for releasing anger energy from your body.

Using these tools, you're not just breaking a pattern. You're releasing the frozen energy blocks in your nervous system. You're reclaiming parts of yourself that were silenced, shamed, or suppressed. You're freeing yourself from the trapped energy that is protecting your grief and sadness. From all the times you felt deeply hurt.

This is where genuine change starts. Now, let's explore another form of anger — a more profound anger that extends across time and space.

## The Deeper Roots Of Anger And A New Perspective

Anger doesn't just reside in an individual's body or lifetime memory. It moves through entire cultures, bloodlines, and families. It is carried in the stories we inherit, the behaviours we witness, and the survival patterns passed from one generation to the next. It is not just an emotion; it is a frequency of energy that can be felt collectively as well as individually.

This kind of anger has deep roots. It dates back to the first time a boundary was crossed, a voice was silenced, or a person or community was stripped of their freedom, culture, language, or way of life. Beneath much of this anger sits grief — grief that was never fully acknowledged, expressed, or released.

Science is only beginning to recognise what many indigenous cultures have understood for centuries: trauma is not only psychological. It affects the body, the nervous system, our relationships, and how we move through the world. Its effects can continue across generations through learned behaviours, family conditioning, and inherited survival patterns.

For many cultures, this anger is ancestral. Beneath the anger lies grief — the grief of stolen land, broken treaties, forced assimilation, and the loss of language, ceremony, and sacred rites of passage. It is also the grief of losing connection to country, community, ancestry, and belonging.

This isn't just about your personal trauma. It is also about the pain carried by families, communities, and cultures. The experiences may be different, but the emotional wounds often echo through generations until someone becomes conscious of them and chooses to heal.

This is about both the oppressed and the oppressors. Trauma leaves patterns on everyone it touches. Some experienced powerlessness, while others learned to suppress empathy, disconnect from their emotions, and dominate in order to survive. The pain may look different, but the survival patterns continue until someone interrupts the cycle.

When you feel that deep anger rise within you — the anger that feels bigger than the moment, the injustice, the unfairness, the fire that seems to come from nowhere — recognise that it may not be entirely about what is happening right now. Sometimes you are feeling the accumulated weight of old wounds, inherited beliefs, and unresolved grief.

This anger is not something to fear or suppress. It is information. It is showing you where pain still exists and where healing is asking to occur. You now have the opportunity to acknowledge it, feel it, and express it in a way that creates change rather than continuing the cycle.

Apply the Drop Your Shoulders® Method and relax your body.

Feel deeply into your body and notice any anger, injustice, or unfairness that arises. You do not need to analyse it or know exactly where it came from. Simply acknowledge what is present. As you release the energy of anger and grief, you are not only changing your own experience; you are also creating a new pattern for the generations that follow.

**Truth.** Ancestral anger and grief were never yours to carry alone.

Take action today; start with the **Drop Your Shoulders® Method Scribbling or Woodchopping.**

# Evolution Of Emotional Awareness

It is important to recognise that you are not your ancestors. Their lives, struggles, and survival experiences were very different from your own. Yes, you carry their bloodline, stories, beliefs, and survival patterns, but their life is not your life.

Many people carry anger, grief, fear, and emotional pain that feels bigger than their own experiences. Sometimes these feelings are connected to patterns that have been passed down through generations.

This is not just a biological inheritance; it is also an energetic one. It exists in your subconscious, your cells, and the frequency of your body.

## When Will It stop?

It stops when you become aware of the pattern and choose something different.

**Truth.** You are not here to carry the emotional burden of previous generations. You are here to learn from it, heal what is yours, and stop passing the pain forward.

## Survival And Emotional Evolution

Consider this. Previous generations were primarily focused on physical survival. Food, shelter, safety, and protection came first. There was little understanding of emotional wellbeing, childhood trauma, nervous system regulation, or the long-term impact of emotional pain.

This does not make their suffering any less real. It simply offers a different perspective.

Many people were doing the best they could with the awareness, knowledge, and resources available to them at the time. Their emotional pain was often expressed through anger, withdrawal, punishment, control, violence, or emotional disconnection because they did not know another way.

The emotions they could not process were often stored in the body and expressed through survival responses such as Fight, Flight, or Freeze. These patterns continue to surface in families today.

## Why Are You Carrying Such Deep Pain?

When you hear stories from previous generations, it is natural to feel sadness, grief, anger, or injustice. Your emotional body recognises suffering in a way that many of your ancestors may never have been taught to recognise within themselves.

As humanity continues to evolve, so does emotional awareness. Today, you have access to information, tools, and understandings that previous generations simply did not have.

The difference is that you now have the opportunity to recognise these patterns, understand them, and choose something different.

I often ask these questions:

*Why would an adult hurt a child when they were also physically and emotionally hurt as a child?*

*How is it possible to have so little compassion for a child's suffering when they have experienced similar suffering themselves?*

The answer often lies in emotional disconnection. Many people simply did not understand the long-term emotional effects that childhood pain and trauma can carry into adulthood.

## The Evolving Emotional Body

The evolving emotional body is the ability to feel, process, and let go of emotional energy. It understands the difference between physical and emotional pain, and that all pain is energy that needs to be expressed and released.

The emotional body is your ability to feel, express, and process energy; it forms part of your human evolution. You are not just a thinking mind or a physical body. You are an emotional being, and like every aspect of human development, the emotional body has had to evolve. Currently, this evolution is still in its early stages; it has not been widely supported or fully understood.

We still believe that talk therapy is the best way to heal from trauma when it targets the part of the brain (conscious mind) responsible for short-term thinking, planning, and analysing. Talk therapy has its purpose and can be helpful in specific situations involving thought processes, especially when it aligns with the experience of being seen and heard. The **Drop Your Shoulders® Methods** complement existing mental health plans and other healing modalities.

When trying to access trauma patterns, memories and processes activated in the subconscious mind, it is logical to conclude that healing from any childhood or past trauma requires meeting it in the part of the brain and body where it is active — in the subconscious and nervous system.

Your subconscious influences how you feel and respond to specific situations, drawing on your long-term memory. The nervous system is the system that activates physical and emotional responses. Depending on the memory or reference point your subconscious connects to, it determines whether your response in the nervous system is positive or negative, based on your own long-term memories and reference points from similar situations and events you have previously experienced.

The physical feeling in your body — whether light, happy, joyful, or heavy, uncomfortable, anxious — is the physical experience that depends on which hormones have automatically been released into your bloodstream.

There was a time when survival meant staying physically alive. Food. Shelter. Protection from the elements, war, and harm. In that world, there was limited time for grief. There was only *"get on with it"* to survive, so the body learned to suppress emotional energy and store it in your cells.

As this energy built up in the body, the nervous system began to awaken to more than just physical danger. Once physical danger is no longer the major priority. It started to recognise emotional threats such as disconnection, rejection, and abandonment as unsafe and developed emotional survival responses.

Safety was no longer only about physical safety; it now extended to emotional safety and the need to be loved, heard, and seen.

The human emotional body began to evolve; however, a gap remains.

The energy of emotion inside the body had nowhere to go and couldn't be fully released. Depending on how open your ancestors, parents, and caregivers were in their personal learning and growth, they didn't know what to do with this energy or how to release it from their own bodies.

Instead, it came out in bursts of anger, rage, withdrawal, grief, and disharmony, projected outward onto others, including you. The intensity of the emotion was often misunderstood.

When something is misunderstood, it becomes feared. When fear arises, it is usually either suppressed or projected outward.

By nature, as a child, you are evolving and emotionally expressive. You scream when frustrated, cry when hurt. You radiate joy, laughter, terror, anger, and grief; raw, unfiltered, unashamed emotions are on display.

In front of an evolving emotional body in its infancy, a parent, a teacher, or a system that does not yet know how to express their own emotions or has not learned how to release energy or to feel safe within themselves on an emotional level, the child's natural expression of emotions becomes a threat to the adult. Something devastating happens. It stirs the suppressed emotional energy inside them, and this energy leaks out, often without their control or complete understanding.

The adult projects their fear, control, and silence onto you, the child. You hadn't done anything wrong; you were simply responding naturally, but the adults around you did not learn how to handle the emotional energy that was rising within them.

This is how you, as a child, were physically, mentally, and emotionally hurt. Their emotional survival responses triggered generations of unhealed emotional pain.

Personally, I carried a lot of unhealed emotional pain that was projected onto me when I was a child. Imagine abuse as a ball of energy projected onto you. You are a child, open and free, with no boundaries. You absorb this ball of energy and start to accept it as your own.

For example, I was sexually abused for many years by my mother's partner, a man much younger than her. For more than thirty years, I carried the weight of self-hatred, feeling unloved and unworthy, as though something was wrong with me. Through my healing and emotional development, I came to understand that the self-hatred and unworthiness were never mine — they were his. His pain, his self-loathing, had been projected onto me through the abuse.

While that pain may have its roots in generations before him, it was still his choice to continue the cycle rather than break it. What I had carried all those years was not my own emotional energy but the burden of a lineage of pain that he chose to pass on.

Once again, my question is: "*Why would an adult hurt a child?*" When a person carries a deep sense of inner pain, shame, or self-rejection, they may project that pain onto a child through their actions and abuse. When someone has been severed from empathy and self-awareness, their unprocessed shame and self-rejection become too heavy to hold, and they seek an outlet. The child becomes that outlet — the place where their unhealed pain is discharged through control, violation, or dominance.

It becomes a self-fulfilling prophecy — when others find out what they've done, they are often met with the same rejection and disgust they already felt inside, confirming and reinforcing their internal shame and suffering. The cycle of projection continues, fuelled by disconnection from self and the absence of emotional evolution.

This understanding may not apply to all perpetrators; however, it does apply to those whose actions arise from deep emotional disconnection, unhealed shame, and generational trauma patterns that were never healed.

Some people project their pain and unhealed wounds outward, repeating the patterns of harming others just as they've been hurt, while others turn it inward, hurting themselves. I have projected this energy inward, hurting myself with negative, self-destructive beliefs and behaviours.

This understanding comes from my own healing journey and from years of working with clients who have experienced childhood trauma.

Whether you personally relate to my experience or not, you can recognise that, during your own childhood, you may have absorbed and carried the energy of someone else's pain — internalising and processing energy that was never yours to process. From those experiences, your beliefs shaped how you saw yourself and the world around you.

When there has been physical, emotional, mental, or sexual abuse, these foreign energies leave a somatic imprint within your nervous system and cellular memory, influencing how you relate to safety, love, and belonging.

Healing is the process of reclaiming your own emotional frequency. As you begin to recognise what is truly yours and what was projected onto you, you start to interrupt the inherited patterns.

This is the evolution of the emotional body — breaking the cycle of unconscious pain by transforming energy back into awareness.

The **Drop Your Shoulders® Methods** in this book are practices that work for everyone. You just need to be willing to evolve your emotional body, regardless of whether you consider your childhood to have been a normal and loving experience, have memories of individual traumatic events, or have endured ongoing physical and emotional abuse.

The process remains the same, and the results improve with continued practice.

Evolving your own emotional body begins with breaking the cycle, releasing energy from your body and nervous system, and creating new reference points for your subconscious.

My personal experience shifted from a constant state of fight or flight and long-term adrenal stress to feeling calm and centred. It began with just a few minutes, then an hour or two of feeling different and calm, gradually expanding over the weeks to a full day, then a week, then months of feeling great before being triggered into old emotional survival responses.

With practice, your body reacts more quickly, and your responses begin to change. This doesn't mean you'll never be triggered into stress or survival patterns again; it's about having the tools to interrupt these patterns immediately by simply dropping your shoulders.

The time and distance before feeling triggered again lengthen, helping you stay calm and centred longer.. Our goal is not to reject or ignore perceived negative emotions that surface but to release the energy of these feelings through various methods, scribbling, acknowledging and releasing it.

# The Consequences Of An Unevolved Or Overdeveloped Emotional Body

Understanding the emotional body is not evolving at the same rate for everyone. We are still in the early stages of transition and must all begin to recognise that some people have an underdeveloped emotional body, while others have an overdeveloped emotional body. We need to consider what this might look like moving forward.

This is not about judging that one is better than the other; it's about acknowledging that we are all at different stages of evolution and emotional intelligence. During the transition stage in humanity, there will be a broader range of stages.

**What we call 'narcissism,' a word that has become widespread, especially in relationships, is not always what we think it is.**

I am not speaking from the perspective of mainstream psychology or clinical authority. I am discussing the field of emotional energy and trauma stored in the body and the potential of a less-evolved emotional body.

In some cases (not all), narcissistic traits may result from a lineage where the emotional body has never had the opportunity to change, with generation after generation learning to survive through self-protection, control, performance, and emotional detachment.

What we see as manipulation or superiority may, at its core, be a profound fear of feeling emotions passed down through generations. This does not excuse harm projected onto another; it does, however, offer an invitation to see the wound beneath the mask. It's a nervous system passed down through DNA that reads, *"If I feel deep emotions, I will not survive,"* and the inner child learns how to block emotion. As an adult, they feel it deeply and suppressed emotions leak out, presenting in forms of control, through a mask of being nice and never losing emotional control. It is hardwired as an identity of power, and appearing strong because being vulnerable is too dangerous.

In these lineages, the ability to feel a wide range of emotions is often shut down early during childhood. Not just feelings of anger and grief, but also joy, tenderness, empathy, and compassion for oneself and others. The nervous system becomes conditioned to operate within a narrow bandwidth, where vulnerability feels dangerous, and emotions are seen as weaknesses to be avoided, suppressed, or intellectualised.

From this place, compassion for another's emotional pain is almost impossible, not because the person is cruel, but because they cannot tolerate the discomfort of deep feelings — either theirs or anyone else's.

Their inner world becomes organised so that physical and emotional survival are linked. As a result, they may live without experiencing the peaks of pure joy or the depths of genuine sorrow. This is where compassion and empathy fail to develop or expand, and self-awareness was never nurtured. Emotional pain is instead diverted into grandeur, blame, control, or complete emotional shutdown and avoidance.

This is not meant to justify abusive behaviour of control and superiority. However, it offers a different perspective on the evolution of the emotional body and its quest to find balance. This transition allows for the existence of both the underdeveloped and overdeveloped emotional bodies, where these two polarities also coexist.

I am not suggesting that clinical diagnoses are invalid or should be ignored. Rather, I invite you to consider an additional perspective. Beneath some of the behaviours and patterns that are labelled and categorised within our mental health systems may also exist an emotional body in transition — one that never felt safe to truly feel, or one that is heightened in awareness but was never given the tools to release the overwhelm of intense emotional energy.

Some people see the world through a very different sensory and emotional perspective. Across a spectrum of human experience, they often navigate life with heightened sensitivity, where the chaos, noise, and unspoken emotional signals of the world can feel overwhelming. It is simply a unique way of perceiving reality.

This is where the concepts of the underdeveloped or overdeveloped emotional body are introduced. The modern emotional landscape is intense, filled with mixed signals, false pleasantries, and unspoken rules. A child or adult who cannot process these emotional undercurrents might shut down — not from disconnection, but from feeling overstimulated or unsafe. While some individuals may naturally experience greater sensory or emotional sensitivity, an overdeveloped emotional body refers to a different dynamic: one in which there is no safe bridge to integrate emotional input or expression.

Both reflect survival responses and nervous system regulation that have fallen out of balance, and both carry emotional pain without the practical tools to release it. I invite you to see all experiences through the lens of love and compassion.

**Deeper Truth.** The evolution of your emotional body is inherited at either end of the spectrum — from a parent who couldn't feel, or one who felt everything with no tools to process or understand it. Generational and childhood trauma directly influence how your emotional body evolves, leaving it underdeveloped, overdeveloped, or anywhere in between.

Some of us inherited both, or swung between the two, raised in households that were both emotionally absent and emotionally explosive, where shutdown and overwhelm coexisted.

What matters now is that you are the one undergoing emotional growth, regardless of where you are in the process. You possess awareness, the tools, and the willingness to feel and release suppressed emotions.

# Drop Your Shoulders® Method 12

## Releasing Suppressed Emotions From The Past

When you feel that deep emotions of anger, grief, fear, shame, or guilt come up within you, it can feel too big or overwhelming because it's not just your energy; it is energy passed down through the generations.

- Drop your shoulders, calm your nervous system.
- Ask yourself:

*Is this emotion mine?* (Write the first answer that comes to your mind)

*Is this emotion, anger or rage, coming from a current experience, such as a boundary being crossed or an injustice I am facing now?*

*Is this emotion triggered by a childhood experience, energy projected onto me from my parents, caregivers, or influential people? Yes/No*

*Is this emotion unresolved grief from those who came before me, from my mother, father, grandmother, grandfather? Yes/No*

- Now you have identified if the emotion is yours or someone else's emotion projected onto you. You have the power to release this energy right now, not by reliving it, or even consciously understanding it, but by releasing the energy frequency of the emotion. You have the ability to say;

*"This pattern ends with me."*

- Now, action the **Drop Your Shoulders® Method Scribbling or Woodchopping** to release the energy stored in your body.

Suffering is a choice, and the root of all suffering is **RESISTANCE.**

You have the power to choose inner peace.

# Chapter Nine

# Your Past, Your Story

Now you have tools to release energy passed down through your own family line, including the silence, anger, disconnection, rejection, grief, guilt, and shame.

You have felt (and may still be feeling) the burden of emotions that never truly belonged to you.

Now we will delve into your personal story, giving you a voice and a moment in time when healing becomes truly personal. It is no longer about your ancestors, your parents, or the collective story of humanity. This is about you and your life, your body, your childhood, and the emotional truths that have shaped how you move through the world.

You might be beginning to feel uncomfortable, like you want to stop here and avoid moving forward.

*Do you notice your stomach tighten as fear rises and the repetitive questions in your mind start to surface? Yes/No*

The overthinking starts to take hold with continuous questions;

*What if I go there and it's just too much?*
*What if the truth ends up worse than I remember?*
*What if I can't handle it and I fall apart?*

These fears are genuine, and they trigger resistance.

RESISTANCE is at the core of all suffering.

**Truth.** You have already explored expectations versus reality equals anger. You have also started using the **Drop Your Shoulders® Method Scribbling and Woodchopping**, practical tools to release the energy of anger. There is nothing to fear now. You already have the tools to move forward.

## Reflection

You have now explored the patterns, survival responses, and emotional energy that may have been passed down through your family line. You have begun to understand how silence, anger, disconnection, rejection, grief, guilt, and shame can be carried from one generation to the next.

Now it is time to explore your own story.

The questions that follow are not designed to judge or blame anyone. They are intended to help you identify the patterns, experiences, and emotional responses that have shaped your life. As you answer them, notice what you feel in your body. Pay attention to any tension, discomfort, resistance, or emotions that arise.

This is where healing becomes personal.

*Do you recall moments in your life when you felt disempowered? Yes/No*

*Did you suppress your anger or other emotions in order to be loved? Yes/No*

*Do you feel silenced, dismissed, or ignored by your parents and caregivers? Yes/No*

*Did you hear your parents yelling at each other, or were they yelling at you? Yes/No*

*Did you learn to hide your feelings to keep the peace, protect others, or simply to get by? Yes/No*

*Do you carry shame and guilt for expressing your own emotions (do you apologise when you cry or get upset)? Yes/No*

*Did you learn to please others and to smile, be nice, and stay small? Yes/No*

*Did you learn to avoid confrontation by staying out of the way and tiptoeing around tension? Yes/No*

*Did you learn to take responsibility by becoming a childparent to your carers or siblings, or by becoming an adult too soon? Yes/No*

The answers to these questions provide insight into the patterns you are personally carrying today. Some may belong to your own experiences, while others may reflect survival patterns passed down through your family line.

You may recognise themes of silence, anger, disconnection, rejection, grief, guilt, shame, people-pleasing, hypervigilance, or the need to stay small in order to feel safe.

Awareness is the first step. What you can now see, you can begin to heal.

Beneath your memories of these experiences lies an unspoken truth. You felt hurt, disempowered, rejected, alone, helpless.

Now is the time to give it a voice through the **Drop Your Shoulders® Method Scribbling.** Feel into your body, notice the places of tension, contraction or pain. Start scribbling, relaxing your muscles in these areas and calming your nervous system.

Allow yourself to speak aloud.

*"I surrender and let go".*

*"That was not okay."*

*"I needed to feel loved, held, nurtured."*

*"I deserved better than the abuse, the betrayals, the lies."*

*"This should never have happened."* Add any other statements here.

This is not about blame, nor is it about playing the victim. This is your truth, and your truth is the key to your healing.

When you let fear hold you back, you deny what you feel and disconnect from the part of yourself that knows the absolute truth.

What happened to you in the past was not okay; there was a crossing of a boundary — your boundary. You know the truth and sensed the injustice, not because someone told you, but because you felt it in your body.

Your intuition and your heart are speaking to you now.

You are witnessing your own truth and personal experience, and by allowing yourself to speak your truth out loud, something begins to unravel. Your body starts to relax.

Now add this simple process to create distance between the past and now; this simple process allows you to become present in this moment.

Say the following three times:

*"THAT WAS THEN, AND THIS IS NOW,"*

*"THAT WAS THEN, AND THIS IS NOW,"*

*"THAT WAS THEN, AND THIS IS NOW."*

This is your story, and you have the power to reshape it and let it go.

Again, should emotion surface, continue to scribble until it dissipates, breathing in for 4, out for 4.

Emotions are your personal compass.

They reveal where something once mattered to you deeply, where things went awry, and where your soul said NO but that NO went unheard. This is the sacred space where truth and compassion start to meet. Where your experience and personal story are honoured. Where the emotional energy within you is no longer feared; it is felt and released.

## Your Personal Emotional Triggers and Responses

You have often experienced annoyance, frustration, and anger; you feel it in your body, and others frequently project it onto you. You now understand the fundamental concept: expectation vs. reality = anger.

However, you have a default pattern hardwired into your subconscious on how you express anger. What is your default pattern?

Before I practised the **Drop Your Shoulders® Methods** to release emotions, my usual pattern was to go quiet and withdraw. Then, like a volcano beneath the surface, I would erupt suddenly — without any control — going from 0 to 100 in milliseconds.

*How do you express annoyance, frustration and anger?*

*Do you explode, letting your anger take over and affect everyone around you? Yes/No*

*Do you withdraw, retreating into silence and coldness, punishing others with your absence? Yes/No*

*Do you tend to be passive-aggressive, expressing your anger through sarcasm, quiet resentment, or subtle sabotage? Yes/ No*

*Do you become the peacemaker, smiling when you want to scream, saying yes when you want to say no, hiding your truth to keep the peace? Yes/No*

These responses are survival techniques, the way you've learned to cope with intense emotional pain inside you. These strategies keep you disconnected from your truth, your power, and your ability to fully express who you are.

Each of these responses shows you where your boundaries have been crossed, where your needs have been ignored, and where your truth has been silenced.

Anger is your body's way of telling you that something is wrong, something needs to change, or something needs to be seen.

Now you have the power to release the energy of anger through the **Drop Your Shoulders® Methods.** You can stop pretending anger does not exist, and you can stop fearing it will be out of control without any warning.

You are encouraged to channel your anger without causing harm to yourself or others.

Beneath unmet expectations lies your pathway to grief and deep sadness. This is the end of the line for unexpressed emotion, which is why it has taken so long to even mention it in this book. Anger is the most feared emotion, and grief is the most protected and avoided emotion.

You now understand the fundamental concept: expectation versus reality equals anger.

# Chapter Ten

# Understanding Grief

## The First Separation: Where It Began

Grief starts long before you knew its name, before language, and before memory, in the earliest moments of your life.

Your first grief may have been the shift from the safety in the womb to being born into the world we live in — feeling the warmth and connection inside the womb, where you were held, nourished, and content, to the cold air outside — separate and alone — as your nervous system activated to ask for what was once effortlessly provided: food, nourishment, safety.

This initial grief resides in your body, nervous system, and subconscious. It leaves an imprint, a feeling that something has changed or been lost, which many people carry without ever understanding why.

Your next introduction to loss and grief happens with any change, like when the milk didn't come quickly enough, or your cry was ignored. As you start to grow, this grief is when someone first told you to *"stop crying,"* instead of holding you.

None of these were perceived as *"big events"*; they are what is considered normal, especially when we look into controlled crying techniques and other processes used to manage behaviour as you grow up. This is particularly relevant for an evolving nervous system when you are forming perceptions of the world, and deciding if it is safe or dangerous.

You naturally adapt, and your subconscious forms a default pattern within your nervous system to keep you safe; now, it's not just physical safety but also emotional safety.

Grief is the sacred emotion of the heart, as you were told to stop crying, internalising that crying is wrong. You began to see grief as something to fear, to suppress, to avoid. You even started to apologise for crying when crying is a natural release for grief.

The grief — the deep sadness — is still there, sitting inside your heart, protected by your anger. It can feel like an ache in your chest when there are changes in your life or when triggered, a heaviness against your chest and a lump in your throat as the tears threaten to spill out.

Grief expressed through the heart is your greatest gift; it embodies what it means to be human. When you no longer fear releasing the energy of emotions, you no longer fear the energy of grief — you are truly free.

## Suppressed Grief In Childhood And Beyond

As you grew up as a child navigating the world with your own words and thoughts, grief had already started to shape your nervous system into something perceived as dangerous and best avoided.

Suppressed grief now intertwines with your emotional survival responses. You held it in when you were disappointed, pushed down the sadness when your parent forgot something important to you or told yourself it didn't matter that your best friend suddenly stopped talking to you, or that the teacher embarrassed you in front of the class. All the disappointments build up, and the energy feels heavy.

**Truth.** It always mattered — it mattered to you. Every disappointment, unmet need, and moment of change that felt out of your control meant you lost something. Each time, you decided that change equals grief and sadness.

Now your subconscious and nervous system are both hardwired to fear death and change, as both are seen as loss, grief, and deep sadness. Again, as you develop your emotional body, the adults around you had not yet learned how to connect with their own hearts in grief; they could not help you meet or understand yours.

You begin to learn and imitate how the adults around you manage their emotions through anger, withdrawal, numbness, avoidance, and disconnection.

You learned that showing sadness made people uncomfortable. That speaking up and asking for what you needed or what mattered to you was labelled as dramatic, selfish, or needy. That if you kept crying, you would be rejected, abandoned, and the love you seek would disappear.

## Reflection

*Do you smile when you are hurting, responding with "I'm fine" even when your heart is breaking inside? Yes/No*

*Do you apologise when you cry in front of others? Yes/No*

*Do you try to avoid feeling sad by putting up a wall around your heart and pretending your needs don't matter? Yes/No*

*Do you feel embarrassed when you cry and think that crying is a weakness? Yes/No*

*Do you cry in secret to avoid bothering someone or making them uncomfortable? Yes/No*

*Were you told that crying is only for babies and that you should stop? Yes/No*

These responses have become common in our society, where expressing anger and grief is seen as something wrong with you that needs fixing, even though it is a normal reaction to loss and life changes.

As your emotional body continues to evolve, shutting down or avoiding fear and loss can feel like the safest option in a constantly changing world.

Labelling these emotions as negative and bad suggests that feeling them intensely means something is wrong. Many of us are now hardwired to avoid these emotions, so when they arise, we try to fix them or help those experiencing them. The common belief now is that only positive emotions are valid and worth experiencing, and that negative ones must be eliminated by any means necessary. Remember the emotions chart and the polarities? When you reject the negative emotion, you cannot fully rise to meet the positive emotions.

Grief is a natural emotion; it is valid and needs to be acknowledged and heard, offering a way to release the energy that accumulates in your body. It originates from the feeling of love, connection, and safety of the womb. A part of you knows what it feels like to be loved, held, met, and seen. It is the ache of your heart trying to return to wholeness. Grief is natural — when change happens, you grieve the loss of what was, so you can embrace what is now.

When I began exploring grief as the core emotion that is both valid and needs to be expressed, I realised that change in your life always offers an opportunity to grieve what once was. This is especially clear during significant life events like moving to a new place, when you grieve the changes — in location, friendships, familiarity, support, safety, past memories, and more. When you grieve, you create space to welcome the new — a new home, new friendships, new experiences. This applies to both large and small changes in life, and it is important to make time for grief and grieving. Since we have avoided grief for so long, it can feel overwhelming, like something too big to face.

When my son first started school, I remember wanting to honour the process of change and the grief that comes with it. Instead of keeping myself busy after dropping him off on the first day — which was both a joyful, exciting occasion and an inner sadness — I went to the beach to grieve and make space for the change.

I cried for what this shift meant to me; I had been a stay-at-home mum and had literally spent 24 hours a day with him since he was born. For five years, he was part of every moment of my life, and now that had changed. I grieved for the loss of time and energy that he no longer needed from me. I let go of my own identity, opening myself up to becoming more than a full-time mum at home with him. I also grieved for the times we spent painting, dancing, and laughing — not because those moments were gone, but because they would be different now. This process honoured our connection and allowed me to be fully present and embrace the new life ahead. A life where my role changed dramatically, and where his life altered just as significantly.

Taking time to grieve change is essential for creating balance both internally and externally.

## Grief As A Layered Energy: Why Loss Feels So Much Larger Than the Moment

When you've suppressed loss and grief out of fear of the emotion itself, letting it surface can feel overwhelming.

When you avoid taking time to grieve and only confront it during a major event, like ending a relationship or moving house, grief can seem overwhelming. Without understanding what is truly happening, you can activate your fear-based survival responses and shut it down.

This is why these major events like marriage breakdown, changing jobs, a child starting school, or a shift in routine trigger a sadness within you that feels disproportionate. You're not just grieving what is happening now; you're grieving every moment when you had to keep moving forward without the time and space to feel the sadness — when you pushed it down, held back the tears, and swallowed the lump in your throat.

# Grief and Deep Sadness

Grief lies at the heart of all humanity. The emotion of the heart. Protected at all costs, the deep grief of humanity is perceived as dangerous to acknowledge. To accept grief and loss would mean recognising that humanity is capable of the atrocities that we have all endured. You would have to admit that we, as a species, have caused unspeakable harm.

To do so, you must accept that your ancestors were not only survivors but also perpetrators. That rape, war, slavery, destruction, and domination are not merely historical events.

They are imprints within the human energetic field passed down through generations, residing in your DNA and cellular structure. Through your lineage, perpetrators, victims, and rescuers all exist. All of them, depending on the situation, and you must accept within yourself that you have played each role in different situations to varying degrees.

People tend to avoid grief at all costs because accepting it means embracing the contrast between love and hate, life and death. You would have to accept that all humans are capable of these polarities, as we are biologically wired for physical survival — survival of the fittest. As the emotional body evolves and develops, the heart breaks with grief over what humanity has inflicted upon itself.

Now you are entering awareness of what it means to hold an unevolved emotional body — accepting that your ancestors were in physical survival mode, unable to contain the increasing energy of an evolving emotional body.

The energy of grief was suppressed within them, and they lacked the skills to process emotional energy, so they projected it outward like a child screaming to be heard.

They took from the earth, destroyed everything around them with their anger, protected grief, and we are all still doing it now.

When we, as a collective, suppress grief, shield it with anger, and refuse to accept responsibility for the pain we've caused others, we fracture the very progress of our emotional evolution.

## Grief And Forgiveness Are Connected

You have spent a lifetime avoiding it, managing it, pushing it down, or mistaking it for other things. Grief is the truth — the real truth, the hard truth.

It is the heartache of truth that lies beneath your anger, beneath the frustration, beneath the stories. It is when your expectations, your deepest hopes and needs, do not match your reality.

The voice of anger says, *"This is not fair."*

The voice of grief says, *"This hurts me."*

Grief is disempowerment, helplessness, and hopelessness, and it hurts — it's unbearable even to think about. It asks you to accept what you cannot change. It doesn't ask you to fix, justify, or explain it; it only asks you to feel it.

This is where resistance starts, and fear gets activated. Anger rushes in to protect you. Not because you do not want to heal; you do, and your body knows how to grieve, cry, and release energy.

The evolving emotional body experiences intense emotions in a world where there is little or no compassion, and where empathy and nurturing are not readily available; it doesn't feel safe to grieve the pain of the past. So, you protect the grief and keep it hidden.

You may feel connected to a deeper collective grief — an awareness of the suffering, loss, and pain that humanity has carried throughout history.

Whether through your family lineage, cultural stories, personal experiences, or the emotional energy passed through generations, these feelings can sometimes seem bigger than your own life experience.

Drop your shoulders to calm your nervous system. You have just touched something ancient within you — a truth that may have never been named before. Grief is at the heart of love and compassion. The tears that rise are not weakness; they are sacred, a release of the deep pain of humanity. The collective grief, grief that you know exists but has no context.

Your body is wired to cry; as a child, you cried to signal you needed food or warmth to survive. When you cried, energy was released, and your needs were met. But what happens when you cry, and your needs aren't fulfilled? This marks the start of grief — feeling the loss when your needs go unmet, and recognising that what you need isn't available.

To truly feel grief is to allow your heart to break for everything. For the child who was never embraced. For the land that was taken.

For the wisdom that was lost. For the violence that remained unhealed. For the love that was taken too early.

**Truth.** You are connected to your ancestors and the stories that came before you. Every family, culture, and lineage carries experiences of loss, grief, change, resilience, and survival. While the stories may differ, the human experience of grief is universal.

Deeper Truth. Human beings carry the capacity for both great love and great harm. When we understand the conditions, wounds, fears, and survival pressures that shaped previous generations, we can begin to see the complexity of the human experience with greater compassion.

This is not a moral judgment; it is about recognising the complexity of humanity evolving through your emotional body.

As the emotional body continues to develop, you are now able to feel what previous generations expressed through violence, projection, addiction, and silence. The emotional pain they did not know how to process.

Now here you are, with a heart that can feel everything. You can sense the full range of emotions, including anger, frustration, sadness, grief, shame, guilt, as well as love, joy, excitement, freedom, and acceptance.

You are moving forward to evolve your emotional body for yourself and all of humanity. What you learn spreads through your lineage both backwards and forwards as you break the patterns.

When acknowledged and given a pathway, emotion leaves quickly. The body does not want to hold onto emotional pain, and you do not need to relive past experiences.

Your body only stores emotion because no one has shown you how to intentionally release it.

When sadness is triggered, you feel it in your body; tears well up in your eyes, your throat contracts, and each time you shut it down or pretend it isn't there, you suppress it. Sometimes, your tears spill over, and you apologise for what is a normal release of emotional energy. Emotions, when felt safely and fully, do not want to stay stuck in your body; they will leave with ease and grace.

Just like a baby who cries and sobs with their whole body, two minutes later they are laughing again. The emotion doesn't hurt them; it leaves the body easily and effortlessly.

That is your natural state to feel, release, and feel peace.

You don't need to fear the depth of your emotion; it's nothing you cannot handle. You just need to create a safe enough space for the energy to leave.

And right now, you are learning to do exactly that.

**Truth.** Grief is sacred.

It presents an opportunity to release stored energy in your body — energy that could become a physical illness if it remains unexpressed. Unexpressed grief sits on your lungs and may manifest physically as cold and flu symptoms; this manifestation is a natural way for your body to release the stored energy through coughing.

Your body knows how to release grief. When given the opportunity, this energy will flow out of you with ease and grace — it just needs your permission. It can come in waves, sometimes feeling out of control; however, it can also be consciously released without needing to relive each experience of loss and change.

Practice **Drop Your Shoulders® Method Scribbling** as an effective way to release grief and sadness from your body.

*Have you ever watched a really sad movie and found yourself tearing up? Yes/No*

This is a good moment to consciously release your grief. When tears come, tell yourself, *"I am releasing my grief through these tears."* By intentionally allowing the tears to flow, you can release the frequency of energy of grief. You do not need to cry for hours — just 2 to 10 minutes without resistance will suffice.

Crying is an intense release of energy that can leave you feeling exhausted, tired, and fatigued even after a few minutes — like you need a nap. Sleeping after crying plays an important role in integration, providing the rest your body needs to process the grief that was released without having to relive it. You might also experience relief and a sense of lightness in your body and chest.

This is your body's natural method of releasing grief and sadness.

This ongoing grief is a natural part of life, part of the cycle of birth and death, and part of the cycle of change and letting go, allowing yourself to grow and evolve. Making time to acknowledge and release grief through the **Drop Your Shoulders® Method Scribbling** is a powerful way to create inner peace.

This book is not specifically about the grief that occurs when someone you love passes away; however, we will touch on it, as this type of grief differs from our everyday experiences. Working with clients, I can share that after someone dies, there is a sacred period of grief that cannot be interrupted, and how each person experiences this varies.

When someone passes away, you are grieving more than the person's passing.

When someone you love passes away, the first point of trauma is SHOCK — the initial moment you realise that something significant has changed, and it's this moment that causes frozen energy in your body. We've already covered shock in the first chapter. After the initial shock, the grieving process must run its course.

As a practitioner, I respect this process and generally encourage people to allow space for the natural grieving process in the early weeks following a significant loss. During this time, the initial **Drop Your Shoulders® Method** can be helpful for calming the nervous system while allowing grief to move naturally through the body.

Allowing the energy to flow through your body is a crucial part of healing. You may find yourself in a haze where nothing seems to make sense, and you either remain in shock or feel waves of grief flowing through you. I'm not here to guide you through this process. It's a sacred time for each person, and everyone will experience it differently as the energy moves through.

As the grieving process unfolds, there often comes a point where grief begins to take on a different meaning. There is no set timeframe for this shift; it occurs differently for each person and in their own time. I mentioned six weeks as a minimum timeframe, during which there should be no interruption to the natural process. There is no strict time limit; it can be extended until each person feels the shift within themselves, only when they are ready.

I will speak directly to you to give real context. In the event that this has happened to you and you are ready, for many people, after the initial period of grief, deeper layers of personal grief may begin to surface. The loss can activate unresolved sadness, disappointments, and emotional wounds that were already present beneath the surface, bringing them into awareness so they can finally be acknowledged and released.

This is when your lifetime of unresolved or suppressed grief starts to come to the forefront. It's about your perception of grief and your belief that you have lost something, and now every unprocessed experience of loss and grief in your own life has nowhere else to hide. Your nervous system has been activated, and the energy of grief has started to flow differently. This can feel too big and overwhelming, causing fear and anxiety to activate for your protection. Anger also arises here to protect you.

Now you are grieving perceived loss that has occurred throughout your life, layered on top of the loss of someone you love.

Since you do not truly own anything or anyone, you cannot genuinely lose anything or anyone. Yes, they have changed form and moved into a different state depending on your belief systems; however, when you tune into the person and remember all the times you spent together, the gifts and the moments you shared, this remains unchanged. It is still present. This is when grief transforms into a celebration of life.

When you think of the good times, you will remember them and feel them in the same way you did when they were alive. Your memories hold no time or space and can feel real in a moment if you allow yourself to experience the memory, not from a place of loss but from a place of love, connection, and gratitude.

For example, if you are at home thinking of someone in another state, you can connect with them energetically even though you are not physically together.

*Have you ever experienced it when you think of someone you love and they call you? Yes/No*

If you have, you will now understand that you can feel their energy activate in your energy field, the memories, the feelings, and connect with them even after they are no longer physically here with you. This has not changed.

There is another factor to consider here: when grief follows a death of a loved one, and you find yourself caught in it, unable to move or breathe for a long time afterwards, this is the energy of shock. Feeling stuck is the shock that hits your nervous system the moment you find out. It's that instant when everything freezes, your heart stops for a split second, you hold your breath, and your body freezes to protect itself. This one moment of unresolved shock triggers an emotional repetitive pattern known as PTSD. Unless shock is consciously released, you may find yourself repeatedly reliving that single moment of shock, questioning why you can't 'move on'.

Shock triggers feelings of disempowerment, helplessness, and hopelessness, making it difficult to change how you feel and respond. This is where the **Drop Your Shoulders® Methods,** the practical tools you have already learnt throughout this book, can now be used to clear the energy of shock from your subconscious and nervous system.

Once you have identified and cleared the shock moment, remember that expectation versus reality can lead to anger, and beneath anger lies grief — the meaning that expectation held for you.

Now, this is the grief that is surfacing and requires your attention.

Now is the time to let go of the grief you've been holding in your whole life.

The times you did not feel safe, when you felt unloved, unseen, or unimportant. The times you said goodbye to a friendship or a relationship, and all the times you hid from the grief of change.

You do not need to lose a loved one for grief to surface this way, although if you have suppressed grief for a long time, this is usually when it happens.

For me, all my suppressed grief surfaced when my marriage ended. The ending itself triggered deep shock, frozen energy now activated and ready to move. The shock I did not see coming. It felt like a death, and it was a death — the death of a dream, a life, and a family I had worked so hard to create.

The grief was intense and overwhelming. It wasn't about the relationship itself; change is part of life. This was about what it represented — the loss of stability, the dream of family unity, and the sadness of knowing my son would now experience divorce and separation. The situation amplified the hidden and unprocessed trauma and shock energy I had carried since childhood, resurfacing layers of emotional pain I had long forgotten and suppressed.

This sadness had always been beneath the surface, hidden by fear of this kind of grief. I fluctuated between shock, anger, and profound sadness. I had already done significant healing in my personal journey and was grateful to have developed the **Drop Your Shoulders® Methods** — tools that continue to support me.

As I recognised the connection to my long-term childhood shocks and trauma, along with the generational and ancestral patterns embedded in my subconscious and nervous system, I realised these emotions were surfacing so they could finally be released — suppressed so deeply within me that nothing short of this kind of shock could have reached them. With love and compassion for myself, I was able to evolve my emotional body far beyond what I ever expected.

This kind of grief is deeply personal — shaped by your own life experiences. It arises every time life doesn't turn out the way you needed it to, when expectations fail to meet reality.

It lives in the love that never arrived, the years spent waiting for change, the illusion that understanding or an apology would one day come — that somehow, things would be made right.

When there has been a significant event that activates grief, you have the opportunity to grieve and release all the moments that were taken from you, not just by circumstance but by people who couldn't love you in the way you needed. By the silence that was louder than words. The chaos that became your normal. The people who were meant to protect you and didn't.

This grief is ancient; it is not from what is happening today.

It is the grief that lies dormant, carried through generations. Knowing it sits beneath the surface, hidden behind patterns of being strong and of pretending everything is fine.

It is the deep sadness of your inner child who never got to cry. Your inner teen who never felt safe. Your adult self who's been holding it together ever since. Now, you are also grieving what never even existed – the loving, caring family you always wanted, the safety that never came, the moment the people you love would finally see you, hear you, love you the way you have always dreamed.

Most importantly, you are grieving for the part of you that had to shut all of this down just to survive – the part of you that kept going through trauma, loss, and constant change, through abandonment, rejection, and criticism, because you had no other choice, because it was not safe to grieve and fall apart.

On top of everything, you are also grieving the stories of your lineage. You are mourning what your mother never got to feel. What your father buried so deep it turned into anger. You are carrying the grief of generations of being shut down, told not to cry, and just to get on with it. Where their emotional bodies were unevolved and unable to process energy shifts, loss, and grief. Then, on a deeper spiritual level, you are grieving the atrocities humanity has inflicted upon itself.

Grief is both deeply personal and ancestral
— a thread connecting every human heart.

It is the feeling we avoid most and the one that brings you to deep inner peace.

**Truth.** All emotion is energy that wants to leave the body. When given a safe passage for it to flow, you don't get stuck in grief or frozen in time. Over a short period, when provided time and space, it leaves gracefully and easily, without replaying or reliving past trauma or pain.

Now I ask you, *if you broke your leg, would you go to the hospital? Yes/No*

You might need surgery, and you would put everything on hold, take time off work to let your body recover, and allow yourself to rest and heal.

When you experience significant changes that trigger loss and grief, activating deep emotional pain, the same care and nurturing are needed for healing. Taking the time to heal your emotions in the same way as you would recover from a physical wound is important here. You don't need to take months off work as you would with a broken leg; however, allowing 10-15 minutes a day to release suppressed emotions somatically from your body can be beneficial. This can be done by using the **Drop Your Shoulders® Method Scribbling or Woodchopping.**

You can spend a few minutes each day dropping your shoulders to relax your nervous system.

You are not here to process grief through constant tears and stories, talk therapy, reactivating, reliving, and re-experiencing.

You are here reading this today to allow the energy to move through you quickly and cleanly, flowing through the body without resistance and without suffering.

Energy shifts quickly when faced with truth. This energy can exit the body within seconds.

I invite you to somatically and energetically heal your past using the **Drop Your Shoulders® Method Scribbling.** Breathe into the areas of your body where grief and sadness dwell, and deepen your breath into your heart with love and intention — whether that's through scribbling on a page or engaging in a profound healing exercise like woodchopping. If tears surface, take 5-10 minutes in the shower to truly cry, make intense faces, and release the frequency of grief and sadness, letting go, creating space for new energy to flow in.

Yes, this can be intense for a moment in time, and then it is gone.

Grief and sadness are not things that are too big or overwhelming to move through, nor do they take years to heal. Crying is not something to avoid, and there is no need to apologise for it. Feeling grief deeply doesn't make you weak — and there is no timeline for when it should begin or end. These are the lies that keep you trapped in fear and close your heart.

Grief is an emotion, a frequency of energy, and when you give permission and a pathway without fear, it leaves easily.

Grief is the emotion of the heart. Allowing grief and sadness to flow freely instantly opens your heart and unlocks compassion and love in its purest form. Opening your heart also makes it possible to forgive — both yourself and others — and to accept the human condition. Through this process, you are free to experience deep inner peace and a profound sense of truth.

It is here that you can trust your intuition and listen to your heart.

# Drop Your Shoulders® Method 13

## Grief And Loss

Note: this is not the same process for grief of the loss of a loved one.

- You can start by recognising the grief stored in your body — begin with everything you feel sad about, even things not personally affecting you, e.g., *"I feel sad for the people affected by the floods, I feel sad for the man on the train who always looks lonely, I feel sad that my friend is going through a divorce, I feel sad..."*

- Say to yourself or out loud;

  *"I release the energy of deep sadness from my body and my cells."*

- Start writing;

*"I feel sad because..."* Continue writing all the things that make you sad, including those closest to your heart, until you run out of things to write.

- Safely burn the paper or rip it up and put it into the bin when you are finished.

- Feel into your body, into your heart, experience the sadness, start the **Drop Your Shoulders® Method Scribbling**

- Scribble with the intention of releasing all the energy of grief and sadness from your body.

- Drop your shoulders, calm your nervous system, do not analyse, overthink it, or re-read it.

- If tears flow, I recommend having a shower or a swim and letting the water wash them away. Set the intention to release all the suppressed grief and sadness held in your body — you're not required to relive every experience, just to focus on releasing the grief. After a few minutes, get out of the shower. The process of movement, such as getting dressed, helps shift your energy and allows you to continue with your day.

- After releasing the energy of grief, which often comes after crying, you may feel tired or a light, relieved feeling wash over you. Allow yourself to rest.

# Part II

## Self-Love And Healthy Relationships

# Chapter Eleven

# A Daily Practice.

## You Do Not Need To Relive The Pain Of The Past To Heal It

Take a moment now to acknowledge how far you have come. Allow your body to register what you have already learnt, how it is being integrated into your daily life, and how you have the power to change how you feel each day. Start with the **Drop Your Shoulders® Method.** You have already achieved so much in a short time. Let's review how far you have come.

**Drop Your Shoulders® Methods** include daily and weekly practices for emotional health and wellbeing, as follows:

1. **The Drop Your Shoulders® Method.** Interrupt your subconscious emotional survival patterns and calm your nervous system as naturally and effortlessly as brushing your teeth.

2. **Calm Your Nervous System.** Expanding to include feeling safe and loved in each moment.

3. **Releasing Tension and Pain.** Designed to help you let go, release pain and tension, and relax your body even further.

4. **Active Affirmations.** Go deeper to discover what you need to feel safe and loved.

5. **Transform Subconscious Overthinking.** This process rewrites fractured statements that cause disharmony within you.

6. **Connecting with Your Inner Child.** Connect and start a dialogue of reassurance with your inner child.

7. **Scribbling.** Releasing physical, mental, and emotional pain. The most profound somatic release method that allows you to let go of tension and pain in your body.

8. **Recognising Emotions and Releasing Blocked Energy.** Effective for Anger, Grief, Shame, and Guilt.

9. **Identify Your Realistic and Unrealistic Expectations.** Anger arises from the gap between your expectations and your reality.

10. **Woodchopping for Anger Release.** To release suppressed anger from your body and reclaim your personal power.

11. **How to Release Anger in the Car.** Another version of an anger-release technique that can be done in the car for convenience.

12. **Releasing Suppressed Emotions from the Past.** Suppressed emotions create blocked energy in the body. Releasing this energy makes you feel lighter.

13. **Grief and Loss.** Acknowledging and releasing grief.

You are here, ready to integrate and experience the outcomes of embracing healing through somatic exercises that work directly with your subconscious and nervous system.

These practices are no longer just tools for emotional wellbeing. They are now part of who you are, practices you were never taught as a child or while growing into a teenager. These practices teach you not only to release emotional energy from your body but also to create inner peace somatically and energetically, and the opportunity to pass this on to your own children.

As you incorporate **Drop Your Shoulders® Methods** into your daily routine, those around you, including your own children, will notice the changes in you. They will see you managing emotions, big events, and changes, and taking responsibility for your emotional wellbeing. They will observe you using practical tools to better understand that emotions are energy and how easily you can release this energy from your body.

Now, the more you practise, practise, practise every day, the quicker you will see and feel the results in your life.

Why? Because each time you practise, you work with your subconscious and nervous system to reprogram emotional survival patterns, belief systems, neural pathways, generational trauma, and your own life experiences that have caused disharmony.

When you use all the methods regularly as a way to maintain inner peace in a chaotic world, you are in your personal power. These practices become your daily self-love and self-care routine, just as you automatically get dressed each day or go to the gym to build muscle. You are building emotional safety.

Before you go any further in exploring how **Drop Your Shoulders® Methods** can improve your relationships, let's take a moment to feel the joy of your own achievement. You did not just read these pages. You showed up for yourself every step of the way, experienced the methods, and felt the changes in your body, thoughts, and emotions. It is not easy to hear, read, or feel the truth; however, when you know your own truth in your heart and feel it in your body beyond logic, that is your truth. You felt the changes in your nervous system, can see the outcomes in your reactions, and feel the inner peace growing within — this is integration.

You are now achieving self-empowerment, knowing you can change how you feel each day. You are empowered to free yourself from emotional chaos, the internal struggle you have been battling for years.

This marks a crucial stage in the development of your emotional body, where you begin to understand polarities. It is the point at which you no longer reject or judge negative emotions; instead, you give them a voice, acknowledge them, release them, and then carry on with your day.

Stress, anxiety, depression, emotional trauma, and survival patterns may still be triggered; they are part of your life journey.

True empowerment occurs when you no longer ignore, fight or reject negative emotions and experiences, but instead use **Drop Your Shoulders® Methods** to create a different experience. This practice takes less than 5-10 minutes each day.

*Can you allocate 5-10 minutes each day to free yourself and enjoy the rest of your day? Yes /No*

Yes, it is this simple. You no longer need to suffer each day from emotional turmoil. You now have a choice. While your emotional or stress survival responses may be activated and responses from past wounds may be triggered, you no longer have to stay trapped in automatic reactions like fear, anxiety, or depression for hours, days, weeks, or even years. You can now use these various methods to break the stress response, calm your nervous system, and create a different experience. You can now find moments of inner peace and deep relaxation.

These practices are now integrating into your cells. When you practise them daily and incorporate them into your life, you'll feel the difference immediately. Over time, the gap between emotional trauma and suffering and feeling safe, happy, and free widens.

For example, you have been experiencing long-term adrenal stress for years, including anxiety, depression, PTSD, and trauma. You feel as if there is an inner war going on inside you every day — something no one else can see — and this has become your normal. As soon as you start integrating these practices into your daily routine and feel an hour of calm, centredness, and happiness, you create a different subconscious reference point. This marks a significant shift from a constant state of adrenal stress to feeling calm, centred, and happy.

After a short time, you will notice you've had a whole day free from overthinking, anger outbursts, or discomfort in your body. As you continue, you will see that by adding these practices to your daily routine, feeling good will become normal. While life's ups, downs, and chaos will still come and go, you're now able to navigate them with ease and grace, and you can change how you feel within minutes of noticing you are triggered.

## You will not remember all the tools at all time.

It is normal not to remember at first because you are changing patterns that are automatically activated in your subconscious and nervous system. This is why it becomes a daily practice that gradually integrates into your new automatic nervous system response.

Let me show you how simple it is to bring these practices into your everyday routine. For me, as soon as I wake up in the morning and am still lying in bed, I take 4-5 deep breaths — inhale for 4, exhale for 4 — focusing on breathing into my body and relaxing any areas of tension, tightness, or pain. This helps me feel grounded in my body.

In the shower, I imagine the water cleansing my energy, letting go of negative energy and releasing tension from my body.

I activate the **Drop Your Shoulders® Method**. I say "activate" because after you have applied this and practised dropping your shoulders, it becomes a normal subconscious response, so you only need to think of it, and your body will respond. You will immediately notice the areas of tension in your body and start relaxing the muscles in these areas. I then expand and breathe into my body, and say, "*I am safe. Right now. I am standing in the shower.*" This alone resets my nervous system, helping me start my day feeling calm and centred.

**Drop Your Shoulders® Method Scribbling.** I keep a pen and a small pad in my car and another in my bag. When you begin this practice, you will need to scribble at least once a day, whenever you feel triggered into an emotional response or experience discomfort in your body.

As this becomes a way of life, you will make time to scribble and release tension and emotion from your body as soon as they are activated. You will notice the tension start to build, often felt in your stomach, chest, or throat, from the little frustrations and disappointments that happen during the day. Your emotional survival patterns will be on high alert; now you stop, drop your shoulders, and calm your nervous system.

When you are triggered, especially when you feel confronted at work or with your partner, it is easy to say in that moment, *"I am just going to the car to get something"* or *"I am going to the bathroom,"* and then you can simply drop your shoulders to calm your nervous system. Breathe into your body; release the tension, and return to your centre and then continue with whatever you are doing. This only takes a few minutes.

One of my clients suggested downloading a whiteboard app on their phone, so that he could scribble anytime, anywhere, and that works too.

These practical tools are now yours to adapt however works best for you. It's not about doing them perfectly or exactly as I have shared, but about having the intention to release built-up emotional energy and to interrupt your emotional survival responses. This approach encourages you to take responsibility for your own emotional wellbeing.

You no longer need to analyse why, where, or when something happened in your life. Sometimes understanding is helpful; however, when overthinking and analysing become destructive and cause long-term adrenal stress, it is more effective to release tension and energy from your body and create a new emotional-somatic reference point for lasting change.

The **Drop Your Shoulders® Method Woodchopping** practice is recommended once a week, even when you are not angry. You do not need to be angry to release the energy of anger from your body. You can do this practice when you start to feel tension building, or after a big day when you need to release it.

For those of you who say *"I never get angry"* — woodchopping is the best exercise for you. Why? Because there is not a person on this planet who does not carry anger in their body. Anger is the difference between your expectations and your reality. Every single person carries anger; it is part of being human. You have expectations of yourself and others, both conscious and subconscious, and more often than not, those expectations are unrealistic. So this isn't about not getting angry; it is about having learnt to suppress your anger as something unsafe or unacceptable to feel or express.

I had an experience where, after a big fight with my partner at the time, I was scribbling and thoughts of anger towards my father came up. I realised the fight had nothing to do with the present moment; however, it had activated unresolved anger from my childhood. I released the emotional energy of anger through scribbling and immediately felt calm again.

These are potent tools, especially when used on a daily or weekly basis.

Miraculous results are now within your reach.

I have seen my clients heal from chronic physical pain; neck and back pain have vanished, and chronic immune disorders have returned to balance.

Others report they are more patient, compassionate, and understanding, and no longer project their emotions onto their loved ones.

I have had clients report that, after using these practices to heal from childhood trauma, they have reconnected with family members and experienced improvements in their relationships.

I have also had clients report significant reductions in anxiety, PTSD symptoms, and depression after just a few weeks of using the Drop Your Shoulders® Methods.

The power of somatically releasing emotional energy from the body to create greater balance within yourself can lead to profound changes, and your experience will be unique to you.

## Reflection

*How has your experience been until now?*

Take a moment to reflect on your own experiences with the **Drop Your Shoulders® Methods.** Notice what is different, not what is the same. Notice whether you move through situations with greater calm, or respond differently to moments that may once have triggered anger or tension. Become aware of how often your shoulders are tense, and how your body now responds under stress. Focus on what has changed, rather than what has remained the same.

The **Drop Your Shoulders® Method** is a living practice. Each time you allow your nervous system to soften and your subconscious to rewire, you might not see the change immediately — but it is occurring on a physical, mental, and emotional level.

Every time you drop your shoulders, tune into your body instead of reacting, stop analysing and listen to your heart, or release suppressed emotions through scribbling or woodchopping, you are creating a new pattern.

Integration unfolds in its own rhythm, over time, as it becomes part of your everyday life. If you had been taught these tools as a child, they would have prevented years of emotional pain and confusion. It is my hope that these tools will continue to be shared with the generations to come.

Integration is not a task to focus on; it is a natural process — and you have already activated it; it is already happening.

Notice what is different, not what is the same. Notice when you are calmer, lighter, freer. Notice when you no longer react with anger where you once were triggered — how you automatically drop your shoulders and calm your nervous system.

**This is the beginning of your evolving emotional body — where awareness becomes embodiment, and healing becomes your natural state.**

Integration is a natural process.
It has already happened.

## Reflection

*Do you believe healing has to take a long time? Yes/No*

*Do you fear the unknown? Yes/No*

*Do you know what it feels like to be happy? Yes/No*

*Have you felt happy for long periods of time in the past? Yes/ No*

*What would it be like to feel peaceful, happy, joyful, and excited?*

Healing does not have to be painful or a lengthy process focused solely on making the negative disappear. Healing and growth are ongoing parts of life, about evolving and moving forward. There is no start or end; it is just part of your journey. Expressing emotions as a somatic energy release isn't painful — in fact, without resistance, the energy flows, and you will feel lighter, happier, and calmer. A sense of relief naturally comes over you when you release energy in this way.

# Chapter Twelve

# Becoming Your Own Inner Parent

Your inner child is not something separate from you. It is the part of you that still remembers what it felt like to be a child. The part that carries your unmet needs, emotional wounds, fears, hopes, and dreams. It is the younger version of you that still longs to feel safe, loved, seen, heard, and understood.

Self-love involves becoming your own inner parent — the parent you once needed — by showing up for yourself in a way no one else can every day. It is about learning to love and accept the parts of you that were abandoned, not with pity or as a victim, but with personal power and a practice that opens the door for love to flow in.

It involves hearing the silenced voice and giving it a voice. It means safety, not just as a concept but as a tangible experience.

Practice the **Drop Your Shoulders® Method Active Affirmations.**

Consciously affirm and reassure yourself: *"I am safe. I am loved."*

When you practise every day, you will rewire your nervous system to feel safe and loved.

You start to feel calmer and more centred, stopping the habit of scanning your relationships for danger, rejection, or abandonment. You cease the compulsive patterns of seeking love or trying to control your external environment to feel safe. Instead, you find yourself present in the moment, laughing and observing, no longer seeking a parent's love in your friendships or in your partner.

You are the love you've been searching for, the parent you've been wanting, the best friend, the lover.

Your past trauma no longer defines your life or your identity.

You now have a choice about how you respond in any situation.

Your emotional wellbeing and reactions are within your control; they are choices you can make.

You now understand the parts of yourself that were hidden, including bodily sensations, grief, anger, and the power of your emotional survival patterns and nervous system responses.

Healing and growth are not about becoming someone new or rejecting the pain of your past. You no longer need to suffer from your past wounds.

Now you are empowered to recognise that you did not receive the love and support you needed during childhood, in the way you expected or needed. Your emotional survival responses were established during this time, and your inner child now requires reparenting with your love and support.

It is not that your parents did not love you; they loved you within the limits of their capacity at the time, given their own generational trauma patterns and life experiences.

You can now reparent your inner child with love and compassion, offering care to the parts of you that once felt unloved, unsafe, hurt, shamed, rejected, abandoned, disempowered, helpless, and hopeless.

In my life, there were people who saw I was struggling and wanted to help me. They often said to me, "You just need to love yourself."

**What does that really mean?** For me, I didn't know what love was; I had never truly felt loved and safe, either inside or out. I had a distorted view that love equated to chaos, abuse, and trauma. Without healthy emotional and somatic reference points for love, it seemed like an impossible task.

It is very common not to know how to love yourself, especially if you did not feel loved and safe during your childhood.

This is where loving yourself takes on a deeper meaning.

*Is it possible, on a subconscious level and based on your childhood experience, that love equals chaos, abuse, drama, and trauma? Yes/No*

If the answer is Yes, *are you ready to explore that love as kind, gentle, nurturing, and caring? Yes/No*

If your answer is No and you already have emotional somatic reference points that love is kind, gentle, nurturing, and caring, you will use these reference points when connecting with your inner child, reactivating feelings of love during times when you have felt unloved as an adult.

Either way, this is about loving the parts of you that have felt unloved at any given time. This involves reparenting and loving your own inner child, as well as rewriting the belief patterns formed during different developmental stages in childhood so that love is always gentle, kind, caring, and nurturing.

Giving yourself the love your inner child needed and did not receive. It can also mean offering love to any part of you that felt shocked, fearful, unloved, or unsupported. This could be your inner teenager or your adult self in moments when you felt unloved and unsupported.

I have experienced several unhealthy and abusive relationships in which my unloved inner child was seeking the love and nurturing she missed out on during those early years, and then seeking it externally through primary relationships as an adult.

If this has happened to you as well, know that seeking love and connection is natural and human. Two distortions may be contributing to this: one is linking love to chaos, trauma, and abuse; the other is seeking a parent's love instead of an adult's love.

Seeking love and connection outside ourselves in relationships is an experience everyone goes through. As you develop your emotional awareness and realise that adult love is a balanced exchange of energy, you'll begin to explore healthy, adult relationships with clear boundaries.

However, when you have experienced childhood trauma or carry generational trauma patterns, whether known or unknown, your inner child still seeks the unconditional parental love of a mother or father that he or she missed out on, leading to confusion in adult relationships. This confusion can result in unhealthy and abusive relationships.

Trauma bonds and co-dependency are common when one or both people in an adult relationship seek the parental love they missed out on during childhood.

When I started facilitating couples therapy where one or both partners have childhood trauma, anxiety, depression, or PTSD, the core issue is often the inner child seeking parental love in the relationship, which contributes to the disharmony.

Introducing the tools provided through the **Drop Your Shoulders® Methods** helps interrupt emotional survival responses. Learning to calm the nervous system is the first step towards healing, which extends to releasing suppressed emotions and reprogramming subconscious survival patterns. Each individual can learn to reparent their own inner child and understand how to give and receive love in adult relationships.

Exploring self-love through reparenting your inner child and filling your own cup with self-love that overflows fosters a balance of giving and receiving love in an adult relationship. It invites love between partners rather than overlaying expectations or expecting your partner to offer the unconditional parental love they cannot provide, nor is it their responsibility to do so. The time for unconditional parental love is from birth to age 18, and this period has passed.

Loving your inner child is not a product of your imagination; it is a real part of you. Your inner child resides in your subconscious, nervous system, memories, and emotional survival responses. It appears whenever you are triggered into an emotional survival response. The severity of your emotional pain and your reaction to it depend on your core childhood wounds.

Your inner child has unresolved shock and trauma, which you have already been addressing and releasing with the **Drop Your Shoulders® Methods.** Now, we are going to explore how these unresolved shocks and traumas express in an evolving emotional body and how they are now affecting your relationships.

Whether you believe you had a happy childhood or are aware of instances of abuse and trauma, you have previously examined the fractured statements (subconscious overthinking) formed from a child's perspective and how these statements evolved into core wounds.

## Reflection

*What are your core childhood wounds?*

Here are some examples you might relate to feeling:

*Betrayal*

*Rejection*

*Abandonment*

*Not Enough*

*Unloved*

*Unheard*

*Unseen*

Write a list of what you believe are your core childhood wounds that are being repeated in your current adult relationships.

You are now responsible for giving yourself love. You become the original source of love for yourself without seeking it externally. We will explore the dynamics of healthy relationships and of giving and receiving love in future chapters.

When your core childhood wounds are triggered, you have an automatic, default emotional survival response.

Your emotional survival responses are not random behaviours; they are unique to you and part of being human. They remain consistent each time your core childhood wounds are triggered. The way you express anger is the same every time, regardless of who or how it is triggered. What you feel in your body is consistent — the tension in your stomach, chest, throat, and hands. It doesn't matter whether you are cut off in traffic or having an argument with your partner; your physical and emotional response to confrontation is the same every time. You might yell, become violent or abusive, or withdraw, go silent, or become overly busy.

Let's be clear: silence can be just as aggressive as yelling. Often, people think that if they remain silent, they are not being aggressive or showing anger — but using silence or withdrawal to express anger can be equally aggressive and damaging.

Emotional subconscious survival patterns are not creative; they are consistent each time.

When you are triggered into your emotional survival responses, it is like reverting to a five-year-old tantrum. Your inner child takes over and makes the decisions. These responses are a mix of learned behaviours based on how your parents or caregivers responded to you as a child.

Your unique pattern might include the same behaviours your parents or caregivers exhibited — if they yelled, you might yell too; if they withdrew, you might now withdraw. Either way, a default pattern was formed within you, and it influences how you respond now.

What is your default emotional survival pattern? Circle all that apply on each line; you may choose more than one. For example, you might yell and withdraw, or eat and become busy.

1. *Yell, withdraw, or become abusive or violent.*
2. *Overeat, drink alcohol, take drugs, and avoid being busy.*
3. *Blame internally, blame externally.*
4. *Seek attention, avoid it.*

When your emotional survival responses are triggered, it's your inner child reacting out of fear or simply not knowing another way to respond. As a child, feelings such as overwhelming anger and grief were hard to process or hold, or you were shut down and told to toughen up, stop crying, or that emotions were bad. Now, you've suppressed these feelings, and whenever you start to feel overwhelmed, your default emotional survival responses are triggered.

There is a deeper layer here that depends on your core childhood wounds. These are emotional survival patterns that can become hyper-vigilant, always looking out for danger. When activated, you might feel that your entire foundation is unstable. Hyper-vigilance means you're constantly triggered into perceiving that you're being attacked, rejected, betrayed, or abandoned. It is similar to CPTSD, where the subconscious activates pain from the past in the present moment.

During one of the Alchemy of Men retreats, a man shared that whenever his partner walked away mid-argument, slamming the door or shutting down, he felt completely dismissed. *"It's like she does not even care,"* he said. "I*t feels like punishment.*" As the group sat with this, something more profound began to shift. Another man reflected, *"That is what I do too, and it is not because I do not care. It is because I don't know how to respond when I feel like I have already failed."*

The realisation that emotional shutdown or reactivity is not always about power, control, or manipulation; it is about protection.

We discussed how many men were raised in homes where expressing emotions wasn't safe, where conflict meant rejection, and where there was never space to understand what was really happening beneath the outburst. These patterns now appear in your adult relationships. What seems like anger, control, or detachment in adulthood is often just a younger version of yourself who has never learned how to process emotional energy.

I also explained that if your partner were a child behaving this way, you would not take it personally, get defensive, or attack back. Instead, you would approach with love and compassion, clearly seeing that the child is in pain and responding in the only way they know how. When someone is yelling at you, it is their emotional survival pattern kicking in — their inner child tantrum.

These patterns, learnt in childhood, are still activated; they are mimicking how they were taught to respond to confrontation. These patterns did not change just because we grew older and got bigger bodies.

When you see someone yelling or withdrawing instead of reacting to feeling attacked, and your own emotional survival responses are activated, it is helpful to stop, drop your shoulders, calm your own nervous system, and see through the external drama to recognise that the person in front of you is in a state of emotional survival and pain. When you are in a state of emotional survival, you need love and kindness.

*Can you offer yourself love and compassion in these moments? Yes/No.*

Unfortunately, we are so used to punishing ourselves and others for being human and for having these emotional survival patterns. Instead of repeating these patterns, there is another way forward — one based on self-love and on giving and receiving love.

**Truth.** You are not stuck in your childhood story; you are not destined to relive the pain.

As your emotional growth deepens, so do your survival responses, giving you the power to change how you respond in any moment. You have choices. You have the opportunity to break the cycle of generational abuse and trauma responses. You can choose to have a different experience. Reparenting your inner child is a form of self-love. It involves love that is compassionate, understanding, kind, and nurturing. This is true love.

You can go back in time and work the parts of you that need love and safety. You can reshape the past by adjusting the energetic and emotional reference points for love and safety within you.

This is not about pretending your past trauma did not happen, avoiding it, or making it disappear. Now, you can give your past a voice by entering into the memory or the somatic feeling. You can rewrite your past as an adult who is open to healing and who provides your inner child with the love and safety you missed in those moments.

When you do this, something profound occurs. Your nervous system recalibrates to a new pattern, your neural pathways align with your adult self, and you are empowered to change your thoughts and emotional survival responses. When you view your emotional pain through the lens of love and compassion in your heart, everything changes. You retain a memory of the past without the emotional charge. You develop a new pattern that, with practice, can become an automatic response and integrate easily into your nervous system. You have the choice to respond differently to yourself and others.

At this moment, you have begun to rewrite the meaning of the past and offered the love and nurturing your inner child has always needed. You have shifted your automatic emotional survival responses from trauma to an act of love and compassion, where love is kind, gentle, nurturing, and caring.

These practices build on the **Drop Your Shoulders® Method Active Affirmations** *"I am safe,"* now going deeper by directly addressing your Inner Child. This creates a pathway to self-love, compassion, inner peace, and genuine freedom.

*"I am safe, I am loved"* becomes your ultimate truth. Expanding this active affirmation to connect with your inner child, subconscious, cells, and DNA, your active affirmation *"I am safe, I am loved"* becomes true on a physical level, aligning your subconscious and conscious minds. When both minds are in harmony, you will feel inner peace; when the words you speak match the feelings in your body, that is inner peace. I am safe, I am loved.

When you reparent your inner child this way, you are rewiring trauma patterns at a subconscious level through your nervous system, which in turn alters your automatic emotional survival responses, healing your past, present, and future in a single moment.

You are dissolving the subconscious beliefs and patterns that equate love with trauma, abuse, abandonment, rejection, and chaos. Reframing love as kind, gentle, nurturing, and caring.

As you continue to offer love to your inner child, you strengthen the relationship you have with yourself. Over time, love replaces fear, compassion replaces criticism, and feeling safe and nurtured becomes your new subconscious pattern.

This is your life now, and you get to decide. Today, you have made that decision.

My kinesiologist (a very wise man) once told me this, and it reshaped my life:

*"Everything is exactly as it is meant to be, or it would be different."*

This simple statement changed how I viewed my life. I realised that resisting reality was creating much of my suffering. It didn't mean I agreed with everything that had happened, nor did it make painful experiences okay. It simply meant accepting that what had already occurred could not be changed. In that acceptance, I found peace. I stopped fighting the past and began focusing on what I could choose now.

# Drop Your Shoulders® Method 14

## Loving Your Inner Child

Loving your inner child is simple and will happen naturally.

- Start with the **Drop Your Shoulders® Method Scribbling.**
- Notice areas of tension, tightness, or pain, whether physical or emotional. Emotional pain may manifest as anxiety, with discomfort mainly in your stomach, chest, or throat. Depression can feel like numbness or dissociation. Focus on these areas.
- Continue to scribble as you imagine yourself as a small child, at any age that comes to mind. Visualise this part of yourself the best way you can, standing in front of you; give them permission to express their emotions. Is he or she angry or sad, yelling or crying? Continue to scribble as you visualise this image and calm your physical body. Note: if you have trouble with visualising, that is ok; just the intention is enough.

- Now soothe your inner child as if they were your own child; in your mind, talk directly to this part of you.

*"You are safe, I love you, I am here for you now, and I will keep you safe now."*

- Imagine hugging or holding yourself as a child while you continue scribbling, relaxing your muscles and calming your body.

- When you feel your physical body is relaxed and your nervous system is settled, picture your inner child as calm and bring the image and energy of your inner child into your heart centre, merging together as one.

- Say to yourself:

*"THAT WAS THEN, THIS IS NOW."*
Feel the distance between the past and the present.

- Burn your scribble paper safely and let go of all attachment to the experience. Drop your shoulders and get on with your day.

- Initially, do this when you feel triggered into an emotional survival response. If you do not feel triggered, you can still connect with your inner child to reassure them that they are loved and safe. It only takes a few minutes with intention to reassure your inner child. Drop your shoulders and say your active affirmation, *"I am safe. Right now, I am...."*

Note: When you are visualising yourself as a small child, this can come across as a small baby, a toddler, a young child, a teenager, or a young adult, ranging from 0 to 18 years old. Often, the age you remember is the moment when the shock or trauma first triggered your emotional survival response. You do not need to understand the details or even remember that moment; you just need to accept the connection between the age and the tension in your body. By expressing and releasing the energy through this method, your body will let go of the tension, helping you feel calmer and lighter.

To truly reparent your inner child, it is important to come to terms with those who could not parent or care for you as you needed when you were a child.

**Forgiveness is not about forgetting or excusing someone's behaviour.** It's about choosing today to stop carrying their energy. You stop carrying their energy, their story, and their pain in your body, and you stop confusing survival patterns with love.

# Chapter Thirteen

# Forgiving Your Parents And Caregivers

Regardless of what happened in your childhood, your parents and caregivers did the best they could within their own limits. Refer to the previous chapter on ancestral trauma patterns.

This is not about excusing trauma and abuse, nor about minimising what happened to you. It is about understanding why it occurred in the first place. We touched on this earlier when discussing the evolving emotional body and the polarity between the underdeveloped and overdeveloped emotional bodies. For many, your parents were not emotionally capable, nor did they have the skills or knowledge you possess now to provide the love, care, and nurture you needed as a child. In terms of realistic expectations, they were not emotionally capable of behaving differently; otherwise, they would have.

The day I realised my parents were not capable of self-love and nurturing before I was born, and in turn were not capable after I was born. They were trapped in physical and emotional survival patterns, default patterns passed down through generations. They did not have the tools or practices I now have to calm their nervous systems or heal from past traumatic experiences and events. Their nervous systems were wired for physical survival. Their hearts were broken long before I arrived, and the generational patterns of abuse, betrayal, rejection, and abandonment were overwhelming for them to navigate.

I assume the generational patterns that were repeated on both sides contributed to my own programmed belief that love equals chaos, abuse, and trauma, and therefore I carried these survival patterns in my DNA.

This does not determine whether it is right or wrong; it simply states what happened. Your parents did their best with the information they had, and it fell short of what you needed while growing up. It was not entirely their fault; they were also repeating patterns of shock and trauma passed down, patterns of anger, and fractured statements ingrained in their subconscious. Your parents may also have endured difficult childhoods themselves, perhaps even worse than what you experienced. To them, these behaviours were considered normal.

Again, if there is no specific traumatic event you can recall, there are subtle trauma patterns of absence rather than presence. Neither is worse than the other; however, all people develop and enact emotional survival responses from childhood.

When you drop your shoulders now and breathe into your heart, you can calm your nervous system and see through your heart of compassion. You can feel that they suffered and may still be suffering deep emotional pain, disconnection, and avoidance. Their behaviours stem from their own life experiences.

As you continue to reparent your inner child and heal your past, you will notice that your inner child sees the world through a child's eyes, not an adult's.

Your parents were not gods or perfect; they were wounded children in grown-up bodies, carrying generations of pain that had never been addressed.

They projected these behaviours outward, and you are now learning to calm your nervous system and release the energy without projecting onto others. Breaking free from the trauma cycle, you can identify which ones your mother played out and which ones your father played out. Identifying these behaviours without judgement or punishment is the first step towards understanding that what was projected onto you was not yours to carry.

Do this exercise for both of your parents. *What is their default emotional survival pattern?* Circle all that apply on each line; you may choose more than one, for example, you might yell and withdraw, or eat and become busy.

1. *Yell, withdraw, or become abusive or violent.*

2. *Eat, drink alcohol, take drugs, avoid by staying busy.*

3. *Blame internally, blame externally*

4. *Seek attention, avoid attention*

**Truth.** They did and still do love you in the best way they know how, given the limits of their emotional capacity. It is true that they were still doing their best, even if that best hurt you deeply.

You are not forgiving them just to *"let them off the hook."* You are forgiving them because you no longer want to carry their wounds in your body.

For me, I had to sit with this. I was angry that my parents did not create a safe or emotionally loving environment for me. Understanding and accepting the truth that they were not capable of giving me what they did not have themselves allowed my anger to soften and my heart to open to forgiveness. It was not personal; they would have behaved this way anyway. On some level, I believe I (my soul/spirit) chose to be born into this family rather than another.

*Have you ever wondered why you belong to this family?*
*Why you were not born into another family in a different country?*

I believe the parents I chose gave me the life lessons and insights I needed to do the work I do today. I chose to break generational patterns and evolve my emotional body, not just for myself but for the next generation and to share these learnings with you.

Now you can understand the concept of forgiveness for those who came before you; you are free to heal from the past and give yourself the love you did not fully receive.

# Drop Your Shoulders® Method 15

## Forgiveness, Dissolving Contracts, And Cutting Cords

- Drop your shoulders and start the scribbling method
- Now expand into the **Drop Your Shoulders® Method: Loving Your Inner Child.** Connect with yourself as a child, imagine this part of you expressing emotions, and then offer reassurance and nurturing.
- Now picture your parents or primary caregivers in front of you and say the following to each of them in turn.

*"I cancel, nullify and void all contracts, agreements, cords, hooks, and bindings on all levels across all space and time."*

*"I cancel, nullify and void all ancestral and generational patterns that are not mine to carry."*

*"This is my free will and choice, and must be respected on all levels."*

*"I see you now; I see you did the best you could at the time."*

*"I forgive you. I forgive you. I forgive you."*

*"I resolve, dissolve and release all that is not love."*

- Now, imagine a blue-and-black cord linking you to them, and picture cutting it. (These cords can attach anywhere on your body, such as your chest or throat, front or back. Trust what comes to mind; what you imagine is perfect for this exercise.)
- Now say in your mind or out loud,

*"You no longer have access to my energy circle; you no longer have the power to hurt me, and I choose not to hurt myself."*

- Take a deep breath in, then release it with a sigh. Imagine pushing the image of your parents and caregivers out of your energy field.
- Returning to your energy circle, imagine a circle of energy surrounding you, with a silver boundary at the outer edge. A bubble of light completely surrounds you.
- Connect now with your inner child and imagine they are happy, playing with you and laughing. Reassure your inner child, *"You are loved, and you are safe."* Now bring your inner child into your heart centre and merge as one.
- Drop your shoulders, calm your nervous system and carry on with your day.

Remember, this forgiveness process does not excuse abusive behaviour; it aims to release you from the energy you are holding on to.

When you choose to love yourself physically, mentally, and emotionally, you return to your original state of wholeness. It is your birthright to feel loved and safe, and as an adult, it is your responsibility to love yourself first.

# Chapter Fourteen

# Self-Love Is A Sacred Practise

Self-love is not just a concept. It is a sacred practice, a somatic experience, and a commitment to giving yourself love.

You are enough right now, not when you have healed or when you think you are better. Right now, in this moment. Yes, you have wounds and scars, but you don't need to relive the past to heal them, and you definitely don't need to keep picking at or reopening your wounds.

To love yourself fully, it is essential to understand how you receive love. *A well-known framework is the 5 Love Languages, developed by Gary Chapman*. We will look at them not as strict rules but as invitations to nurture love within yourself and others. Each offers a unique way of giving and receiving love.

Your love language is not random. It is a direct reflection of your earliest experiences of love or its absence. It speaks to the part of your subconscious that learned what love was like through repetition. Sometimes that wasn't through warmth and nurturing, but through absence, silence, withdrawal, or inconsistency.

You figured out what to expect based on what you were provided with, and what was missing.

This is why discovering your personal love language is not just about self-awareness; it is a step towards self-responsibility and self-love.

When you do not know how love feels in your nervous system, you will keep searching for it in places that cannot provide it, such as your adult relationships. You can keep chasing the idea of love without truly understanding how to receive it.

The old saying "you must love yourself first before you can receive love" is true. When you do not know how to love yourself, it can feel overwhelming. Even thinking about it can activate rejection and abandonment patterns that trigger deep emotional pain within you.

Before we go further, I invite you to pause for a moment and tune in not to what you think your love language is, but to what your nervous system actually craves. The love languages are explained in more detail later; however, right now, if I asked you the question,

*"What do you need to feel loved?"*
*"What would your response be from the following options?"*

- Time
- Acts of Service
- Touch
- Gifts
- Positive Words and Affirmations

I encourage you now to honestly and openly explore your own love language. Take a quick online love language quiz to discover the key to loving yourself. You will have one primary love language, or two that are equally strong. These are the pathways your nervous system uses to determine whether you feel emotionally safe, seen, and heard.

It is your primary human need to feel loved and safe. When your core love languages go unmet, your nervous system kicks into overdrive, activating emotional survival responses such as fear — a fear that subconsciously equates to death — and this response can feel intense.

Receiving love is not optional; it is essential for survival. If you do not receive love, whether through self-love or from your environment, your survival responses are triggered and stay on high alert. You feel rejected, unseen, or abandoned — not because those around you are intentionally hurting you, but because your most basic emotional need for love is not being met, and your nervous system remains on high alert to keep you safe.

Understanding which of the five love languages offers a pathway to emotional safety is the first step towards learning how to receive love.

Love languages are not about being in love, physical attraction, or chemistry. They are about whether your nervous system and body feel safe and open to giving and receiving love. When your love language is met, whether through self-love or from your partner, family member, or friend, you feel safe, seen, and heard. From this place, intimacy becomes possible; intimacy is not about desire or performance. It is a place of vulnerability where love is shared, and intimacy is the physical, mental, and emotional expression of love in action. When your love language is honoured in relationships, attraction deepens into something real; feelings of love and safety are then shared. Your nervous system receives the message, *"I do not need to fight or run right now."* Your two core human needs — love and safety — are finally felt. Oxytocin rises, changing your body's chemistry; your nervous system begins to settle, and cortisol has less of a grip. Over time, higher oxytocin can lower cortisol levels, shifting your body into the parasympathetic (resting) state and opening you to love, intimacy, and regulation. Your shoulders naturally drop without trying; your body relaxes, and you are no longer in emotional survival responses.

Intimacy, love, and attraction are truly possible only when you feel loved and safe within.

To achieve this, we will explore the energetic templates of the five love languages. As you read them, do not just read the words—feel into them. I often tell my clients that your love language is the one you complain about the most. For instance, if your love language is time, you will frequently complain that the people closest to you aren't spending enough time with you, and you'll also automatically feel rejected and abandoned by them. This not only causes trauma for you but also challenges those who want to love you and don't know how.

I feel it is important to distinguish between your expectations of love and your actual experience. Movies have played a big role in shaping a picture of what love should be, not just in romantic relationships but also in family and friendships. This has created unrealistic expectations, creating a gap between the ideal image and real-life experience.

For someone like me, who did not receive love and safety in childhood and spent years searching for them externally, I can clearly see how movies became the blueprint for what I thought love should look and feel like. I did not have a somatic reference point for love and safety, so creating one through movies happened naturally.

If you are still searching for love in your relationships, your inner child is holding on to those cinematic images, projecting them outward and using them as a guide to ask, *"Does this person love me?"*

In those movies, the storylines are familiar, with all five love languages often displayed, especially after conflict, reinforcing the idea that love involves chaos, neglect, and confrontation, followed by grand romantic gestures, apologies, and reconnection that make everything perfect again. This is fantasy disguised as love in relationships; however, what you're seeing in these movies is unresolved child-to-parent dynamics playing out in adult relationships. The love languages are shown, but not in their true, healthy form, nor within a healthy adult-to-adult connection. Similarly, when they depict the ideal family or friendships, these are distorted images.

This can lead to unconscious patterns of layering fantasy over real people, expecting them to meet needs you did not receive as a child and to play roles they never agreed to. It is natural to believe in love and romance; however, when this belief is based on fantasy, it can lead to destructive relationships, co-dependency, survival patterns that become abusive, and a repetitive cycle of re-experiencing your childhood wounds in adult relationships — whether with a partner, friend, or family member.

When you learn to love yourself, you understand that it is not your partner or friend's responsibility to provide the parental unconditional love you that you seek; it is yours to give yourself.

Giving and receiving love is a gift and an opportunity to invite the people in your life to love you in ways you can receive it. It is not an expectation or a requirement. We will explore this further later, as we delve into relationships and connections.

Let's explore the five love languages now. No matter what your love language is, when it is received, you either hear *"I love you"* or *"I don't love you."*

**Words of Affirmation** – You do not just hear words; you absorb them. For you, words equal love. When someone truly sees you, speaks to you as if you matter, and offers positive encouragement, your body softens and settles, and you feel loved and safe. The opposite is when there is no kindness in their voice, a harsh tone, no recognition in their eyes, and the words are received as criticism and blame. In such moments, your emotional survival patterns are immediately triggered. You feel attacked and hear *"I don't love you,"* and respond defensively. To you, words are not just words; they are an expression of love.

**Quality Time** – You do not need constant attention; you need presence, eye contact, and undivided attention. You feel loved when someone chooses to be fully there with you — not distracted or rushed — just with you. You appreciate being invited to events and spending time with people, and you value simply sharing the same space without distractions. Without this, you may feel invisible, rejected, or unimportant, leading you to believe that those who do not spend quality time with you do not love you.

**Acts of Service** – Love feels genuine to you when it is demonstrated through actions. A cup of tea made for you or an offer to help with a task shows care. You feel secure when someone demonstrates they care by doing or fixing something for you, not just by saying they will, but by actually doing it. Inconsistency or unreliability can feel like betrayal to your nervous system, leaving you overwhelmed, having to do everything yourself and feeling unloved.

**Physical Touch** – Your body communicates through sensations; a hand on your back, a hug, or a gentle touch can say more than a thousand words. This isn't sexual intimacy; it's loving touch without expectation. Without safe, loving touch, your system might go into a quiet freeze — disconnected, feeling unloved, and longing for connection. You may feel unloved and believe you're unworthy of love.

**Receiving Gifts** – You feel cherished when someone puts thought and intention into giving gifts, and this is not about materialism. It is about feeling considered, remembered, and honoured. It could be something they made for you, a flower picked from nature, or a chocolate bought for you at the store. A gift says: *"I was thinking of you."* Without this, you may feel forgotten, unseen, dismissed, and unloved — that you give so much and it is never returned.

Once you know your love language and how strongly it connects to your nervous system, you can start to respond to it with presence.

When you understand that it is your responsibility to give love to yourself and have a clear path to do so, that love becomes an action within your control. This is where emotional safety begins — when you no longer rely on others as your primary source of love, because you can give it to yourself.

It is in this moment that you reclaim your personal power. Love is available to you in every moment, and you can give it to yourself; you no longer need to depend on the emotional capacity of those around you to give love to you.

When you learn to love yourself, you will be able to invite others to love you in a way you can truly receive it.

Self-love is about understanding that there is nothing wrong with you, recognising that you're doing the best you can at any given moment, and accepting that is enough. As you begin to genuinely love yourself in the ways you've longed for, you develop your emotional resilience. You stop expecting rejection and start receiving love in ways that feel safe, complete, and natural. You can then establish emotional boundaries that allow you to feel loved and secure within. It is clear that self-love is essential for your emotional health and wellbeing.

When your cup is filled from within, love no longer feels elusive or something you need to seek from others. You will no longer rely on receiving love from those who cannot give it to you, and you will set realistic expectations for your relationships. When you focus on self-love, and you feel loved and safe within, this is when adult relationships become enriched, and love is a shared experience.

Self-love is about GIVING your own love language to yourself.
It is a priority and not negotiable for your own health and wellbeing.

# Drop Your Shoulders® Method 16

## Giving Love To Self

- Drop your shoulders, begin to scribble and calm your body.

*What is your love language?*

- Make a list of all the ways you can express your love language to yourself.
- **Take Action**. Choose one item from your list and give it to yourself. One action each day.

Here are some examples.

**Words of affirmation:** explore how you speak to yourself. Negative self-talk is not self-love; it is heartbreaking. Words are important, so listen to positive podcasts or music. Writing in a journal is a form of self-love. Engage in anything inspirational: paint positive words, dance to them, and sing them.

**Acts of Service:** When you do not love yourself, you are always doing things for other people, not for yourself — cooking, cleaning, fixing, running around for them. Now is the time to make a list of what you can do for yourself: make food you like, not always what they like; clean a room in the house that is your special place, a sacred place. Do it for you.

**Physical touch** isn't about intimacy; it's about sensory touch and caring for your physical body. Take a bath with bath salts, book a massage, exercise, and look after your physical wellbeing as part of self-love. Eat well.

**Receiving Gifts** — go shopping and buy yourself something you love. This is regular self-gifting; it doesn't need to be expensive. Crafts and making something for yourself are great, too. Even a small treat is still a gift.

When your love language is **Time,** make space for yourself each day — whether it's time in nature, a creative activity, journaling, or simply enjoying time alone.

Remember, self-love is not negotiable. Expressing love to yourself every day, in your own love language, is true self-love and will change how you give and receive love in relationships.

## What occurs when there is resistance?

For all the years I did not love myself, I was plagued by self-hatred, negativity, emotional pain, and survival-based imprints that equated love with chaos, trauma, and abuse — all playing in the background, unbeknownst to me. I hated being alone; when I was alone, all my negative thoughts and emotions surfaced, and I kept reliving the deep pain of emotional trauma.

I avoided being alone, filling my time and space with others, parties, dinners, and events. The fear of being alone kept me in relationships far too long. I tolerated things I should never have, ignored my needs, and made myself smaller just to keep the peace. Their comfort came before mine, and when drama arose, it somehow felt familiar — my nervous system knew how to respond.

By understanding that my own love language is time, I realised self-love meant spending time alone. Initially, it was challenging. I dropped my shoulders to interrupt the stress response, wrote my affirmations repeatedly to reach my subconscious, scribbled and released energy, then scribbled some more, and practised woodchopping. I practised daily, and within about 4 to 8 weeks, something profoundly shifted. At first, it was subtle, but I felt lighter and freer, and I began to enjoy having my own time. I started making different choices about how I spent time with myself, viewing it as a way to love myself.

I went hiking, booked massages, went to the movies alone, painted in the middle of the night, danced and sang when no one was watching — I began to give love to myself. I started to own my own love language. Now, I enjoy time with myself as self-love.

You have one or two main love languages, but giving love to yourself can involve all five. There are no strict rules; the key is to intentionally give love to yourself first. This will quickly bring a deep sense of peace within you, and you won't need to seek it from outside sources. When you do receive love from others, it becomes a gift that you accept with warmth and gratitude.

Another example: if your love language is words of affirmation and you are not loving yourself, every negative thought becomes an attack on yourself. You are essentially bullying yourself and self-harming. It can be challenging to recognise that you don't know how to love yourself through positive words, and it's normal to let negative thoughts overpower you. Self-love involves changing the narrative you tell yourself; therefore, loving yourself means speaking kindly and offering yourself the positive words and encouragement you need to feel loved.

Ask yourself: would you speak to someone you love with the same harshness, criticism, and judgement you direct at yourself? The answer is usually no — that would be cruel. It's about changing your self-talk to phrases like *"I am doing my best in every moment"* or *"I love and accept myself."* Use active affirmations, positive podcasts, and music to help shift your inner dialogue.

Acts of service, when you are not loving yourself, can look like over-responsibility, always putting others' needs first, running around after people, making food, and always offering to do things for others, leaving you feeling alone and depleted of energy at the end of the day. When you shift this to self-love, you take the time to prioritise your needs, make food you enjoy, and allow others to fix things for you, or even pay someone to do it — all of which are acts of self-love.

As you can see, not giving yourself your own love language can leave you feeling unloved, and this has nothing to do with whether the people around you love you. This is about you and how you choose to treat and love yourself. Making these changes is easy; when you know your love language and give it to yourself, you will feel it.

## Why do people stay in abusive and toxic relationships?

Your nervous system tends to move toward safety. When there has been childhood trauma or traumatic events that were not safe, it creates neural pathways where love equals chaos, abuse, and trauma. Your nervous system tends to seek what it knows rather than what it does not. Even though you know it is unhealthy, you respond to these situations subconsciously with a sense of familiarity and safety. You haven't yet begun to love yourself in a way that can change the subconscious and somatic reference points, so the patterns continue. This is a form of self-betrayal; it is not loving yourself.

# Chapter Fifteen

# Parental Love Masked As Adult Relationships

If you did not feel deeply loved as a child — safe, seen, and unconditionally held — your nervous system is still searching for that experience. You might continue to search for parental love in your adult relationships.

It begins subtly at first. You might tell yourself you just want to be loved, cherished, and to feel chosen. If you were honest, you would realise that underneath it all, it's not adult-to-adult love you are seeking. It is the love you never received as a child.

The kind of unconditional love that would have said, *"No matter what, I am here. You are safe. You are everything I ever wanted; I will love you no matter what; I will never leave you."*

This creates a strong emotional projection, often rooted in fantasy. It reflects your inner child's desire for unconditional love and to feel loved and safe.

You may unconsciously look to a partner, friend, or even a sibling to play the role of a loving parent. Unknowingly, you push boundaries to see if they love you and will stay no matter what. This distorted pattern of seeking a parent's love in an adult relationship demands unconditional devotion from the other person.

You can seek it in any relationship, but mainly in your primary relationship with the person you feel closest to.

This is usually a romantic partner; however, if you are single, it can be transferred to a friendship or a sibling relationship.

In some cases, you may still seek it from a parent who was unable to give it to you initially, hoping they will step into the role of a loving, caring parent.

These relationships can be dangerous, especially when both people are seeking parental love from the perspective of a wounded child. You can lose your identity, experience ongoing physical, mental, or emotional abuse, and repeat the rejection and abandonment patterns you faced as a child. You might find yourself trapped in fight-or-flight patterns in a chaotic environment where your emotional needs are not met, keeping you in a constant state of emotional survival.

While it is deeply human to seek love and connection in relationships, it can also be risky when it turns your adult relationship into a reenactment of childhood trauma. A place where old wounds are replayed rather than healed, leading to codependency, imbalanced communication, and emotional trauma.

No matter how loving someone is, they cannot heal your childhood wounds or fill the void left by your unmet needs. Only you can reparent and love your inner child, and expecting someone else to do it creates a trap for both of you. Remember, expectation versus reality leads to anger, and beneath anger lies deep grief.

When your inner child seeks parental love externally as an adult, it's important to accept that the time for parental love has passed and to let go. This may trigger a grieving process (see the chapter on Grief).

The period for parental love is from ages 0 to 18; after that, you are the adult responsible for providing this love to yourself. It can feel unfair, especially if you did not receive unconditional nurturing love from your parents and caregivers, but now it's an opportunity to offer this gentle love to yourself and your inner child. That's why self-love begins with reparenting your inner child with the love you crave.

Continue with the **Drop Your Shoulders® Method Giving Love to Self.** Choose one item on your list and take action now.

Self-love is an action. You break the cycle when you give yourself your own love language and turn inward to re-parent and love your inner child with reassurance:

*"I'm here now. You are safe. I love and accept you just as you are."*

You won't need to seek love from outside sources anymore. You don't need to test whether people will love you or leave you. You become your own parent, loving yourself and your inner child as you always wanted to be loved. Reassure your inner child,

*"I'm not going anywhere, and I'm here with you."*

Until you stop seeking parental love in adult relationships, you will keep feeling disappointed, not because love does not exist for you, but because you are asking for a parent's love to appear in an adult relationship.

For a long time, I did not realise it. I was living through the lens of my inner child, chasing unconditional parental love in my primary adult relationships, hoping to be chosen and loved no matter what.

As a child, I became an adult far too early, emotionally parenting myself before I was ready and also emotionally parenting my mother. That role has never left my body, so it makes sense that as an adult I entered relationships still carrying that same weight — emotionally caring for others and quietly wishing someone would finally look after me.

This story is not just mine; it belongs to many of my clients, and you may have had a similar experience. When you've been the child-parent in your own family — caring for yourself, your siblings, or your parents in any way — taking on physical and emotional responsibility too young, due to the absence of proper adult guidance, you develop survival patterns for emotional resilience. You lack clear emotional or physical references for healthy love and, as a result, struggle to give love to yourself, seeking it externally instead.

For me, this meant: If they needed something, I showed up 100%; if they pulled away, I leaned in; and if they could not love me, I worked harder to be worthy of love and gave more.

All the time, my childhood wounds are being replayed — rejection, betrayal, abandonment. I did not know I could leave the relationship because, as a child, I was unable to leave.

Of course, this is not a healthy adult relationship or partnership. It's a child seeking a parent's love in disguise. This is the inner child running the show, trying to rewrite the past through the present.

**Truth.** The more I over-gave, the more I attracted people who took from me — time, energy, money, joy. Not necessarily knowingly, as they were emotionally unavailable themselves; it was because my energy radiated, *"You do not need to take responsibility; I will carry it all."*

Beneath the surface, I was still enduring emotional pain, feeling unsafe and unloved. Moving between exhaustion and burnout, then picking myself up again to give more. A cycle of self-destruction.

It was not until I began re-parenting my inner child that I truly started meeting my own needs, loving myself, and giving myself my own love language of time and positive words. I listened to my heart and chose myself repeatedly. This is when I fully understood the imbalance and that breaking this pattern comes from self-love and re-parenting my inner child by giving myself the love I never received as a child.

I stopped chasing love that could not love me back. I stopped trying to fix people, hoping they would finally notice me. I stopped over-giving, hoping to be enough, and taking full responsibility for how others felt and behaved.

I distanced myself from those who could not offer an equal exchange of giving and receiving. I began valuing my own love language, my time, my energy, and what I gave to others.

Most importantly, I stopped expecting my partner, friends, and family to give me the love my parents never provided. I also stopped expecting my parents to step into the role of loving, caring parents.

Through forgiveness, I was able to accept them as they are now. I was able to establish a new relationship with them — one grounded in healthy boundaries and an adult-to-adult connection.

I took responsibility for loving myself, and you can do the same.

## Adult Love Is Not Unconditional, Unlike A Parent's Love.

Adult love is a choice and a mutual agreement; it is not owed to you. It is offered as a gift and a shared relational experience.

When you start to recognise the difference and stop demanding that others give you what your parents could not, you set yourself free. You free yourself and your relationships from the impossible and unrealistic expectations created by your inner child. You free yourself from constant disappointment and emotional chaos.

Most importantly, you free your inner child from waiting at the door for someone who is not coming. You are now the parent (the mother and the father) of your inner child, and these self-love practices will help you build healthy adult relationships.

## Love Languages As A Path To Emotional Maturity

Your love language is not just a discussion point or an online quiz. It mirrors your emotional needs, reflecting what your inner child longed for most and what your adult self requires to feel safe and loved.

Understanding your love language involves learning to meet your own needs first and to clearly communicate an invitation for others to love you in this way. This is not about seeking unconditional parental love but about inviting and experiencing adult love.

## How Did It Become So Confusing And Misinterpreted? What Happened

First of all, you did not understand love languages, so you naturally give others what you need to feel loved, hoping to receive it back. When your efforts and energy to love someone are not received as love or reciprocated in the same way, you begin to believe there is something wrong with you — that you are unlovable, not enough, or unworthy of love.

For me, this happened in childhood — not just because of the traumatic experiences and environment I grew up in, but also because the people around me did not love themselves and therefore did not know how to show love, or offered me their own love language, which was different from mine and which I did not receive as love. Early on, I believed I was unlovable. My situation was more complex; however, for you, it might be as simple as your parents giving you their love language without understanding that your love language was different and that you needed something else from them to feel loved.

Where are your shoulders right now? Practise the **Drop Your Shoulders® Method.**

You have assumed people do not love you because they haven't given you your love language, but they have been giving you their love language.

They are loving you in the way they know how; they are giving you their love language instead.

When you feel unloved in any of your relationships, ask yourself the question.

*Do they have a different love language than I do? Yes/No*

*Have I told them what my love language is and what I need to feel loved in this relationship? Yes/No*

*Are they showing me love in the way they know best, i.e., are they giving me their love language? Yes/No*

Alternatively, if the people in your life do not know how to love themselves, they will find it difficult to give love to you, even if they understand your love language. They will also find it even harder to receive your love and support.

You will notice this in people who perform acts of service; when you offer to help them in any way, they say no. Or when you give a compliment or encouragement, the person whose love language is positive words downplays or pushes it away. This indicates that the person isn't giving themselves their own love language, and when it is offered, they deny themselves the gift of receiving love as well.

It's important to recognise this. Dr Marshall Rosenberg, the founder of Nonviolent Communication, explained that when you ask your partner or someone close to you, *"How can I love you?"* and they reply, *"I don't know,"* they may not be in a place to receive love at all, no matter how you try to give it. In one of his talks, he noted that when someone can't identify or communicate how they receive love, your efforts may go unnoticed.

The message was clear: sometimes the most loving thing you can do is step back, as they will be seeking love externally, from you, to fill the void inside them.

When you continually give your own love language to others in the hope that it will be returned, you may feel unloved and start complaining that you do not feel loved in the relationship — that your partner does not spend enough time with you if your love language is *time*, that he/she is always criticising or putting you down (*positive words and affirmations*), or that your partner never helps around the house and you have to do everything (*acts of service*).

It is easy to see, through the complaining, what your own love language is and to identify the love languages of those around you. The disharmony in your relationship could be as simple as them having a different love language than you.

*What does this look like in reality?* For years, I felt unloved and rejected, mainly because I did not know how to love myself and therefore couldn't receive love in any form. Additionally, I lacked a healthy somatic reference point for receiving love.

When I changed my understanding of giving and receiving love, I realised that the people in my life truly loved me; they just expressed it in different ways. This realisation changed everything and transformed my fractured statement, *"I am not lovable."* For example, my love language is time, and a close friend of mine has the love language of gifts. I was always upset when this person was not available to spend time with me, not because she did anything wrong, but because I did not receive my love language.

I also didn't understand her love language, and as a result, didn't fully reciprocate through gift-giving, which is how she receives love. When there's a mismatch in love languages, both people can feel hurt and unloved. Even though we love each other deeply, we express love differently. Now that I understand the depth of the love languages, I can see how much she loves and how she has expressed it over the years — she would always send me wonderful gifts to show her love.

Another example of Dr Marshall Rosenberg's work. In a previous relationship, after recognising our love languages, I discovered that my partner's love language was words of affirmation. However, he had very little positive self-talk. He struggled to maintain his sense of self-worth without constant reassurance from others.

Even when I offered words of support or encouragement, he couldn't accept them as love. His nervous system was always on high alert, waiting for an attack. A simple comment like "You forgot to put the bins out" wasn't received as a reminder but as rejection. His mind would echo, *"I am not good enough, I am not loved."* From there, his emotional survival responses would activate. No matter how gently I spoke or how much I cared, everything was filtered through the lens of criticism.

With my own unhealed trauma patterns, the space between us became a battleground. Two nervous systems caught in survival mode, fight-or-flight, trying to protect rather than connect. It doesn't take long in that dynamic before both of us feel misunderstood, unloved, and exhausted.

I came to realise that no matter how much love you give someone — even if you are offering them their love language — if they do not know how to love themselves, they will not be able to receive it from you.

**Truth.** Self-love is when you give yourself your own love language and reparent your inner child.

A woman I worked with was loving and generous in her relationship. Her love language was acts of service; she expressed love through actions. She would cook, clean, run errands, and anticipate her partner's needs. That was her way of saying, I love you, I am here, I see you. It came naturally to her.

Her partner, on the other hand, felt love through physical touch. He would reach for her hand, initiate affection, and want to cuddle on the couch or sit close at dinner. That's what love felt like to him — safe, close, reassuring.

She felt exhausted, unseen, and taken for granted. He felt unloved, pushed away, and unwanted. She grew frustrated when he did not help around the house or show love in a way she could receive it. He felt rejected when she kept moving around him, always "doing" but never pausing to sit beside him or soften into closeness.

Neither of them was wrong. They were both offering their own love language in the hope of receiving it in return. But because their love languages were different, their nervous systems didn't recognise what they were receiving as love.

This mismatch led to a slow build-up of resentment and confusion. Their emotional survival patterns began to take over. She would yell and complain. He would shut down and withdraw. Arguments began over small things, but what they were really fighting for was love and safety in the relationship.

When I worked with her, she realised that, even though her partner was showing up as he knew how, she couldn't receive it as love, and he couldn't feel her love.

It was not about fixing each other. It was about understanding and learning to give love in a way that could genuinely be received.

When you understand that your love language is how you feel and receive love, and that other people have different love languages, you realise it is your responsibility to give that love to yourself daily. Then you can give their love language in a way they can feel and receive it.

When your love language is time, make time each day to be fully present with yourself. If your love language is touch, nurture your physical body with tenderness, even in stillness. If positive words are your love language, pay attention to how you speak to yourself. If acts of service are how you show love, do things like cooking lovely meals or tidying your space for yourself. If gifts are your love language, create or buy items that brighten your day or make you feel great. Start by giving yourself one act of love each day, aligned with your love language.

When your cup is full, and you love yourself in this way, you no longer seek love externally, nor do you come from a place of lack or a sense of being unloved. You learn to give yourself your own love language.

This overflowing love can then be shared with others, and when you are in a relationship with a partner, friend, or family member, you can give them their love language as a gift.

The invitation to give and receive love becomes very straightforward.

When you love someone and understand their love language, you will want to give it to them not because it comes naturally or easily to you, but because you want them to feel loved by you. This is the point where emotional maturity and mindful communication come into play.

# Chapter Sixteen

# Love Is An Inspired Form Of Giving

Love is an action; it is a gift, not a duty or obligation. It is a gift to yourself and to others.

Love, as an inspired form of giving, flows through presence and small actions—in how you show up—not just for others but for yourself. When you understand your love language, you can start giving it to yourself each day rather than waiting or hoping someone else will.

You also begin to speak it clearly, not as a demand or expectation, but as an invitation to those in your life. It isn't their responsibility to love you this way, but if they genuinely want you to feel loved by them, they will meet you there. They will give you your love language, and you will naturally give them theirs.

This is where love begins to feel safe, where giving and receiving become a natural rhythm, not a transaction but a deeper expression of care.

Alternatively, when someone you love cannot give you your love language for any reason, they may have chosen not to or may be unable to meet you in this way. This is their truth, and once again, it is not their responsibility to fill your cup of love. You can let go of the fantasy that one day they will wake up and love you in the way you need to receive love.

Not receiving your own love language in a relationship creates an imbalance and, over time, will lead to feeling unloved.

That said, when you love yourself and do not rely on your relationships to fill this space within you, you will surround yourself with people capable of giving and receiving love in an adult relationship, where there is a balance of giving and receiving.

When sharing your love language with your partner, family, and friends, it is vital to own it.

You learn to communicate, *"This is how I feel loved. Would you like to love me this way?"*

Note: Be specific about the action you need to receive love, so the other person knows exactly how to love you. For example, my love language is positive words and affirmations. You can say,

*"I love it when you call and text me during the day or when you acknowledge the little things I do for you."*

Then it is the same for the other person. Ask them.

*"What is your love language, and how can I give love to you?"*

If they do not understand their love languages, share what you know, then give them space and time to discover what they need to feel loved in the relationship.

That question alone can transform all your relationships. It opens the door to deeper connection, where both people feel loved, seen, and heard.

When you clearly communicate your own needs, you no longer make it the other person's responsibility. Instead, you take ownership of it by giving meaning to an action. This is important because the other person might not realise that positive words mean love to you or that quality time makes you feel loved, especially if their love language differs from yours; they can't connect the two.

For example, if your love language is acts of service and you are always complaining to the other person that they do not do what you ask or help around the house, they see the tasks as jobs, not as an expression of love—especially if their love language is something else. Once you both understand that the meaning of the task or action is an expression of love, it becomes a gift of giving. It is no longer a chore or task; it is a gift of love. It is a choice to give you love in this way.

*Have you assumed your love language is the only one and wondered why the people you give love to don't recognise your efforts as love or return them in the same way? Yes/No*

Giving your own love language to yourself and offering others theirs is true love. Receiving love then involves inviting the other person to gift you your love language in a way that you can receive it as love, as an action.

No one knows your love language; only you know what makes you feel loved.

When you communicate your love language and what it means to you, you invite love into your life.

When you do not clearly, and with an invitation, explain what you need to feel loved in relationships — specifically, how the other person can show love to you — your relationship can quickly turn into a push-pull dynamic. Both you and the other person may then be trying to receive love without truly giving it in a way that can be received. As a result, both of you may start to feel unloved in the relationship.

This is when you start demanding love and trying to change the other person to get your love language and have your needs met. You might begin to complain and reject the other person, and feelings of anger and resentment may arise, making the relationship unhealthy.

Many clients have told me, *"If I have to tell them, then it does not mean anything."* Again, this reflects how movies and cinematic portrayals shape your perception of love — that the other person should automatically understand and know what you need. The truth is, they cannot know unless you tell them.

When you tell your partner, friends or family members, *"this is what I need to feel loved by you"*, and they make a conscious effort to express your love language so that you do feel loved by them, this is the greatest gift of all.

They are saying, *"Your love language does not come naturally to me; it is different from mine. You matter, and I want you to feel loved by me, so I will show up for you the best way I can and give you what you need — not what I think you need, but what you actually need to feel loved by me."*

Again, if they choose not to love you in this way, it is their choice. Often, it's not because they do not love you, but because they lack the capacity to give love in that way. Usually, this is because they are not yet loving themselves and find it difficult to love others.

Another scenario is relying on one person, for example, your partner, to meet all your needs for love. It is not one person's responsibility to give you all the love you need; this is an unrealistic expectation.

Your primary responsibility is to love yourself first. When you fill your own cup with self-love, receiving love from others becomes a bonus, and you can then accept it from everyone in your life in different ways. It's not just about relying on one person to provide that love.

Now you can take responsibility for self-love and communicate your needs to those in your life from the adult within you who is ready to build a healthy adult relationship. The more you give yourself your own love language, the more you start to create your own emotional and somatic reference points for healthy love. You have more love to give.

# Drop Your Shoulders® Method 17

## Giving Love To Others

- Begin with the **Drop Your Shoulders® Method**.
- Write a list of all the ways you can show love to another person (partner, friend, family member)
- What is the other person's love language?

Partner:
Family Member:
Friend:

- Action one of the items on your list each day to give love to one of the people on your list.

## Giving Yourself Permission To Forgive Yourself

I encourage you to be honest and to forgive yourself for your past decisions and behaviours. The moment you genuinely forgive yourself for all the times you abandoned your own heart, ignored your intuition, or didn't listen to your body when it told you this was unsafe or didn't feel right is a vital step.

This includes forgiving yourself or others for what happened and recognising when you ignored your own truth. When you judge and criticise your past without considering all the information available at the time — such as what was happening, your age, your mindset, your emotional state, and external circumstances — you overlook the full picture.

You can also forgive yourself for having survival-based imprints that equate love with chaos, abuse, and trauma. With this running in the background of your subconscious, behaving differently in the past would have been impossible. Now you can stop judging the decision not to leave an abusive environment earlier, or for all the times you responded with emotional survival responses. You can create new somatic reference points and shift your energy frequency.

This is the day when self-forgiveness allows you to let go of your own judgements and criticisms.

*Are you aware of how your negative thoughts and self-talk are harming you? Yes/No*

This practice reconnects you with the parts of yourself from the past that still carry the imprint of shame, guilt, and grief. By becoming the one you forgive, you dissolve self-judgement, criticism, and negative self-talk.

Self-forgiveness is the foundation of emotional safety; it is not an external process. When you return to the truth that the deepest abandonment, betrayal, criticism, and judgement came from you, you realise you have been harder on yourself than anyone outside could ever have been. You can open your heart to self-forgiveness and compassion.

**Truth.** Whatever age you imagine yourself, you did your best at the time with the information you had—physically, mentally, or emotionally.

When emotional pain goes unprocessed, it transforms into energy that is projected outward onto others, often towards those closest to you. This projection occurs through yelling, withdrawal, violence, control, perfectionism, chaos, or physical, emotional, or sexual abuse.

However, when it is projected onto children or other vulnerable individuals, it transfers this energy into their energetic field and activates survival patterns in those it touches.

Cycles of abuse can be passed down through generations, repeating again and again until someone in the family says "No" and decides to break the cycle.

I wasn't born with self-hatred; it was energetically projected onto me. This is how the energy of emotional pain is transferred. That projection influenced how I viewed myself and how I experienced the world around me, and it created a frequency within me of self-abuse.

As I became a teenager, I did not outwardly show this pain; instead, I turned it inward. It was not separate from me; it was part of me. I judged myself harshly, holding myself to impossible standards. I didn't directly criticise others, but I expected a lot from myself and from the world around me. This was more than a survival strategy — it was a survival-based imprint. I was learning to control my external environment to feel safe.

Throughout my 20s, I was hyper-vigilant, and my emotional survival patterns didn't present in the way you might expect. I was high-functioning, driven, focused, and reckless at the same time. I was motivated to survive; I worked for large corporations for most of this period, building financial security as a foundation for my own sense of safety.

Beneath this, I was unable to accept that my life was filled with emotional trauma. I was also motivated to find answers, break the cycle, and change the world so that what happened to me wouldn't happen to others. I knew this energy and pain weren't truly mine. I searched and searched for a way to be free of it. I journaled, tracked my patterns, and monitored my automatic emotional responses, yet I still couldn't stop the process that felt out of control. I was continuously on high alert and unable to rest.

I had to forgive myself for being a child who could not protect herself, for carrying the weight of self-hatred that wasn't mine, and for the years of self-abuse.

I also had to give myself permission to stop carrying the burden of self-hatred. For years, I believed that if I let go of the self-judgement, criticism, guilt, and self-hatred, I was somehow letting everyone else off the hook. I thought holding onto the pain protected me. In reality, I was the one still suffering whilst those who hurt me had moved on without a second thought.

**Truth.** You cannot judge your past decisions through the awareness you have today. At every stage of your life, you responded with the knowledge, emotional development, survival patterns, and resources available to you at that moment.

You do not need to forgive the person who hurt you to free yourself from their energy (although you may or may not choose to do so; it is not necessary). This is about reclaiming your personal power and releasing the energy that was projected onto you. It involves cutting the energetic cords that connect to your energetic field and closing the holes.

Forgiveness is not about forgetting what happened; it is about embodying truth in action. Self-forgiveness involves refusing to hold onto the energy of those who hurt you and refusing to perpetuate the cycle of abuse, whether directed towards yourself or others.

**This is how you break generational cycles of pain and abuse. Self-love and forgiveness enable you to break the cycle.**

Forgiveness helps you see clearly and make a conscious choice to stop passing emotional pain on to others and to prevent turning that pain inwards.

You were and always are doing the best you can with the information you have physically, mentally, and emotionally. Therefore, practising self-forgiveness frees you to see through the drama of the roles you have played, and now you have a choice in how you want to respond and behave.

Yesterday, you did not have this information, so you cannot judge or criticise yourself for what you did then, even though you now have new information and can make a different choice today. The same applies to others; you will see the roles they are playing. It's important not to judge or criticise them and to remember that they are also doing their best with the information they have at any given time, along with their own physical, mental, and emotional state.

Revisit the **Drop Your Shoulders® Method Expectations Versus Reality** to set realistic goals for yourself and others.

When you do not feel emotionally safe, it can feel like repeatedly reopening your wounds. It can be overwhelming and leave you feeling out of control.

Forgive yourself for all the times you did not know how to protect yourself or say "No" when your heart pleaded with you to stay, when your inner child believed that love meant chaos and abuse. You did not know how to walk away when your nervous system was already in a constant state of survival. You did not know what you did not know. And now you do.

This is the moment when you stop blaming the people who hurt you and start recognising the ways you have been hurting yourself. Recognising the small, subtle ways you have created unhealthy attachments in your adult relationships. The times you said "Yes" when you truly wanted to say "No". The times you've stayed silent to avoid conflict. The times you've prioritised another person's needs over your own to feel a moment of connection, even if it cost you your dignity.

No one has the power to hurt you without your permission. That doesn't mean the pain you experienced was not real; it means true strength comes from within. When you give that power away, you become dependent on someone else's approval or behaviour to feel loved and safe. You might believe they rejected you, betrayed you, or criticised you.

**Truth.** No one can betray you more deeply than you betray yourself by staying in relationships, environments, or situations that don't feel safe, by silencing your truth to avoid conflict, or by overriding your own needs to be loved or accepted.

This is not about blame.

There are times, especially during childhood or in situations involving coercion or entrapment, or when your nervous system is frozen in survival mode, when you're unable to choose differently. In those moments, you are not betraying yourself. You are simply surviving.

But outside those dramatic circumstances, if you continue to ignore the part of you that knows the truth, keep choosing what is familiar over what is safe, or hand your power to people who cannot hold it, that becomes a pattern of self-abuse.

This is the harsh reality of betrayal because you already knew it. Healing begins the moment you stop ignoring your own knowing. The moment you decide what is right for you, regardless of what that looks like.

When there has been betrayal, I ask my clients, "Did you already know?" 100% of the time, the answer is yes — I felt it, I already knew. The betrayal here is not what the other person has done to you; it's about ignoring your own truth and intuition and not acting on them.

This is where self-forgiveness comes in, not for what they did to you, but for what you did to yourself in the absence of knowing another way. This is the moment you take responsibility and connect with the part of you that you have been secretly punishing or blaming through negative self-talk. Now you can reconnect with this part of yourself — whether it's your inner child or the adult you were at a different time — and offer love and acceptance.

For example, *"Can you love and accept the naive 20-year-old self who was doing their best with the information they had at the time?" Yes/No*

Consistent with clients and myself, I have found that it is easy to overlay self-punishment or judgement onto a younger part of yourself. It is important to recognise that your past decisions and behaviours were shaped by your age, knowledge, and physical, mental, and emotional capabilities at the time.

Now that you are older and have more information, knowledge, and capabilities, you can easily find yourself judging and blaming your younger self without recognising that you did not have the same understanding back then as you do now.

*Is it acceptable for a 40-year-old brain to judge and criticise the decisions and behaviours of a 20-year-old brain without considering their knowledge, stress levels, and environment at that age? Yes/No*

It's the same if you're judging and criticising yourself for not speaking up as a child, without understanding that you were just a child and not in a position to speak up or make a different decision.

When you realise that your negative self-talk and self-judgement as a child or young adult are what hurt you every day, self-forgiveness — for the decisions you made or didn't make, for your emotional survival responses, and for simply being human — becomes an opportunity to create freedom within yourself through self-love and self-acceptance.

I believe that each person is doing the best they can at any given moment. Imagine a person addicted to drugs; they are doing the best they can in that moment. Their body craves the substance, and their emotional state is overwhelmed. This does not make it right or wrong, nor does it mean they are incapable of hurting another person. It is about recognising the truth through external judgements and then establishing energetic boundaries, which we will explore in more detail later.

When you understand, without judgement, that your decisions and behaviours were influenced by your age, life experience, and mental and emotional state at any moment, you can show compassion for yourself and others.

I always say that when people behave badly, it is usually because they either lack the knowledge or understanding to make a different decision, or they are responding from emotional survival patterns. Either way, they are doing the best they can in that moment.

Remember the difference between expectations and reality: when you're under extreme pressure and triggered into emotional survival responses, you cannot respond as well as when you feel loved, safe, and empowered. Self-forgiveness is the process of forgiving yourself for whatever you still blame, judge, or criticise. When you genuinely recognise that you were doing the best you could at the time, you are acknowledging the truth.

The moments when you hurt another person — whether through tone, words, silence, distance, blame, or even violence — often don't stem from malice. They arise from emotional pain already within you, from your nervous system and subconscious survival patterns. They stem from unmet needs that lacked a language or a safe way to express themselves. However, there are unique situations in which harm may be intentionally caused.

When you recognise the unintentional nature of your own pain-driven actions, you can offer genuine compassion to the parts of you that have been carrying guilt. Through self-forgiveness, you begin to heal the parts of yourself that have held onto emotional pain — and choose not to project that pain onto others.

# Drop Your Shoulders® Method 18

## Self-Forgiveness

This practice originates from Ho'oponopono, an ancient Hawaiian prayer of forgiveness and reconciliation, as shared with the modern world by Morrnah Simeona and Dr Ihaleakala Hew Len. I use it here to approach yourself with compassion and let go.

- Start with the **Drop Your Shoulders® Method Scribbling**
- Scan your body for areas of tension, tightness, contraction, or pain. Breathe into these areas to relax the muscles. Now take your pen and paper, and let your hand move, scribbling on the paper.
- Picture yourself at any age that comes to mind. This is the age you will be forgiving yourself for. (Over time, I recommend you do this for all ages.)

- See yourself through the eyes of compassion — the part of you that you have judged, criticised, or blamed for actions born out of pain, fear, shutdown, or for hurting others while trying to survive. The part of you that you blame for what others did and carries guilt and shame. Let that part of you stand before you now.

- Look at yourself with love and compassion.

- Begin the Ho'oponopono phrases, one at a time. Speak them out loud or silently, directed towards the version of you in front of you.

*"I'm sorry. Please forgive me. Thank you. I love you." (Ho'oponopono)*

- Repeat it three times or more if you feel called. Continue scribbling until you feel calm in your physical body. Let your body guide you. Allow tears to come.

- In addition, use your own words. Here is an example.

*"I'm sorry for judging you and not understanding the pain you carried. For keeping you frozen in the story. "*
*"Please forgive me. For the times I turned away from you, for the shame, for the silence, and for thinking you were wrong or broken."*
*"Thank you for surviving, for trying, and for showing me where i still need love. I love you. You are not separate from me. You are me, and I am you. I am not leaving you behind."*

Another option;
*"I'm truly sorry I abandoned you; please forgive me. I apologise for ignoring you and putting you in danger; thank you, I love you. I'm sorry I stayed in a relationship while you were hurting; please forgive me. Thank you, I love you. I'm sorry I ignored the red flags and you; please forgive me. Thank you, I love you. I'm sorry I called that love when it was actually fear; please forgive me. Thank you, I love you."*

- Continue to add whatever comes to mind here.

- Let the tears flow as you let go of the energy, or as you imagine your inner child crying out all the pain of years of feeling abandoned, betrayed, criticised, and judged by yourself.

- Now bring the image of your younger self into your heart centre.

- Now, drop your shoulders, coming back to your centre and continue with your day or evening.

Feel the love and compassion for yourself and acceptance of the human condition. You are always doing your best in any moment, unlike the past when you responded subconsciously, mainly through emotional survival patterns or imprints. Now you have the ability to choose. You can use the **Drop Your Shoulders® Methods** to experience emotional health and wellbeing and respond differently in any situation.

# Chapter Eighteen

# Inner Child Attachment Styles

## When The Safety You Seek Is Within Yourself

There are two fundamental human needs that cannot be negotiated: the first is love. We have discussed self-love, loving your inner child, and how to give love to yourself, as well as how to give and receive love in relationships. The second is safety—how do you feel safe within yourself and in relationships?

### What Is An Attachment Style?

Attachment theory was developed by John Bowlby and expanded by Mary Ainsworth. In this chapter, I explore these styles through the lens of the inner child, the nervous system, and healing.

An attachment style is the emotional and behavioural blueprint you unconsciously develop in early childhood, shaped by how your parents and carers responded to your physical and emotional needs for safety, connection, and soothing. This is an imprint on your subconscious, your nervous system, and the way you respond to closeness. If your early environment was attuned and consistent, you will develop a secure attachment, a sense that love is safe and that you are worthy of connection.

When love feels unpredictable, distant, or overwhelming, insecure attachment patterns form, including anxious, avoidant, or disorganised attachment strategies for survival.

It primarily relates to your primary relationship with a partner or any relationship where your vulnerability is evident; when you feel vulnerable, your attachment style becomes apparent. It reflects your childhood relationship with your primary caregiver or parent.

Knowing your attachment style at the start of a relationship, especially your primary relationship with a partner, is essential. This isn't about labelling attachment styles as better or worse, but about recognising the unseen patterns that influence intimacy, conflict, and the desire for closeness or control. Your attachment style will emerge during a disagreement, through silent withdrawal, or in an argument that seems disproportionate to the situation.

This is another opportunity to re-parent and reassure your inner child. Your inner child learnt to attach in a way that felt safe at the time, even if it wasn't actually safe. With this awareness, you can once again provide your inner child with the safety and security they missed out on.

Now is a good time to reassure your inner child with the **Drop Your Shoulders® Method Reparenting Your Inner Child.**

## The Four Attachment Styles

*Are you aware of your inner child's attachment style? Yes/No*

*Are you aware of how your inner child's attachment style manifests in your relationships? Yes/No*

No matter what your attachment style is, it is not wrong; it is part of you and will be a pathway to feeling safe both inside and out.

There are four attachment styles, each expressed through your subconscious patterns and nervous system. Your aim is to feel safe — not just physically, but emotionally as well.

Here is how you naturally experience each attachment style in your life.

### 1. Anxious Attachment (Inner Child's Story: "I'm not safe when I'm alone")

- Anxious Attachment (Inner Child's Story: "I'm not safe when I'm alone")
- You discovered that love can disappear at any moment.
- You look for signs of impending abandonment.
- You feel overly sensitive to delays in replies.
- You might become clingy, over-communicative, or rush to fix things — because any space feels like rejection.

Your inner child is panicking and feeling afraid, asking questions like *"Are you still there? Are you going to leave me?"* When triggered, you might overshare, over-apologise, or lose yourself trying to keep the peace, all to soothe the fear of being left behind.

### 2. Avoidant Attachment (Inner Child's Story: "Closeness is not safe")

- You realised that love often involved pressure, criticism, or unpredictability. So you protected yourself by retreating.
- You might appear independent, but deep down there's a fear of being overwhelmed, trapped, or consumed.

When things become too emotionally intense, your inner child shuts the door and pulls away: *"It's safer if I do not need anyone."* You withdraw, go silent, or rationalise your way out of connection, even when you care deeply.

### 3. Disorganised Attachment (Inner Child's Story: "Love is both safety and danger")

- You experienced love, but it wasn't consistent.

*Did the same person who held you also cause you pain?*

- Your system experienced confusion: *"I want love, but I do not trust it."*
- You draw people in and then push them away.
- You might feel overwhelmed by intimacy one moment and terrified of abandonment the next.

There's often a deep internal struggle: *"I want closeness, but I do not feel safe there."* This is your inner child, trapped in a trauma pattern and unsure of which way is safe. Your inner child is in chaos.

### 4. Secure Attachment (Inner Child's Story: "I am safe and lovable as I am.")

- You have learned — or relearned throughout this book — that love is consistent and trustworthy with self-love practices.
- You can handle space without spiralling and enjoy closeness without falling apart or losing your sense of self.
- You express your needs and listen to others.
- You know how to self-regulate and stay grounded, even when the other person is triggered and you don't take it personally.

Of course, we all want to have a secure attachment; it is available to everyone because your attachment style is not fixed. It is rewired through self-love, establishing a secure attachment by connecting with your inner child and developing new emotional and somatic reference points for love and safety. This builds awareness, self-regulation, and trust in your heart to guide you into relationships that are safe enough to support healing.

## When Your Inner Child's Attachment Style Gets Triggered

The moment you feel yourself slipping into familiar patterns of clinging, withdrawing, overthinking, and blaming. Practice the **Drop Your Shoulders® Method Loving Your Inner Child.**

Your inner child needs your attention, self-love, and self-soothing. While focusing on self-love, you need to feel emotionally safe.

When you are seeking emotional safety in your primary relationship and projecting your attachment style onto your partner, the relationship can quickly become unhealthy, especially if it triggers the other person's attachment style as well. I am referring to situations where both individuals are activated into their survival patterns.

For example, your attachment style is anxious, while your partner's is avoidant. These two attachment styles come together, creating chaos. The anxious person always feels abandoned, and the avoidant person always feels trapped. Once both attachment styles are activated, you are both in emotional survival patterns. Not only is your inner child seeking parental love, but you are also reenacting your attachment style.

In this situation, neither person has a secure attachment, and no adult is present. Both individuals are responding from emotional survival patterns formed in childhood. This relationship can quickly turn abusive as both try to push and pull to have their needs met, seeking love and safety externally.

Emotional safety is not just about your childhood experiences. It's also about what has been happening inside you since then. Often, depending on your attachment style, you may have unknowingly become the one who triggers the imbalance.

Think of the times you have criticised yourself with harsh self-talk, judged your needs, rejected your feelings, stayed silent to avoid conflict, or given away your power. The times you settled for breadcrumbs and called it love.

Or the times you have chased someone who could not meet you, hoping they'd finally see you, choose you, and stay with you.

These are not signs of weakness; they are your emotional survival patterns, rooted in early attachments and still playing out in your adult relationships. These patterns confirm that you are not safe emotionally, mentally, or physically. The imprint in your nervous system—your subconscious wiring—says that love equals chaos, trauma, and pain, and that closeness equals danger.

The journey to emotional safety begins with self-love and self-forgiveness. Show deep compassion for your inner child, who only wants to feel loved and secure. Forgive yourself for every moment you've replayed this pattern and been hurt, for every time you've mistaken chaos and abuse for love, and for every time you've ignored your heart's call to protect yourself.

We have discussed how an adult relationship is a balanced exchange of giving and receiving. In this situation, both people practise self-love, no longer seeking love and safety externally. They then learn to give and receive love and safety with each other, creating a healthy adult relationship.

When you develop a secure attachment within yourself, you hold the frequency to experience secure attachment in your relationships.

This is what it means to take back your power: to stop seeking externally the love and safety that now reside within you.

Your emotional health and wellbeing no longer depends on your external environment, your partner, friends, family, or anyone else in the room. Love and safety are no longer something you need to find outside yourself; they live inside you.

# Drop Your Shoulders® Method 19

## Secure Attachment

- **Drop your shoulders, calm your nervous system.**
- Focus on areas of tension, tightness, or pain,
- **You can start scribbling to release tension.** Now connect with your inner child at any age that comes to mind. Imagine yourself at that age, feeling scared and alone. Then ask yourself a few questions.

*Does your inner child want to run or to fight? Yes/No*
*Are they angry or sad?*
*Disempowered: Helpless or hopeless?*
*Confused or fearful? Separate or alone? Frozen or numb?*

Reassure your inner child: "You are safe. *I love you. I am here for you now. I will keep you safe."*

- Now picture your partner or the person who is now your primary relationship standing in front of you. Speak with your inner child and explain that this person is not your mother, father, or carer. Ask your inner child to let go of their attachment, and imagine cutting the blue or black cord between your inner child and the person you have chosen.

- Hold your inner child and let them feel safe with you. When you feel calm and centred, bring this image of your inner child into your heart centre and merge as one.

- Burn your scribble paper safely and let go of all attachment to the experience.

*"That was then; this is now. I am safe within, and I listen to my heart to make decisions."*

- Drop your shoulders, continue your day or evening feeling safe, calm, and centred.

Use the **Drop Your Shoulders® Method Secure Attachment** as often as you need, until safety is felt in your body. I suggest doing this whenever you start to feel insecure or avoidant in your primary relationship. Sometimes, you need to do this process several times at various ages. For example: a baby, a toddler, a young child, a teenager, or a young adult, anywhere between 0 and 18. Often, the age you recall is the time the attachment was created.

Your Energetic Circle is part of you that you cannot see; you can only feel it. It's the space around your body, an intelligent layer of energy that extends beyond your skin. Some call it your aura, while others refer to it as your energetic field.

We will call it your Energetic Circle.

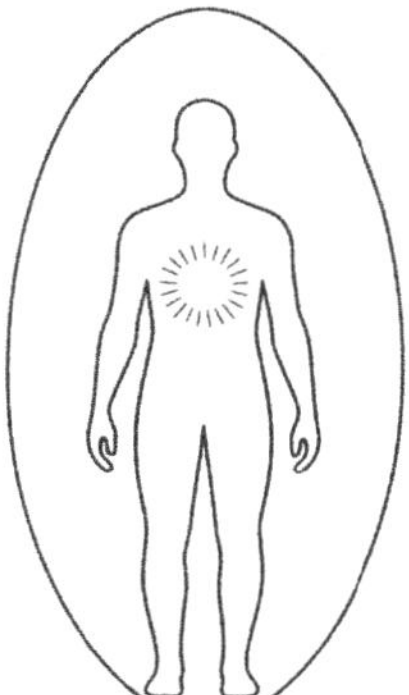

# Chapter Nineteen

# Your Energetic Circle And Emotional Boundaries

Your energetic circle is as real as your physical body. I find it fascinating that we protect our physical body at all costs while leaving our energetic circle open. It holds the frequency of your entire life and directly connects to your subconscious, which stores data and memories that then link to your nervous system, activating your physical, mental, and emotional responses. It is also a combination of geometric shapes that form a blueprint of your life—like a DNA template. It is the vibrational container and the first point of reference for your life experiences and all the versions of you that still live in memory.

You know this field is real because you have already felt it. You have walked into a room after a fight and felt your body contract and withdraw without hearing a word. You have hugged someone in deep grief and carried their sadness home with you. You have sat with a friend unloading their traumatic experiences and drama and left feeling exhausted, unwell, and unsure why. This is your energetic circle — the part of you that constantly interacts with others, whether you are consciously aware of it or not.

When I started working with clients, I quickly realised that when I worked with their energetic circle, the results would filter down into their physical experience, leading to lasting changes.

As an energy practitioner, I focus on your energetic circle and patterns. I understand the power of your energetic circle and how it directly connects to your subconscious and nervous system. To achieve permanent change, you need to work with the patterns in your energetic circle, the original point of activation.

Throughout this book, you have explored working somatically with the body to calm your nervous system, express emotion, and release tension. Now, you will learn to work with your own energetic circle and DNA templates to clear inherited generational patterns and establish healthy emotional and energetic boundaries — within yourself and in your relationships.

# Drop Your Shoulders® Method 20

## Activating Your Energetic Circle and Boundaries

- Apply the **Drop Your Shoulders® Method** to somatically connect with your body, scribble the tension out and calm your nervous system.

- Imagine yourself surrounded by a cocoon of light, a bubble with a boundary on the outside, coloured blue or silver. Like a reflective film facing outwards. Its function is to return any energy projected onto you to its source.

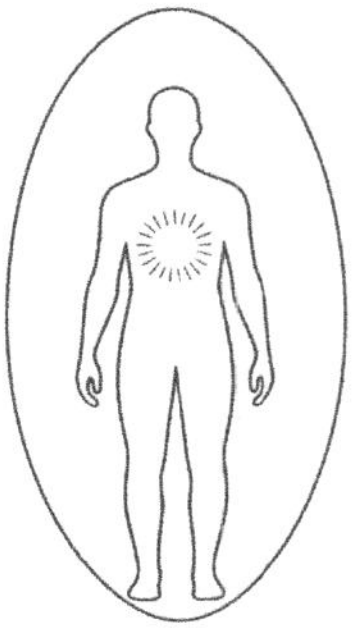

- Now feel into your own energetic field, your personal bubble of light. Imagine light radiating all around you, at arm's length in every direction. This is your energetic circle and boundary; you cannot see it, but you can sense and feel it.

- You feel safe within your energetic circle, when others are angry or projecting energy onto you, you no longer absorb it as your own. You're not triggered into emotional survival responses, and you don't take it personally. This is your energetic circle, and your energetic boundary.

- From here, state (either aloud or inwardly):

*"I call all my energy back to me and return any energy that isn't mine to carry, sending it back to its source. My energetic circle is intact, my boundaries are strong, and I am safe and protected."*

- Feel the shift. Your energetic boundary is not a wall; it's alive and fluid. Every time you intentionally activate your energetic circle and boundaries, it is already done.

This is a daily practice.

# Inherited Energy

## How The Patterns Of Your Parents and Ancestors Are Passed Down Through Your Energetic Lineage.

From the moment you are conceived, you exist within your mother's physical body and energetic circle; you also have your own energetic circle, but it is enmeshed with hers. Her body becomes your home, and her emotions your first language. When she feels fear, your developing energetic circle begins to contract and adapt to danger. When she feels loved and safe, it expands. Her emotional landscape shapes your experience of love and safety.

You are not separate from her in any way. Inherited energetic and emotional trauma patterns are passed down through your energetic fields from the moment you are in the womb. Why? Because there are no energetic boundaries; you are energetically one.

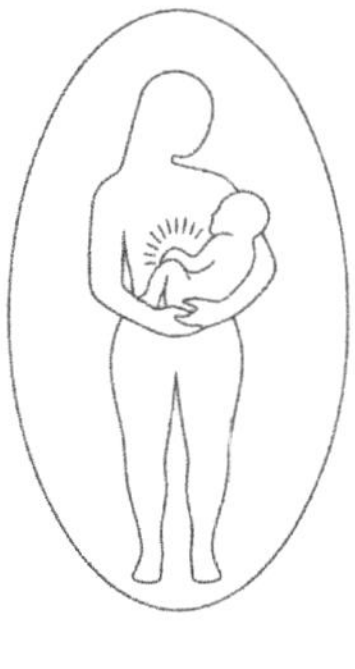

After birth, your energetic circle remains merged with hers, forming an enmeshment of energy, and then also merges with your father or any other primary caregiver.

These energetic bonds with your primary caregivers form part of your earliest energetic imprints and blueprint for your nervous system. As a child, you do not yet have physical, mental, emotional, or energetic boundaries. You do not have energetic borders.

You are a sponge for the physical and emotional world around you.

Every stage of your early development leaves a unique energetic imprint. From birth through adolescence, your energetic circle evolves alongside your brain and nervous system. Your relationship with safety, love, connection, and identity shifts. These changes are not just physical or emotional; they are also vibrational shifts within your energetic circle as it develops. To understand how your adult patterns formed, we explore the energetic stages of growth. From 0 to 8, then 8 to 12, and into the transformational years of 12 to 18, each phase offers insight into how your energetic circle was created, imprinted, shaped, fractured, or forgotten — and how you can now begin to reclaim it.

Between the ages of 0 to 8, your subconscious mind and nervous system are wide open, absorbing everything around you without a filter. There is no discernment yet, no conscious understanding of *"this is mine"* and *"that is yours."* There is only the physical sensation in your body, and appropriate reactions shaped by your mother's stress, joy, love and emotional landscape.

In response, you move, contracting and expanding. After birth, that connection persists, and her emotions become your external energetic environment. If she is anxious, you feel it, and your body contracts; the same goes for anger, grief, shame, guilt, joy, excitement, calm, and neutrality. You contract or expand with these emotions, mirroring her energetic responses and making them part of your environment. When she is calm and present, you begin to feel safe in the world, expand, and feel free.

You cry when you are hungry, sleep when tired, and begin to laugh. Everything that occurs or doesn't occur in your external environment with your primary caregiver is directly imprinted on your energetic circle, subconscious, and nervous system.

At this stage, your energetic circle has not yet formed, and you lack an energetic boundary. You remain entirely merged with your mother, both physically and energetically.

Initially, your focus is on your mother; however, as you grow between the ages of 0 to 8, your field becomes fully porous. You begin to form energetic bonds not only with your primary caregivers but also with anyone else in your home or outside it that you spend a lot of time with.

Your energetic circle is open and merges with theirs.

You are gathering data; you feel it in your body — loud noises or silence—and you are aware of the difference between harmony and disharmony in the energetic field. This shapes your attachment to love and safety, and you begin to learn the default patterns for physical and emotional survival that will eventually become your attachment style.

At this age, you lack the words to describe what is happening; instead, you feel it, and your body remembers. Your energetic circle absorbs your environment, which is why, when your parents were upset, you as a young child might have acted out or shut down. Not because you were misbehaving, but because you were mirroring the emotional tone of your surroundings and responding accordingly. You do not yet have energetic boundaries to separate other people's emotions from your own. Therefore, the emotional tone and energy of your environment become yours to process, express, release, or act out.

As an adult now, if you haven't yet learnt how to establish your energetic circle from someone else's and to activate your own emotional and energetic boundaries, you'll keep absorbing others' emotions, feeling them in your body, processing and expressing them without even realising that the emotion or experience is not your energy.

The most common cause of emotional trauma in adult relationships is a lack of energetic boundaries.

It was during those early years that the template for your attachment style began to form. In those initial moments of life, before the development of logic or language, your body recorded emotional patterns as truth. When your parent or caregiver was angry, you, as a child, did not understand the context; you felt it in your energetic field and concluded, I must have done something wrong.

Why? Because every energetic interaction you have with your environment affects you. In those early years, your parents and caregivers are your whole world; they are your only source of survival, safety, and love. So anything happening to them on an energetic and emotional level also happens to you.

*Remember those core fractured statements from Part 1 of this book? Yes / No*

These fractured statements arose when your parent or caregiver withdrew emotionally or projected their emotions onto you. You lacked the capacity to understand the complexity of adult stress, emotions, or overwhelm. You felt the anger or disconnection and concluded, *'I am not lovable," "I am not worthy," or "I am not enough."* These are not mere thoughts; they are energetic imprints that quietly shaped the subconscious patterns of your emotional life and the functioning of your limbic and nervous systems. To stay safe, you adapted by becoming quiet, overly helpful, or invisible.

Your attachment style and love languages also developed during these moments, through subtle repetitions and patterns of people-pleasing, over-giving, emotional shutdown, and perfectionism, all formed in your attempt to stay safe and feel loved.

Their stress responses become an imprint on your nervous system. Their reactions becomes your story, and their emotional state begins to shape how your body reacts to life. This is the moment when your subconscious is fully open, and the emotional tone of your home, including your parents' and caregivers' voices, how they handle conflict, love, and uncertainty, forms the blueprint from which you develop your entire sense of self.

You do not yet have a clear sense of where your parents end, and you begin. At this stage, there is no separation — neither physically, emotionally, nor energetically. You live within their world, and they 'ARE' your world.

You feel what they feel and respond to what they cannot express. You do not question this because there is no concept of good or bad, right or wrong; there is no judgment, only the felt experience. You perceived their moods as your own and learned to energetically read the room before you could read a book. You responded to joy with the same energy as you did to sadness. You absorbed the lightness of excitement, the safety of calm, the harsh tone of anger, and the grief that had no words.

As a child, you do not know how to recognise abuse, neglect, or abandonment. These understandings develop much later as you grow. At this stage, love and connection, no matter how it arrives, are simply accepted. You adapt your behaviour to receive love and feel safe.

This is also where we started this book, in that first moment of shock, that initial jolt through the body when the nervous system silently registered that something had changed. It might have been subtle — a raised voice, extended silence, or a sense of contraction and tension. Or it could have been a sudden trauma, such as a death, violence, or loss. Whatever it was, your body remembered. These shocks and traumas from ages 0-8 become your nervous system's default template.

These are a natural part of human growth and your own development. They are brilliant, embodied responses; your nervous system was doing exactly what it was meant to do. It was doing what it had to do to stay safe and connected, and it was what you needed at that moment. You were adapting to the environment that shaped you, in the only way a young body knows—through the intelligence of survival.

For myself and my clients, it was not just emotional undercurrents shaping the field; it was trauma. The kind that does not just pass through but crashes in. For example;

Death

Abuse

Addiction

Mental illness

Domestic Violence

These events do not occur as isolated moments in your childhood; they become the ultimate reality. The nervous system records them as permanent, solidified events, leading to a build-up of frozen shock energy in your body. This is when survival-based imprints become entrenched, affecting the development of your neural pathways, energetic circle, limbic system's subconscious patterns, and nervous system default settings — all hardwired to believe that *"THE WORLD IS NOT SAFE. Love cannot be trusted. Love equals chaos, trauma, and abuse. I must protect myself at all costs."*

They do not merely pass through; they become hardwired into your survival-based imprints, which begin to shape every future event and relationship, every boundary, every moment of trust or closure.

You did not learn through conscious reasoning; you learned through repetition. The patterns that kept repeating around you — raised voices, lack of warmth, sudden mood swings, or moments of soft laughter and affection — became your baseline. Your nervous system remembered what it experienced most often; repetition played over and over, becoming familiar, expected, and even comforting in its predictability. What you learned during this time laid the foundation for how you give and receive love, and how you now protect yourself.

If you are a parent reading this, it is not an invitation to blame yourself for how your emotional survival responses and trauma may have influenced your children, their energetic circle, or their subconscious survival responses.

Just as your parents were shaped by their parents, this too is part of a long ancestral lineage, passed from one generation to the next. It is part of human evolution. What matters now is awareness; through awareness, the patterns that cause disharmony do not have to persist. You can choose now to break the generational cycles.

Suppose your children are older and their energetic circle and emotional survival patterns are already established. In that case, it is okay for them to access the **Drop Your Shoulders® Methods** now, and as the next generation, it is easier for them to clear **energy passed down to them.**

## WHY?

1. Because they have not yet repeated the patterns as often as you have, they are not as firmly established or intertwined within their energetic circle, subconscious, and nervous system.

2. Because it is not their own personal energy; it is ancestral or generational energy passed down. This energy can be easily removed through **Drop Your Shoulders® Methods Clearing your Energetic Circle,** allowing them to regain control over their own nervous system.

3. Because you are already changing the patterns, working on yourself, you are clearing generational patterns both backwards and forwards. You can create new emotional and somatic reference points where love is kind, gentle, and caring, and pass them on to your children in real time.

# The Development of Your Own Energetic Circle

As we move into the next stage, ages 8 to 12, you begin to separate from your parents and caregivers. Your energy field starts to take shape, and your sense of identity begins to form. Something new awakens — the realisation that you are a separate being with your own thoughts and feelings. Your conscious mind becomes active for logical thought, analysis, and planning, and you come to understand that your energetic circle is not the same as your parents' or caregivers'.

Something profound is occurring within you, something invisible yet deeply felt. Your personal energetic circle is expanding and evolving. Until now, since birth, it has been intertwined with your parents and caregivers, but it is now gradually, instinctively, beginning to separate. This is a natural process, just as your body grows taller and your bones lengthen, your energetic field expands into form, forming your own distinct energetic circle.

During this time, your brain begins to change; the prefrontal cortex develops, and with it, your capacity for reflection and self-awareness emerges.

As you grow, it is a time of curiosity, wonderment, and quiet exploration, not yet rebellion or pushback. You are not asking, 'Who am I?' in words, but your energy is beginning to reach out, noticing the world around you in a new way. You start to sense yourself as separate, even if you cannot yet name it.

This is a time to notice subtle changes, to sense what feels different, what is in harmony, and what is not. You begin to observe the contrast between your home life and your friends' families. You may not yet question your reality aloud. Still, your energy field is reaching out, absorbing everything — the opinions of teachers, the values of religion, the culture of your school, and the way people interact.

You are gathering information and comparing it with your inner experience. Even if it's not reflected in words, your system begins to respond. It might show up as daydreaming, silence, deep fascination, or overexcitement. You might start taking risks or exploring the outside world more; you want to learn as much as possible and ask many questions. Something inside you is trying to understand the difference between what you have always known and what might be possible.

This period marks the beginning of shaping personal identity. You start developing a clearer sense of 'me' and 'not me.' This is when you learn through trial and error what it feels like to speak your truth, set a boundary, or hold a different opinion. You begin to notice others' reactions when you do this. You internalise events and become aware of your own inner thoughts. During this time, healthy boundaries are established, and your emotional survival patterns start to emerge.

When your early environment was not emotionally safe, especially if your caregivers were reactive, controlling, dismissive, or overwhelmed, this natural separation can be disrupted, creating gaps in your developing energetic circle.

The patterns you learned as a child to survive are now being explored. You are shifting between expansion and contraction, between moments of freedom and moments of fear. Some days you feel alive with curiosity, reaching outward, eager to learn and connect.

Other days, you start to ignore your own feelings to keep the peace, seeking approval, or holding back because you fear that being different might lead to rejection. Even as your body grows, your energetic circle is still taking shape, stretching open in some places while remaining porous in others. These openings leave your system scanning the world for what feels safe and what does not.

When you feel supported, you experience the thrill of discovery and a growing sense of self. When you're not supported, your energy remains entangled with others, uncertain where you end, and someone else begins. This is a time of moving in and out of yourself, testing your boundaries, seeking autonomy, and circling back for reassurance — a delicate dance between enmeshment and emergence as your sense of identity begins to take shape.

## The Awakening Years. Identity, Influence, and Emotional Realisation

We now explore what happened to you between the ages of 12 and 18. You own your energetic circle. When a second wave of transformation begins, the expansion and contraction of your energetic circle becomes more intense, charged, and emotionally complex than anything that came before.

Puberty is a complete rewiring of the brain, body, and energetic field. It is when the subtle shifts that began in early childhood start to crystallise into identity, layered with increased hormones, social mirroring, and emotional awakening. Your own energetic circle and boundaries are not just forming; they are being initiated, tested, challenged, and expanded.

At a neurological level, the adolescent brain is undergoing major reorganisation. The subconscious mind continues to govern survival responses, while the conscious mind — the part that observes, reflects, and begins to make sense of experience — is now coming online.

The amygdala, part of the limbic system, is highly active. It is the emotional command centre, responding to every perceived threat, every change in tone, posture, or energy. Emotions feel intense, immediate, and personal, often prompting a reaction before reflection.

Meanwhile, the prefrontal cortex — the part of the brain responsible for short-term focus, analysis, social awareness, and the ability to pause before acting — is still developing. It has not yet matured enough to provide consistent grounding or perspective.

As a result, although teenagers may appear mature on the outside, their internal capacity for emotional regulation and self-grounding is still developing.

This is a period of significant growth and profound vulnerability.

At this stage, the energetic circle becomes charged and expressive. Teenagers often swing between expansion and contraction, openness and isolation. One moment they want to belong to everything, and the next they wish to disappear. The energetic field is highly impressionable, drawing influences from everywhere—music, movies, friendships, pop culture, religion, and even politics.

Now, with the influence of external factors, something else begins to occur: you start to compare.

This comparison is not superficial. This is a crucial moment and the start of trauma awareness. It is the moment a young person observes how others live, how their friends are treated, how families interact on TV, how other parents apologise, protect, or ask questions, and quietly thinks, "My life is not like that. Why is it different for me?"

This is often the first time the nervous system realises something has happened. Not just that it hurts, but that it was not meant to occur that way. This marks the birth of emotional awareness and emotional pain. It is the result of repeated judgements of right and wrong, good and bad. Long-term programming associates positive emotions such as happiness, joy, laughter, and excitement with good, while anger, sadness, withdrawal, and criticism are seen as bad.

Until now, trauma has mostly existed as a survival mechanism. It shaped behaviours and attachment styles without full awareness.

But now, as consciousness expands, you — as a teenager — begin to feel its impact.

You may not have the words, but your body remembers. Now, the true impact of judgement is overlaid onto those early experiences. The flash of rage when you were ignored is now interpreted as *"this is bad."*

The heartbreak of abandonment, the deep sense of being unsafe, the fractured belief that you are not enough, and the pain of not being seen — these are no longer just sensations.

These are not mood swings; these are memories being recalibrated — early childhood experiences now overlaid with the judgement of good and bad, right and wrong. They become wounds, remembered for the first time as separate and significant events.

It is in this phase that emotional survival patterns truly set in, keeping you on high alert, ready to recalibrate. If emotional pain is met with more dismissal or punishment, you, as a teenager, learn to armour up. Other patterns can develop, such as overachieving, over-performing, adopting people-pleasing techniques, pretending everything is fine, or rebelling by expressing pain through anger, withdrawal, risk-taking, or simply shutting down and numbing yourself to survive the confusion and overwhelm.

The energetic field during this stage is often volatile as your emotional body evolves rapidly. It seeks autonomy but remains deeply focused on the need for belonging, love, and safety. It begins to awaken to injustice and unfairness, still unsure how to make sense of it all. The inner map is not yet fully developed, and you may internalise this emotional confusion, believing that all disharmony in your internal and external environments is your fault.

This is often the point when unresolved childhood trauma begins to make itself known.

For me, it fully kicked in when I was 14 and away from home for the first time on a school camp. I met our school counsellor earlier that day, and looking back, I sensed something different about her; she felt safe. My memories of that time are blurred, but in the middle of the night, I was found in the river, only asking for her. I was suicidal for the first time and couldn't find the words to explain what was happening to me — the realisation that what had happened in my life was not okay, and the emotional pain and thoughts were unbearable.

She had gone home earlier that day, but she drove back in the middle of the night, came to get me, and took me home — an earth angel who could see me. She understood the extent of the trauma and abuse that had occurred behind closed doors in my life — the neglect, the harm, and the survival patterns that had become embedded within me. She recognised that many of the things most people considered normal were not normal for me.

I didn't eat at the table. For the first few days, I barely ate at all. Eventually, she realised that sitting at the dinner table and eating together as a family was too confronting for me. One night, she bought pizza, and we sat on the floor with her children so we could all eat together in a way that felt safe.

I found it strange when she hugged me goodnight. I remember the first time she did it, I looked at her and said, *"Why are you hugging me?"* I wondered if she didn't think I would be there tomorrow.

At the time, I didn't realise how unusual that response was. Looking back, it reveals just how unfamiliar safety, affection, and consistency felt in my world.

Her consistent love, patience, kindness, and faith reached through all the distortion, and to this day she remains in my life, watching from a distance; I am in her prayers. She is the one person who opened her heart and home to me, creating love and stability throughout my life. She never asks for anything in return; she simply holds space and offers unconditional love and acceptance. Her belief in me was stronger than any trauma pattern I carried. She saved my life not just that night, but many times afterwards when life became confusing for me, and I am forever grateful.

This is why adolescence is such a vital time for healing. Not necessarily through grand interventions, as in my case, but through validation. Providing space to feel emotions and a place for honesty. Establishing boundaries that protect without suffocating. Having someone willing to put context around what is happening to you physically, mentally, emotionally, and energetically. Someone willing to say, "Yes, I see you. Yes, it was not meant to be like that, and no, it was not your fault."

This comes from a person, preferably an adult or a mentor, who can hold space for what is happening, or another teenager supported by a balanced adult mentor.

When this is lacking, unresolved trauma from adolescence is stored in the body and your energetic field, attaching to subconscious survival patterns and the nervous system. These patterns reappear in adult relationships as emotional volatility, deep insecurity, or an inability to trust, presenting as the anxious, avoidant, and disorganised attachment styles.

# Chapter Twenty

# Clearing Your Energetic Circle

## From Inherited And Childhood Shocks And Trauma

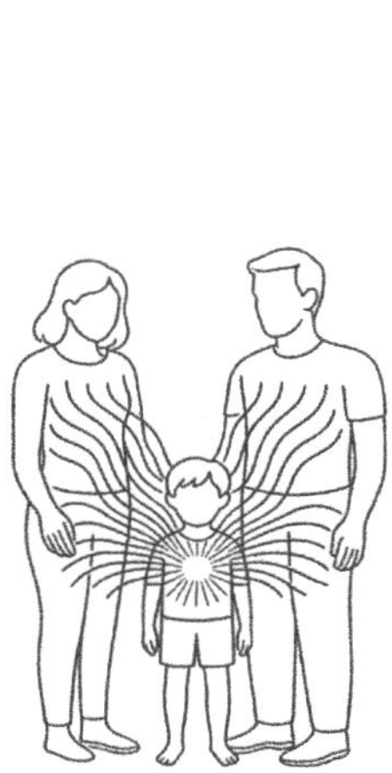

Now you will explore clearing the energy of inherited shocks and traumas, emotional wounds that are no longer yours to carry. You now have the chance to do what no one else could — to meet your younger self with the love, safety, and truth they never received, and to release the weight of energetic cords and debris you have been carrying in your energetic circle. Energy that isn't yours to hold. Energy that has been projected onto you, emotions that are not yours to process. Energy absorbed from your parents that has been stored in your energetic circle and body now connects to your subconscious emotional survival patterns.

This is not about revisiting or reliving the past. It's about releasing the energy that isn't yours to carry and to establish healthy energetic boundaries around your own energetic circle.

This is a deeper invitation to heal your energetic circle. It isn't about erasing the past but about bringing all parts of you into the present moment, where you can finally meet them. It's about returning your energy to its original rhythm of love, connection, and safety — before it was shaped by others' pain. It's about reclaiming your personal power.

Your energy is sacred. It was never meant to carry what did not belong to you.

In a single moment, you can feel this energy stored in your body, nervous system, and energetic field. It is somatic, emotional, and energetic. It connects you directly with your body and nervous system to restore balance, foster deep listening, and cultivate love for the parts of you that were never seen or heard. This is about giving the past a voice.

This is the moment in your journey when your awareness deepens into empowerment, with the realisation that the patterns you have been carrying were never yours to hold.

You might not have realised how much you've been carrying — the fear, the responsibility, the pressure to make others feel better, to stay small, to perform for love, to disappear for safety. But now you know, and you are no longer powerless.

Healing begins with acknowledgement, and now you have the choice to clear the energy that is not yours to carry.

Almost every client I have worked with has spent years processing their parents' or caregivers' emotions, carrying feelings that were never theirs to begin with. They took on responsibility for another person's emotional wellbeing without realising that you cannot process emotions that do not belong to you.

This is mainly caused by the lack of development of physical, emotional, and energetic boundaries—holes in the energetic circle created by trauma.

I often ask, "Is a child responsible for the emotional wellbeing of an adult?" The answer is always no. This applies whether you were a child or are an adult now. It is not your job to carry another person's emotional burden. It's impossible. You can hold space for someone's experience with love, compassion, and kindness, but you cannot feel or process what resides within their system. How someone else feels is shaped by their own childhood, survival patterns, and energetic blueprint. It is not yours to hold, process, or carry.

You are not responsible for your parents' emotional wellbeing.

# Drop Your Shoulders® Method 21

## Clearing Your Energetic Circle

- Drop your shoulders now to somatically connect with your body, scribble to release the tension and calm your nervous system.
- Imagine yourself surrounded by a cocoon of light, a bubble with a boundary on the outside, coloured blue or silver. Like a reflective film facing outwards. Its function is to return any energy projected onto you to its original source
- Imagine a waterfall of light flowing through your entire energy field — a radiant stream of pure energy — with intention, gently resolve, dissolve and disintegrate all energy that is not yours, including old patterns, attachments, or influences from any time or place — especially energy taken on during your childhood experiences or through unconscious agreements.

- Say to yourself or out loud:

*"I cancel, nullify and void all permission I may have given — consciously or unconsciously — to take responsibility for other people's energy and emotions or carry energy that is not aligned with my highest good."*
*"I take back my power — this is my body, my energy field, and I claim it now. This is my free will and choice — across all timelines, dimensions, and systems."*
*"All energy that is not mine must leave now."*
*"My energy circle is clear, whole, and mine alone. I am free. I am safe."*

- Now energetically clear your circle somatically.

- Picture yourself either as your inner child standing in front of you, or, as an adult, imagine they have their own energetic circle. Whatever age comes to mind is perfect. Trust it.

- Observe this part of yourself. *Are you angry, sad, or both?*

- Allow this part of yourself to freely express these emotions. Visualise yourself releasing rage, anger, frustration, grief, or deep sadness. Picture yourself shouting, kicking, punching, crying, or sobbing.

- As the adult you are now, stay in the present, observe yourself releasing emotional energy, and offer yourself reassurance aloud or in your mind.

*"I am here now. You are safe now."*
*"This is not your energy. It is not your burden to carry."*
*"It was never your fault."*
*"You are not alone. I will never leave you." "I love you."*

- Let that grief come. Scribble as the tension leaves your body. Surrender, and let the energy flow out of every cell in your body. Open your heart to compassion for yourself and for how, at that moment in time, the age you imagine, you were doing your best in an impossible situation.

- When you notice your body calming down, when the tension and pain in your physical body have dissolved, shifted, or moved, and when your breathing slows and your heart feels calm, allow yourself to feel deeply relaxed.

- Now imagine this part of you is calmer, laughing, free.

- When you feel the time is right, bring the image of yourself into your heart centre and merge together as one.

- Relax your entire body now as you call all parts of yourself back into your heart centre.

- Imagine your feet as the roots of a tree, grounding your energy into the earth beneath you. As you do this, feel inner peace filling your body.

- Say this out loud:

*"I am safe" "I am loved"*
*"I love and accept myself" "I take back my power now."*
*"This is my life and I get to choose."*

- Imagine your energetic circle is clear, with a clear, silver, impenetrable boundary.

- Say it out loud or to yourself:

*"Nothing enters my energy field without my conscious permission."*
*"I no longer process other people's emotions or carry energetic debris."*

You have cleared your energetic circle, reclaiming your personal power and free will and choice.

When you choose love and safety within, you realise that you gain respect not by what you say *'YES'* to, but by what you say *'NO'* to.

This is the day you set emotional and energetic boundaries in relationships grounded in self-love and inner safety.

# Chapter Twenty-One

# Establishing Healthy Energetic Boundaries

You have been working with your inner child through these pages for some time now; keep reassuring and offering love and safety as often as needed, ideally once a day.

The next step is to learn to protect that presence within your energetic circle, restoring your energetic boundary to its original blueprint before distortion. Your Energetic Circle is not just an abstract idea. It is real, intelligent, and highly sensitive. It has developed and grown with you throughout your childhood and teenage years.

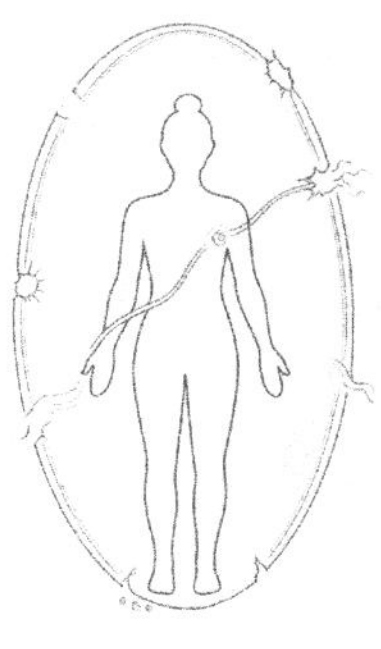

Most people go through life with holes, small tears, or gaping wounds in their energetic boundaries, caused by early childhood shocks and trauma, emotional distress, grief, abuse, or chronic stress. These disruptions weaken your energetic boundary, making you more susceptible to outside influences in adulthood.

You might unknowingly let others attach to, merge with, take from, or project onto you simply because no one ever taught you that you could say NO.

Your main focus has been to protect your physical body, to have boundaries around physical abuse, self-harm, domestic violence, or bullying.

Emotional boundaries were not taught. For generations, emotions were dismissed, feared, or punished, and classified as either good or bad, with the expression of emotions judged as right or wrong.

The emotional body, your inner landscape of feelings, sensations, and intuitive knowing, was not honoured because those before you did not know how. They were living in what we now understand as an unevolved emotional body, a nervous system shaped by physical survival rather than self-awareness. They did not have access to the tools to manage their subconscious survival patterns, nervous system, emotional responses, or energetic circle. They did not have access to the **Drop Your Shoulders® Methods.**

Often, they were not allowed to feel or express their emotions, so neither were you. While emotional abuse and coercive control have always existed as forms of abuse, they are only now beginning to be formally recognised in the legal system. In Australia, laws criminalising emotional and coercive control in intimate relationships were introduced in 2024. Similar legal recognition is emerging across the United Kingdom, Europe, and parts of the United States, finally naming what many people have felt in their bodies all along — abuse is not always visible.

Emotional abuse and coercive control do not discriminate; they are not limited to women or children. Men are just as likely to be on the receiving end, though their stories are often overlooked or minimised. This is not about gender. It is about power, pain, and patterns of control that can exist in any relationship, regardless of who is involved. The silence, gaslighting, withdrawal, control, emotional dumping, and chronic invalidation are just as damaging— sometimes even more so — because they leave no physical bruise but imprint directly on your subconscious, nervous system, and energetic circle.

Emotions are more than thoughts; they are energy that permeates your entire system. They imprint on your subconscious and shape your current life e. They also inhabit your energetic circle—the subtle, intelligent space around your body that perceives what words cannot express.

You were never taught how to protect this part of yourself. You weren't given the tools to manage strong emotions. Instead, you were taught to shut them down — by absorbing, rescuing, and over-giving — leaving your emotional body unevolved and unprotected.

You weren't offered a framework for honouring your feelings, or taught that your emotional energy is sacred. All emotions are — there is no such thing as good or bad emotions. Both joy and anger are essential.

Learning to express all emotions, not just the pleasant ones or those you know as "good," but the full spectrum—from rage to grief, fear to joy — gives you access to more of the truth within you. It opens the door to greater self-awareness, emotional maturity, and a developed emotional body. It offers the chance for deeper connection to love and safety within yourself and in your relationships.

You have been taught to fear your negative emotions, leading you to suppress them and strive only for the positive ones.

When you allow yourself to feel and express all emotions through the **Drop Your Shoulders® Methods,** without shame or suppression, you reconnect with the parts of you that were once silenced. You reclaim your inner world, and in doing so, you become present and powerful within your energetic circle. This is not about being emotional; it is about becoming self- empowered and emotionally intelligent.

Emotional and energetic boundaries are not just helpful; they are essential to your growth, both individually and in relationships.

Emotional and energetic boundaries act as a bridge that reconnects your body, energy, subconscious, and truth, helping you stop abandoning yourself for love. Instead, you love yourself enough to stay whole and complete, calm and centred.

For example, when a child is having a tantrum, there is nothing you can do to stop it because it is not logical; it is energetic. The child is not trying to manipulate you; they are expressing a build-up of energy that needs to flow through their body. You can offer presence and support, but you cannot process the feeling for them.

Once the wave of energy has moved out of their body—often through crying, yelling, or movement—they usually move straight into laughing or playing again. This is how the pure, unfiltered energy of emotion leaves the body.

It was not your responsibility to take on your parents' and caregivers' emotions when you were a child, and it is not your responsibility to manage others' emotions as an adult — whether it's your partner, your friends, or your family members.

You cannot feel, express, or process another person's emotions. You cannot fix, carry, or transmute their emotions on their behalf. When you try to do this, you absorb their emotions into your energetic circle (just as you did as a child); you do not dissolve or release them for the other person. Instead, they add weight to your energetic system, amplify similar suppressed emotions, and trigger your emotional survival responses.

You cannot hold it all; this energy is stored in your body and disconnects you from your own clarity. You do not know what is yours and what is theirs; you have no boundaries, and your energy circles merge as they do in a child-parent relationship.

You learn this pattern early in life; it becomes distorted only when your parents and caregivers project their unresolved emotional energy onto you rather than expressing it themselves.

When they projected anger by yelling or withdrawing love and safety from you before the age of 12, instead of releasing the energy themselves, it entered your energetic circle and your body and stayed there.

As an adult, you still struggle to distinguish where your emotions end, and someone else's begin. If those around you are feeling sad or angry, you tend to feel responsible. Your energy field shrinks, making you feel unsafe and triggering your emotional survival responses. You might think that by taking on their emotional energy, they will feel better and you'll feel secure. However, you are not processing their emotions; you are merging with them. This is where you realise that love equals sacrifice. You believe you can sacrifice your inner peace for theirs.

Emotions can only be released and processed by the person who .

Loving someone as an adult involves respecting their physical, mental, and emotional experiences while maintaining your own physical and energetic boundaries.

Now take a moment to practise the **Drop Your Shoulders® Method Clearing Your Energetic Circle.**

Clearing your Energetic Circle can be done daily or weekly.

## When Your Energetic Circle Is Damaged, Or There Are No Energetic Boundaries

As your emotional and energetic boundaries were developing in childhood, your solidified survival patterns, formed in response to shocks and traumas, interrupted the development of your energetic field. Holes formed in your developing energetic boundary. This is where you feel others' emotions as if they are your own, and where there are no energetic or emotional boundaries.

These holes often become access points. Emotional cords form invisible threads between you and the people around you — those you try to help or fix, those who continually need and rely on you, or those from whom you draw energy.

Some of these cords attach during childhood, from your parents, siblings, and other family members who used you for emotional comfort. It could be a sibling who expected you to be strong, or a family member who crossed your boundaries without taking responsibility. Even if you are no longer in contact with them, the cord can still be active, draining energy from your field. It does not require physical proximity; you grant permission, often unconsciously.

Over time, these cords grow in your adult life. They can come from friends, partners, clients, or even strangers you have spent time listening to or helping. If your default pattern is to please, rescue, fix, or carry other people's emotional energy, your energetic circle will naturally remain open with little or no protection. You may mistake this openness for love, thinking that love means sacrificing your own energy and sense of self for theirs. This is not love; it is enmeshment, and it drains your life force energy.

This siphoning becomes a way of life; you get used to feeling fatigued. You also get used to carrying the weight of other people's emotional energy and trauma. You attract people who feed off your energy (not necessarily intentionally). You learn that your self-worth and emotional safety depend on having people around you to feel happy and well. You can feel responsible for how others experience life; if they are experiencing anger or sadness, you believe it is your job to fix it, to absorb their pain so they do not have to feel it or suffer.

These are common ways you freely give away your energy, indicating you have holes in your energetic circle.

This is not about giving or helping; it is an emotional survival pattern that helps you feel loved and safe in your external environment. These patterns stem from your earliest childhood experiences — the nervous system's agreement that safety comes from attuning to your surroundings and that it is safer when others feel calm and happy. This leads to giving away your free will and choice.

## Free Will And Choice Are Your Birthright

The most powerful gift you have as a human is free will and choice. How you use it depends on you giving yourself permission. It is the gateway to your life force energy. When you are manipulated, coerced, or conditioned into surrendering your free will and choice, you are actually giving away access to your energetic circle — your life force energy becomes available to whatever or whoever you have unconsciously agreed to.

This happens not through logic but through your subconscious and emotional survival responses — fear, shame, guilt, anger, and unworthiness. These emotional survival patterns are reactive, and during this time you are wide open and have no boundaries. Governments, religions, the media, and relationships can activate your emotional survival patterns, making you easily influenced and unconsciously granting permission.

They activate fear, a physical and emotional survival response that makes it easier to influence and control your behaviour. In a state of fear, you accept the narrative presented to you, often triggering fear of danger or death — whether physical or emotional — and feelings of not being good enough or needing to improve. Fear is used to control you, regardless of who instigates it. Over time, your nervous system adapts to a constant state of physical and emotional survival. When you are in survival mode, your body does everything it can to keep you safe. In such a state, what seems like free will and choice is often just reactive behaviour, shaped by past experiences and emotional trauma patterns.

In this moment, practise the **Drop Your Shoulders® Method Giving Love to Self.** This is your time to practise self-love and self-care.

You are grounded in your body. You are empowered to take responsibility for your emotional health and wellbeing, gain clarity, and reclaim your free will and choice.

## Chapter Twenty-Two

# Reclaiming Your Field — Energetic Clearing Practice

Expanding your energetic practice, you will learn how to call your energy back to yourself and cut these ties with those who have manipulated you.

Throughout this process, you reclaim your personal power. You begin to notice the difference between the energy and emotions that are yours and what is not. You become aware of where your energy is going, where it is being drained, and where it remains tied up in others' beliefs, expectations, and emotions. From that awareness, you exercise your free will and make choices. You are free to make different decisions.

This is where you begin to restore your energetic boundary — not as armour, but as a gentle protective layer that says to others, "I will not process your emotions for you; your emotional wellbeing is not my responsibility; it is yours."

Cutting energetic cords, attachments, and enmeshments, and repairing tears in your invisible energetic circle. Your energetic circle contains your life force energy, which is sacred. When you care for your energetic circle as you do for your physical body, with self-love and self-care, you will notice a difference in all areas of your life. You'll feel alive, energised, free to be yourself, and able to experience joy and make choices freely. There are many pathways to reclaim your field. Trust the one you feel most drawn to at any given moment.

These two powerful **Drop Your Shoulders® Methods Cutting Energetic Cords from Your Parents — Womb Healing or Inner Child By The Fire.** Both involve going back to either before birth or when you were a child and cutting the generational cords with both parents. Both processes can be used when working with your inner child, usually between the ages of 0 and 15, to cut the cords not only to your parents and ancestors but also to anyone else who has projected onto you, such as school bullies or other family members.

There is also a general process for cutting cords. The **Drop Your Shoulders® Methods Cutting Energetic Cords with People from Your Past.** Suitable for anyone you feel still has access to your energetic circle, including ex-partners.

When you reclaim your personal power and stand fully within your own energetic circle, you begin to restore the integrity of your physical, emotional, and energetic boundaries.

Remember that your energy was never meant to be scattered or siphoned; your life force energy is always yours to honour, protect, and embody with love.

# Drop Your Shoulders® Method 22

## Cutting The Energetic Cords With Your Parents—Womb Clearing

- Begin with the **Drop Your Shoulders® Method Scribbling**
- Close your eyes. Drop your shoulders. Breathe into your body. Identify parts of your body that are tense, contorted, or in pain. Relax these areas and start scribbling.
- Let your breath deepen in for 4, then out for 4. Allow yourself to journey back to the womb.
- Now imagine you are a baby in your mother's womb. Whatever way you choose to picture this, it is perfect.

- Imagine the embryonic fluid around you as cloudy, with black flecks or other discolourations. Your mother's and father's emotions, the shocks she endured, the family lineage — all of this is present in the embryonic waters. With full awareness as an observer, try to imagine it as vividly as possible. Alternatively, just having the intention will also work.

- Now imagine gentle rays of sunlight entering the womb. These rays penetrate the fluid, dissolving any cloudiness, confusion, or inherited heaviness. The embryonic fluid becomes transparent, like mountain water from a waterfall of light.

- Now observe the umbilical cord and notice any energy flowing through it that no longer supports your highest path. Again, imagine rays of sunlight cleansing the umbilical cord.

- Now visualise the energetic cords connected to you in the womb from both parents and from ancestors through the ages—cords that stretch to people, places, and past experiences—being gently and lovingly cut and dissolved, one by one. With each cut, feel more of your energy returning; feel your physical body softening, releasing, and calming. Imagine as best you can, and whatever you notice is perfect.

- Now as you continue to scribble, say these words aloud or in your mind;

*"I nullify, void, and cancel all contracts and agreements, made consciously or unconsciously, on all levels, in all space and time. This includes all cords, hooks, bindings, energy enmeshments, past-life connections, and ancestral and generational patterns that I now choose not to carry. This is my free will and choice, and it must be respected. I demand that all interference and distortion be neutralised and that further access be denied."*

- Now imagine a new umbilical cord, sometimes called a Vivaxis, forming a line connecting you to the Earth. Visualise this cord extending down into the Earth, to a place where you feel safe right now in your current life. It could be a mountain, a forest, or the ocean floor. Let it root deeply into the Earth and allow the Earth's energy to rise up through the Vivaxis, nurturing you as a baby in the womb with grounding, safety, love, and belonging.

- Now call your soul and spirit fully into the baby's body in the womb. Say the following:

*"I now call my soul and spirit fully into this body — into this form — within the womb. I choose life. I choose to fully inhabit this body with love, trust, and presence. I claim this body as my home, my space here on Earth."*

- Imagine a reflective silver boundary around you in the womb, forming a bubble of light. Any energy that does not belong to you is returned to its original source.

- Take a deep breath in and let go of this image, feeling into your body, to this moment now.

- Imagine that same silver light of protection now surrounding your entire body, your energetic circle, with a reflective mirror facing outward. Any energy that does not belong to you is returned to its source.

- Feel into your physical body now, and feel the inner peace, safety, and love. You can now imagine your energetic circle filled with sunlight and rays of the sun, with a silver boundary around you, complete with no holes. You feel safe within and without.

# Drop Your Shoulders® Method 23

## Cutting Energetic Cords With Your Parents—Inner Child By The Fire

- Activate **Drop Your Shoulders® Method Scribbling**
- Close your eyes. Drop your shoulders. Breathe into your body. Identify parts of your body that are tense, contorted, or in pain. Relax these areas and start scribbling.
- Let your breath deepen in for 4, then out for 4. Allow yourself to journey all the way back into the womb.
- Now picture yourself sitting around a fire pit with a violet flame. The flames are gentle, ancient, and intelligent.
- To your left, your inner child appears at whatever age they need to be today. Invite them close. Hold their hand.

- On the other side of the fire, see your parents or other carers. They might be younger versions of themselves. They might not look as you expect. Trust what comes to you.

- Now, between you and them, see the energetic cords — blue and black — coming into your body and that of your inner child's, into your solar plexus, your heart, your throat, and your head. Feel the tightness in your physical body — where are these cords attached? These are invisible cords that have bound your energy to theirs.

- Now say these words aloud or in your mind:

*"I nullify, void, and cancel all contracts and agreements, made consciously or unconsciously, on all levels, in all space and time. This includes all cords, hooks, bindings, energy enmeshments, past-life connections, and ancestral and generational patterns that I now choose not to carry. This is my free will and choice, and it must be respected. I demand that all interference and distortion be neutralised and that further access be denied."*

- Now imagine you are pulling these cords out of your body and your inner child's body and placing them in the fire; the fire burns away the cords and all the energy attached to them. Let the cords burn completely.

- Speak to the image of your parents and say:

*"It is not my responsibility to process your emotions. I return to the fire all energy, emotions, and patterns I have carried for you. I lovingly call back all of my own energy — my love, joy, innocence, and wonderment. You no longer have access to my energy field."*

- Allow the image of your parents to fade away. Take a deep breath in for 4 and out for 4, dropping your shoulders, relaxing your body, letting go, and relaxing even further.

- Now turn to your inner child. Offer them comfort and reassurance. Hold them and reassure.

*"You are safe now. I am here now. It was not your fault; it was not your responsibility. You are free."*

- When you feel ready, bring the image of your inner child into your heart centre and merge as one.

- Imagine that same silver light of protection now surrounding your entire body, your energetic circle, with a reflective mirror facing outward. Any energy that does not belong to you is returned to its source.

- Feel into your physical body now, and feel the inner peace, safety, and love. You can now imagine your energetic circle filled with sunlight and rays of the sun, with a silver boundary around you, complete with no holes. You feel safe within and without.

# Drop Your Shoulders® Method 24

## Cutting Energetic Cords With People From Your Past

- Always start with the **Drop Your Shoulders® Method Scribbling**
- Close your eyes. Drop your shoulders. Breathe into your body. Identify parts of your body that are tense, contorted, or in pain. Relax these areas and start scribbling. Let your breath deepen in for 4, then out for 4.
- Imagine a stage in front of you. Place an image of the person (or people) you feel have hurt you, manipulated you, or abused you in any way onto the stage. You can also use this method with any former intimate partners with whom you have opened and merged your energy. This process is particularly relevant for family members, for bullying incidents, and for anyone you feel is still draining your energy.

- Now, between you and them, see the energetic cords— blue and black—coming into your body, into your solar plexus, your heart, your throat, your head. Feel the tightness in your physical body—where are these cords attached? These are invisible cords that have bound your energy to theirs.

- Now say these words aloud or in your mind;

*"I nullify, void, and cancel all contracts and agreements, made consciously or unconsciously, on all levels, in all space and time. This includes all cords, hooks, bindings, energy enmeshments, and past-life connections that I now choose not to carry. This is my free will and choice, and it must be respected. I demand that all interference and distortion be neutralised and that they be denied further access."*

- Now imagine you are pulling these cords out of your body, severing everything attached to them.

- Speak to the image of these people and say;

*"It is not my responsibility to process your emotions. I return all energy, emotions, and patterns I have carried for you. I lovingly call back all of my own energy—my love, joy, and happiness. You no longer have access to my energy field."*

- Allow the image of those on stage to fade away. Take a deep breath in for 4 and out for 4, dropping your shoulders, relaxing your body, letting go, and relaxing even further.

- Imagine that same silver light of protection now surrounding your entire body, your energetic circle, with a reflective mirror facing outward. Any energy that does not belong to you is returned to its source.

- Feel into your physical body now, and feel the inner peace, safety, and love. You can now imagine your energetic circle filled with sunlight and rays of the sun, with a silver boundary around you, complete with no holes. You feel safe within and without.

# Chapter Twenty-Three

# Healthy Boundaries in Relationships

Primarily, we will focus on the primary relationship between you and your partner; however, these practices and concepts are applicable to all relationships with family, friends, colleagues, and, of course, your partner.

If you do not have a partner, think of your primary relationship as being with a best friend or a family member. It is more about how you interact in your primary relationships. So if you are not with a partner, replace the word 'partner' with 'friend' or even the name of the person you are referring to.

A conscious adult relationship does not mean you will never be emotionally triggered or that there will be no disharmony. This is an unrealistic expectation; all relationships will trigger emotional survival responses, depending on each person's childhood emotional survival patterns. These patterns are unique to each individual, so differences and conflicts will inevitably arise in relationships.

Conscious adult relationships involve you and your partner learning and growing together, rather than ignoring your emotional survival patterns, attachment styles, or childhood wounds.

It is an opportunity to learn and grow together, to address emotional triggers and develop practical tools to hold space for one another.

Harmony between two people happens when both of you know how to stay present and take responsibility for your own emotional responses, when you both practise self-awareness and show love for yourself and your partner, especially when things feel messy or bumpy.

A healthy relationship allows each person to change and be vulnerable. It's a space where you're free to be yourself, redefine what love means, and learn how to give and receive love within a relationship.

Your inner-child wounds are yours to tend to, just as your partner's wounds are theirs. When both you and your partner understand this, your relationship begins to shift from reactivity to self-responsibility. Your relationship is not about rescuing, blaming, or expecting each other to heal your childhood wounds or to fill the void of not receiving what you needed as a child. Instead, both you and your partner are learning to stay grounded in your own body.

Imagine for a moment that both you and your partner stand alone, each with your own energetic circle encompassing your inner child.

Each person has their own energetic bubble — a space that holds their emotional history, including past trauma, survival patterns, core needs, attachment styles, love language, and inner child. This part of us can still be triggered by stress or conflict.

When you're in your own energetic circle, you feel safe. You can work with your emotions and let them move through you without projecting them onto your partner, family, or friends.

If your anger or grief spills out as blame, shame, or guilt — which it can, because you are learning, growing, and evolving your emotional body while also breaking generational patterns — those unhealed emotional wounds can surface and be projected onto your partner.

This is the moment to drop your shoulders to calm your nervous system. As you calm your nervous system, you learn not to defend or react in those moments.

You stop, drop your shoulders, and shift how you're feeling. You reconnect with your inner child by revisiting the earlier **Drop Your Shoulders® Method Loving Your Inner Child** to reassure your inner child. In these moments, you choose self-love and interrupt your emotional survival responses.

There are no judgements; you are human. There will be times when your emotional survival patterns are activated, and even if you find yourself projecting outward, you now have the **Drop Your Shoulders® Method Self-Forgiveness** as a pathway for growth.

Your partner, friends, and family are not there to rescue you; however, you can invite them to support you when you are activated into an emotional survival response.

Just as you communicate your love language and what you need to feel loved, you can now also share what you require during moments when you are triggered into your emotional survival responses, and what you need to feel safe.

For example, you can communicate in the following way, adapting it to your own words. You can communicate exactly what you need to your loved ones.

Here are some examples.

*"When I am upset, crying, yelling, or withdrawing, I need you to see beyond my emotional survival response. I need you to look past the drama and not take it personally — this is my circle, this is my pain. I need you to hold space for me to be human in these vulnerable moments and to have compassion for the fact that I am in physical, mental, or emotional pain at those times. I also need you to stay within your own energetic circle and, during these moments, ask me, "What do you need?"*

*Or*

*"When I am triggered into my emotional survival responses of fight and flight, no matter why I am triggered, I feel disempowered and vulnerable. Do not try to fix me; I need you to soften and remember who you are. My emotional survival patterns are not about you, nor are they your responsibility. I need you not to be triggered into your own inner-child wounds and emotional responses. In these moments, this is not who I am; it is my emotional survival response. I need you to hold me."*

*Or*

*"This is the time to offer me my love language: a gentle word, a moment of presence, a hand on my back, or simply staying with me. Not because you have to, but because when you express love to me in this way — especially when I am triggered into my emotional survival responses — I can receive it and return to my adult self."*

*Or*

*"When you support me in the moments when I am triggered into survival patterns, I can finally heal from my past wounds, create new emotional-somatic reference points, and feel safe in your presence. These new reference points show that love is kind and gentle and can create a secure attachment between us."*

Practise the **Drop Your Shoulders® Methods** and adapt them into your life—moment by moment—to become a master of your nervous system and reparent your inner child.

When you are triggered, and your inner child begins to spiral or shut down, practise holding space for yourself. Recognise that your emotional survival response is not your true self; it is a reaction that arises when you are confronted with physical or emotional pain.

Ask your partner, friend, or family member to imagine themselves within their own energetic circle. Explain that when you are upset, they need to respect your energetic boundaries, recognising that your emotional responses are not about them and that it is not their role to fix everything.

They too can practise the **Drop Your Shoulders® Method** and say to themselves,

*"I will not make this about me and get triggered into my inner-child reactions. I will not take your withdrawal, harsh tone, or silence as a personal attack. I might feel the impact, but I observe it with curiosity, not punishment. I remember that what I see in you is a moment of pain, not a rejection of me. I hold space for your circle without needing to enter it."*

*When both you and your partner can imagine the other as a child in pain in these moments, would you punish or fight with this child, or would you offer love and compassion?*

This reflects what is happening in your adult relationship. You and/or your partner are responding from an inner child default pattern, also known as a five-year-old tantrum.

If you look beyond the words, the drama, the yelling, and the withdrawal, you will see that these behaviours are a response to pain, and you or your partner needs love and support in these moments. You can hold space with love, compassion, and kindness.

This is how you will practise maintaining healthy emotional boundaries and creating space for each other in adult relationships, with love and compassion.

When two people have the chance to stay within their own energetic circle, they do not need to fix each other to feel loved and safe. They no longer feel attacked or triggered into emotional survival responses.

This is what a healthy emotional boundary looks like — staying in your own energetic circle while holding your own emotional boundaries with love, especially when the other person is in pain, whether physical, mental, or emotional pain.

In a healthy adult relationship, this works when both people know how to hold space for each other. There is an awareness of when to keep your own energetic boundaries steady while the other person is going through something, and the ability to allow space for expression without fixing or interrupting it. You feel safe enough to maintain your adult self. It can be as simple as one person asking.

*"What do you need right now?"* and the other person can answer honestly. It could be *"I need a hug," "I need space,"* or *"I just need you to sit here with me quietly."*

Often, what you need is your love language — either through self-care or by inviting the other person to give it to you. Whatever it is, you can identify it, and the other person can give it to you. They don't need to take your experience personally or make it about themselves. This is what mutual respect and emotional safety look like.

Are you thinking..."*This is great in theory, but what happens when both people are triggered into emotional survival responses at the same time?" Yes/No*

# What Happens When The Pain Is Too Loud?

## The nervous system is already in fight-or-flight mode, and neither of you can hold space for The Other?

These are the moments when everything spirals. When the trigger feels personal, and harsh words leak out. When your own wound is so raw that all you can do is defend or shut down. You feel attacked, so you attack back. They withdraw, so you chase. Or maybe you both collapse into silence or a full-blown screaming match. There is no safety, no clarity—just two inner children fighting for love, understanding, and survival. Your inner child attachment styles are activated, and your emotional survival responses are in full force. Often you will recreate the trauma over and over again with the same fights, responses, and behaviours.

**This is often where many relationships break down.** Or worse, it is where they start to repeat unconscious, destructive patterns when both people are in survival responses, reacting from old pain or childhood trauma rather than the present reality. There is no adult in the room. No one is available to set energetic boundaries and hold space to stay calm and grounded with love and compassion.

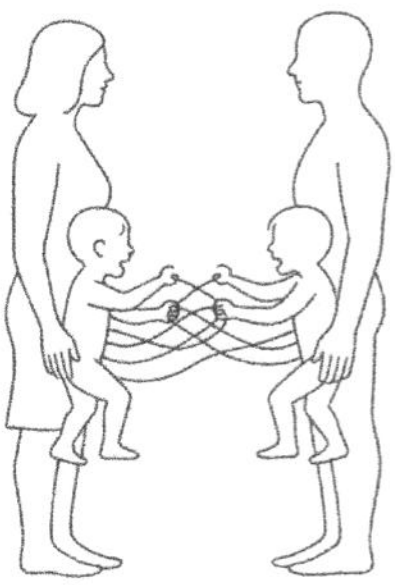

This is how trauma bonds form, which can trigger physical, mental, and emotional abuse in a relationship.

When unresolved childhood trauma meets unhealed attachment wounds, relationships can become reenactments of the very dynamics that hurt you in the first place. It is not necessarily intentional; it is, however, familiar, and your nervous system interprets it as patterns of love because it reflects early childhood experiences. Love becomes fused with chaos, trauma, and abuse. Intimacy turns into pain, and there are no boundaries. As a child, you lacked clear physical or energetic boundaries. Entering adult relationships without boundaries quickly becomes reactive and unsafe—like two children fighting for love and safety.

This is at the core of emotional abuse, where one or both individuals are no longer truly in the relationship but are caught up in their own projections, unmet needs, and fears of rejection, betrayal, and abandonment. The relationship becomes a battleground rather than a loving connection, and both people are fighting their own past trauma memories, failing to see each other or themselves.

You might find yourself subconsciously seeing the parent or caregiver who hurt you, abandoned you, or was unable to provide the love and safety you needed. You see and feel the pain from the past in the present moment. You are unable to see the person in front of you, only the behaviour that triggered the pain of the past and the memory of that pain. Your subconscious confuses the person in front of you with your mother, father or caregiver.

It is important to say now that it is completely normal to be triggered into emotional survival responses. No matter how conscious or self-aware you become, there will be moments when your inner child takes over, and fear hijacks your voice, causing you to say things you did not mean from a place of anger, sadness, blame, guilt, or shame. The nervous system does not respond to growth in a straight line; healing is not linear, and you are human.

The trigger isn't the issue. What matters most is what happens next in the stillness after the argument, when you can calm your nervous system. This is when you learn how to reconnect with yourself and each other using **Drop Your Shoulders® Methods.**

You return to your adult self by tending to the part of you that was just triggered. You start with dropping your shoulders, breathing in for 4 seconds, out for 4 seconds, feeling into your body and acknowledging the pain and uncomfortable tension. You pick up a pen and give the energy of emotion somewhere to go; you scribble, you move the energy. You connect with your inner child or the part of you that is activated.

Reassure your inner child, *"That really hurt. I see how much it mattered. I'm here now. You are safe."*

This is how you become emotionally safe within.

As you drop your shoulders, calm your nervous system, awareness returns. You remember who you are — not the reaction, not the hurt, not the story. You recall the tools you've been practising. You've held the wounded part of yourself, and now, from this place, you can choose how to be present with your partner.

You speak to each other, not to accuse or correct, but to reconnect. You can say, *"I've taken a moment to come back to myself. I want to share what came up for me. I would love to reconnect when you are ready."*

You stay honest. You stay kind. And you do not abandon yourself to manage their emotional reaction.

If they are not yet ready to return, you can now hold space for them. You can see that they are responding from a place of pain and that it is not about you. Hold your own energetic boundary and ask them, *"What do you need?"*

Asking this question allows them to take responsibility for themselves, to communicate what they need in this moment

## You are responsible for keeping your heart safe

One of the most harmful beliefs we can hold is believing it's safe to entrust our hearts to someone who isn't capable of protecting them. Boundaries exist to shield your heart when necessary and to open up when it's safe to do so. When the other person is still in their survival response, they are not capable of looking after your heart. You are responsible for your own safety and emotional and energetic boundaries.

Without healthy emotional boundaries, it becomes all too easy to enter a relationship wide open, exposed, and unguarded. There is an old belief that once in an intimate relationship, you need to blindly trust your partner to have your best interests at heart. However, when your partner is triggered into their own emotional survival patterns, it is unrealistic to expect them to look after your heart or love you the same way they can when they feel safe and empowered. You are responsible for your own emotional safety. It is not that the other person consciously wants to hurt you. In most cases, they do not.

When your partner is still caught up in their own unhealed pain and is acting from their inner child and survival instincts, they are not able to hold your heart safely. They may disregard your feelings, lash out, shut down, withdraw, or manipulate, not out of cruelty, but because they themselves do not feel safe and loved. This can lead to patterns of projecting physical and emotional abuse.

## Reflection

*Do you believe love means giving your heart to the other person? Yes/ No.*

*Do you think loyalty means accepting less than you deserve? Yes/No*

*Do you convince yourself that if you just love them more and sacrifice your own needs, they will stop hurting you? Yes/No*

**Truth.** Without emotional boundaries, you're not just opening your heart—you're allowing yourself to give away your life force energy. You're placing responsibility for your emotional wellbeing on someone else, asking them to care for you in a way you are not willing to do for yourself.

This is not their job or their responsibility. It is yours; it is your heart. This is not about shutting down or building walls; it is about discerning when to open heart and when to set energetic boundaries and look after your own emotional health and wellbeing.

Discernment involves listening to your body, heart, and energetic circle. It means feeling into your body's signals: that tightening in your gut, the shortness of breath, and the urge to over-explain or justify yourself, and recognising these as signs that something within you does not feel safe.

Emotional and energetic boundaries create clarity. They help you recognise what's yours and what's not. They say: *"This emotion is not mine to hold. This is what I need to feel safe."* Your energetic boundaries let you know when it's safe to be vulnerable — and when it's safer to hold a boundary. They are your intuition in motion.

When you honour your emotional and energetic boundaries, you stop ignoring red flags or overriding your instincts to keep the peace or maintain the connection, and you foster self-respect.

True intimacy begins when both people feel secure inside and out

Boundaries do not block love; they strengthen the connection through love and compassion, helping love to thrive.

This is how you establish healthy emotional and energetic boundaries through mindful choice, engaging with people who can meet you in that same clarity.

An understanding of what it means to stand in your own self-worth, to accept the difference between love and longing, between connection and enmeshment. To feel your own value, not as something given by others, but as something you grant yourself. When you love the parts of you that have been hurt, rejected, abandoned, and silenced, and offer yourself presence, care, truth, and love.

When both people in a relationship learn to use **Drop Your Shoulders® Methods** to regulate their nervous systems, establish emotional and energetic boundaries, and recognise when their inner child is online, healing occurs individually and together. Both individuals are willing to take personal responsibility for their own emotional wellbeing.

Sometimes it starts with one person in the relationship. One person who reads this book, adopts the **Drop Your Shoulders® Methods,** and becomes the adult in the room, creating enough safety for the other to follow.

At that moment, everything begins to change. The fight for power gives way to an invitation to love one another in a way that can be truly felt.

This is what a mature, conscious adult relationship feels like.

Now that you have reclaimed your own energetic circle, you are no longer navigating relationships from a place of enmeshment or self-abandonment. You meet others with presence, clarity, and embodiment. You begin to know your own energy so well that you can sense when there is disharmony or a boundary crossing, especially when the lines between you and another start to blur.

No matter how focused you are, you are human; relationships will always be your greatest teachers. They are where real-world practice begins. Where your healing is tested and integrated through the presence of another. Where all you have remembered about your inner child, your nervous system, your emotional body, and your energetic field come into play.

You practise the **Drop Your Shoulders® Methods** to strengthen your boundaries and support nervous system safety.

# When You Have Boundaries, And The Other Person Does Not.

Sometimes it feels effortless, straightforward, mutual, and respectful. Emotional and energetic boundaries are naturally honoured, and you feel safe to be fully yourself, offering that same safety in return. These are sacred relationships, not because they are free from challenges, but because they are grounded in self-care and self-responsibility.

Although this sounds simple, most relationships are not like this, especially when the other person hasn't done the same work you have. When your partner still operates mainly from their emotional survival patterns, their energy will unconsciously try to merge with yours, form a codependent relationship, or develop a parent-child dynamic. They blame, project, manipulate, or expect you to be their emotional anchor. Not because they are bad or unworthy of a healthy relationship, but because they haven't yet evolved their emotional body or energetic boundaries.

They haven't taken the time to learn new skills to express unresolved emotions and trauma.

These unhealthy relationships arise when one person carries the emotional burden. This is a common point of conflict. You do the work, clear your energy, and reclaim your truth. Then you sit across from someone who does not know how to — or does not want to — hold their own emotional boundaries and energetic circle. Their field leaks into yours; they continue to project onto you.

You have a choice to make. This is a moment to accept your own truth — and to confront the uncomfortable reality of what is actually in front of you.

Recognising that we all have free will and choice, not everyone is able or willing to learn and grow, or to put in the effort to build a healthy adult relationship. Some people, whether due to trauma, conditioning, or resistance, simply do not wish to change. This is not something you can control; it is their free will and choice.

You have not failed the relationship, nor are you judging the other person. Another person's free will and choices are not something you can change by being more loving, more patient, or more forgiving. That would only draw you into your emotional survival patterns, the very patterns you are working so hard to clear.

You have done the sacred work throughout this book. Now, as you sit across from someone whose field overlaps with yours and who doesn't yet understand their own emotional responsibility and energetic boundaries, you face more than just a choice.

You are being asked to honour your own truth, even when it is painful. To stop waiting for another person to become someone they are not ready to be. To accept what is, rather than exhausting yourself trying to change what is not within your control.

## Reflection

Choose a relationship, ask the following questions. Trust your intuition when answering; trust the first answers that come to mind.

*What are my realistic expectations of this relationship?* (refer back to chapter on expectations versus reality)

*Can this person meet me where I am? Yes/No*

*Has this person ever behaved any differently? Yes/No*

*Are they willing to examine their patterns? Yes/No*

*Do they even want to help themselves? Yes/No*

*Am I showing up as an adult and an equal partner, or have I become the parent? Yes/No*

*Is this love, enmeshment, trauma bonds, or emotional survival? Yes/No*

These are not easy questions to answer, and the answers might not be what you want to hear. Use the **Drop Your Shoulders® Method Scribbling** to release strong emotions and the uncomfortable sensations in your body.

## What Is True For Me?

You do not need to make a decision right now. You do not need to walk away, stay, or take any dramatic action. It is your responsibility to accept what is real for you. Accepting the truth without distortion, fantasy, or rescuing is the first step towards building a healthy relationship, whether with this person, another person, or yourself.

You can have a relationship with someone who chooses not to work on themselves or grow, as long as you accept them as they are now, without feeling the need to change them to feel safe and loved. This doesn't mean sacrificing your needs for someone else's comfort.

It is in these moments that your practice becomes valuable. When your inner child surfaces in fear, wanting to hold onto the fantasy — the illusion of the relationship — this is when you reparent your inner child first, before making any decisions, using all the tools you have learnt so far.

This is when you stop taking responsibility for someone else's emotions, stop trying to fix their pain. Emotional and energetic boundaries are not about shutting down or walking away. They are powerful when you can stay present while someone else finds their way back to themselves.

If the other person can meet you there, that's great; you are on your way to a healthy adult relationship. If they are unable to acknowledge their own pain, you can start by changing how you communicate. Reframed in your own words, here are some examples.

*"I can see you are in pain, but I am not here to fix you."* (Remember, it is not your responsibility to carry another person's pain or to try to process it.)

*"I am going to take some space to stay connected to myself."* (It is OK to let the other person sit with their pain and work through their emotions.)

*"I am open to reconnecting when we are both calm and present."*

This dialogue helps you reconnect with yourself amid chaos and confusion. It invites you to take responsibility, be truly present, create boundaries and experience a new kind of love — one that honours the energy of both people involved.

If they do not accept the invitation to learn and grow together, that also provides information. It is their choice not to move forward with you in this way. In your clarity, you will know what to do.

Drop your shoulders, stay present here for a moment, in the stillness after truth. Let your body feel what is real to you and listen to your intuition.

## Compassion And Boundaries

There is often a misunderstanding in relationships that being compassionate means you must feel what the other person feels, carry their pain, and somehow make it better. That if you have emotional or energetic boundaries and prioritise your self-care and needs over their survival pattern, it means you do not care. That you are cold, selfish, distant or unloving.

This is inaccurate.

Compassion is not emotional enmeshment, nor is it about becoming the parent to another adult. It begins with having compassion for yourself and love for the wounds your inner child carries, and then holding space with healthy emotional and energetic boundaries, allowing the other person to take responsibility for their own emotional needs.

Being able to sit with someone, witness their pain and their process, and allow them to have their own emotional experience without trying to fix, control, or absorb it. Compassion is trusting that they, too, have the capacity to move through it. It is about not judging emotions as good or bad, right or wrong; it is about recognising that all feelings are valid.

For example, it is very easy to have compassion for a child without taking their behaviour personally. You can hold space, recognise that they are experiencing a strong emotion, and offer comfort and reassurance. When the emotion becomes overwhelming, you can set a boundary and, when appropriate, provide a consequence to support learning and growth.

Another example: when a child is screaming for you to buy a lollipop, you set a clear boundary and say, "No." You know you cannot stop the tantrum, no matter how hard you try, and you stay firm with your boundary, even in the chaos. You still say "No" to the lolly. The child learns that they cannot expect a lolly every time they go to the shops.

I remember a moment in the shopping centre when my son, who was three at the time, had a massive tantrum because I said "No" to buying a toy car. Instead of triggering my own stress responses — fear of judgement and the urge to make him stop — I sat on the floor next to him. People walked past and stared, but I stayed present, holding space for my son's emotions.

Within a few minutes, the anger (expectation vs reality) shifted to grief, and he climbed into my lap, crying. A few minutes later, we continued shopping — he was calm and content, no longer expecting or even thinking about the toy car.

The process is the same for adults.

When an adult projects emotion outward because their expectations don't match reality, they are essentially having a five-year-old's tantrum. When you hold space with your energetic boundary, don't take it personally, and see through the behaviour, you can recognise what's genuinely happening: the person in front of you is in an emotional survival response — and it's not about you.

You can apply the **Drop Your Shoulders® Method Scribbling** to calm your own nervous system, while someone else is experiencing emotional turmoil. Allowing someone to feel what they feel, without judgment or attempts to change them, is genuine compassion.

If the behaviour continues and does not stop, you need to set a boundary. You and communicate:

*"If you keep speaking to me like that, I will leave the room."*

*How many times do you need to leave the room before the other person realises you're serious? Between 1 and 10.*

Usually, it takes only three times for the behaviour to stop or change. Why? Because you're no longer feeding the tantrum. They're not getting the attention, acknowledgment, or reaction they want or are used to. It is OK to say "No".

Compassion for yourself means choosing honesty over illusion. It means trusting your body and intuition when something doesn't feel right. It also means protecting your energetic circle — even when someone accuses you of not caring or loving them simply because you're not doing what they want while they're upset.

This often happens when they realise they cannot control you, and their unresolved childhood tantrum escalates to get attention.

It is not that you do not care; you are simply choosing not to harm yourself. You now have emotional and energetic boundaries, and you are free to communicate them with love and compassion.

This is a new way of expressing love and integrity. One that says, *"I love you enough to be honest, and I respect you enough not to repeat this cycle of hurting each other. I trust you enough to allow you to have your own emotions and to process them."*

There are times when the most compassionate thing you can do is to walk away, not out of anger or blame but with clarity. With deep respect for yourself and the other person, let go of patterns of co-dependency, enmeshment, and abusive entanglements.

Where you accept the other person and their free will and choice without needing to change them or to sacrifice yourself to make the relationship work.

This is what it means to live with healthy emotional and energetic boundaries.

## The Roles You Play: Victim, Perpetrator, And Rescuer

For many of us, love, compassion, and loyalty have been mistaken for rescuing and fixing what is perceived as negative or uncomfortable.

This is where we introduce a pattern that occurs in nearly every relationship system, often referred to as the Drama Triangle. Created by Stephen Karpman, the triangle comprises three roles: the Victim, the Perpetrator, and the Rescuer. You see this pattern everywhere — on the news, in your workplace, within your family, and throughout society.

Here, clarity becomes your power. It's not about fixing or teaching the other person; it's not your responsibility. Instead, you recognise that the other person needs to be ready for this work in their own time and space.

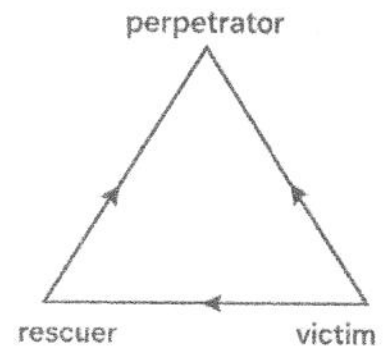


The Drama Triangle requires all three roles to operate. The Victim feels helpless. The Perpetrator shifts the blame. The Rescuer attempts to fix everything. Here is something rarely discussed: these roles are not fixed; you rotate through all of them. The Victim teams up with the Rescuer, becoming the two strongest points on the triangle. Together, they then attack the perpetrator. In response, the perpetrator becomes the victim of this attack and seeks a new rescuer. The cycle of drama continues endlessly. Round and round it goes, repeating a pattern with no boundaries, clarity, or resolution. It is a continuous play of chaos and drama, deeply ingrained in your emotional survival patterns.

You subconsciously play out these roles because they are modelled all around you from childhood. In all the superhero stories, the play is the same every time: there's a perpetrator (the bad guy), a victim (the good guy), and a rescuer (the hero). On the news, when something bad happens, there's a perpetrator, a victim, and rescuers.

When you were young, you may have learned to rescue your parent emotionally, or you might have been cast as the troublemaker—the one blamed for everything—or the golden child, praised for keeping the peace. These patterns follow you into adulthood, into love, into leadership, and into quiet moments when you still feel it is your job to fix, apologise, or absorb.

**Truth.** These roles are not who you are. They are coping mechanisms and emotional survival responses to shocks, trauma, and a lack of energetic boundaries.

When you recognise them as inherited survival patterns, you have a choice:

To keep cycling through the roles of perpetrator, victim, and rescuer,

or

To step outside the triangle and leave the roles behind.

## Stepping Outside The Triangle

Beyond the triangle of drama and the roles you assume, there are only people in pain, repeating emotional survival patterns. The nervous system works to regulate itself to find safety and love.

This is where you begin to take responsibility for your own energetic circle and life experience.

When you realise there are no victims, perpetrators, or rescuers, everyone has a choice, and these choices shape your experience of life.

*Have you been in a situation where a partner, friend, or family member is complaining about someone else taking the victim role, another person playing the perpetrator, and you being in the rescuer role? Yes/No*

Instead of getting caught up in the drama, taking sides, or teaming up against the perpetrator, you centre yourself and focus on the one person in front of you — the person experiencing physical, emotional, or mental pain.

You observe without judgment and empower yourself and others by asking: *"What do you need right now?"* This question opens the door to clarity. It helps the other person connect with their own sense of love and safety in the moment. It shifts the focus from blame to responsibility.

By asking this, you give the other person an opportunity to take ownership of their needs rather than directing their pain outward. If the conversation begins to drain your energy, you can say: *"It's not helpful to stay stuck in the cycle of blame. Let's focus on something more constructive."*

This honours your energetic boundaries and supports you in stepping out of the rescuer role with self-awareness and compassion.

You can expand to "*How can I help you?*" but it's not necessary. If you do ask, when someone tells you what they need, you can choose to say yes, I can do this, or no, I cannot. You're empowered to decide, and they are empowered to own their needs. If you say no, they have the clarity to ask someone else for help or to help themselves in other ways.

It is very powerful to avoid repeating the cycle of drama. You are not obliged to play out these roles.

When you step outside the triangle of drama and choose not to play any role, you create space not only for them but also for yourself. You protect your own energetic circle. You honour your emotional clarity, and you give the other person a chance to step outside the role they are also playing, choose responsibility over projection, and express what they actually need in this moment.

The moment you notice the pattern — the moment you understand the role you have played or may still be playing — you open a doorway to something new. You are not to blame for the emotional pain you inherited, or that was projected onto you during childhood; however, you are now responsible for the role you choose to play—or not play — in any given situation.

You begin to engage from a place of love and compassion, holding space for your own emotional pain and also the other person's pain while maintaining healthy boundaries.

## Chapter Twenty-Four

# How To Communicate Your Boundaries And Feel Respected

Emotional and energetic boundaries are not just a wish list; they are tangible and unique to you. Others do not know your boundaries, especially if they have had completely different childhood experiences, beliefs, and inherited patterns. It is essential to communicate your boundaries clearly, just as you do with your expectations and love languages.

How you communicate your boundaries influences whether the other person responds with respect or resistance. When a boundary is conveyed out of fear or anger, the other person reacts as if they are being attacked. When you communicate from a place of self-love and clarity, the other person can hear you without feeling the need to defend themselves.

Communicating a healthy boundary might sound like this:

*If you speak over me, I will end the conversation.*

*If you keep making decisions without involving me, I will make my own decisions without consulting you.*

*If you criticise or mock what matters to me, I will stop sharing with you.*

*If you raise your voice, I will leave the room.*

*If you cheat on me, I will end the relationship.*

Communicating your boundaries is only effective if you follow through. You need to clearly state your boundary and then stick to what you have said you will do.

*"Say it, do it."*

If you say, "If you speak over me, I will stop the conversation," and then do not follow through, your future words are less likely to be respected. However, when it happens, and you stop the conversation, walk away, hang up, or choose not to re-engage until there is respectful communication, something changes. You receive respect—first self-respect, and then respect from the other person, because they begin to take your words seriously.

This is not about punishment, control, or proving a point. This is about honouring your own boundaries.

*How many times have you set a boundary and then not followed through with it?*

*Do you notice the people around you continuing to ignore your boundary or behaving in the same way towards you?*

When your words consistently match your actions, your boundaries become non-negotiable. They will be heard and respected.

You might only need to do it once or twice before the other person realises your boundary is firm. There is no need for a fight, shouting, or trying to be heard, nor for ongoing negotiation to have your boundaries respected. You are no longer pleading to be treated with respect because you respect yourself.

## Say it. Do it.

This is where the cycle of abuse ends and where your energetic boundaries become real. This is where you cultivate self-respect for yourself and within your relationships.

Yes, this can be easier said than done.

When you've spent years trying to keep the peace or make others comfortable, communication can develop layers of tension you might not have realised were there. It doesn't start with the words. It begins with applying the **Drop Your Shoulders® Methods,** including **Scribbling and Loving your Inner Child.** Calming your nervous system and reassuring your inner child that *"it is okay to communicate your boundaries."*

## Communicating Boundaries Clearly And Thoughtfully

Communication becomes clear when you are present in this moment and feel empowered to speak your own truth without making the other person wrong. You are speaking from a place of self-love, empowerment, and your truth.

This type of communication is about expressing what is true for you at any given moment and ensuring that truth is heard.

When you say, *"That does not feel right to me,"* you are not rejecting the other person; you are honouring yourself. When you say, *"I need a moment; can I come back to you?"* you are not disconnecting; you are connecting with your own integrity. When you say, *"This is not appropriate for me,"* you are not being dramatic; you are naming how you feel.

To maintain this level of communication, you need to stay within your energetic circle, keeping your emotional and energetic boundaries intact. You cannot absorb or process another person's pain, emotions, or reactions.

This is why communication tools like Dr Rosenberg's Nonviolent Communication model are so helpful—not because they provide scripts, but because they remind you to speak from feeling, not blame.

For example, say, *"When this happens, I feel..."* or ask, *"Are you available to hear me right now?"*

Alternatively, when you say *"you never listen or you make me feel this way,"* it sounds like blame or an attack, even if that is not your intention. It triggers a defensive reaction in the other person; they will automatically respond with a fight-or-flight stress response.

Instead, I invite you to speak from your own experience by sharing what you feel and what you need to feel loved and safe, without making the other person responsible for your love and safety.

Changing the way you communicate in relationships is relatively simple; it may take a bit of practice, and this is not about getting it right all the time. Instead of beginning the conversation with the word **YOU** to tell someone how they feel or what they should do, ask a question.

Practice asking;
*"What do you think?" "How do you feel?"*
*"Would you like to...?" "Can you...?"*

This encourages the other person to speak for themselves and gives them space to respond with their own truth. Instead of making assumptions, remember that they are the only ones who truly know how they think and feel, or what they can and cannot do. This is a practice in communication. You won't get it right every time, but if you are aware and remember three out of five times, you are already well ahead of the curve, and the practice will start to show results. It's not about being perfect; it's about learning a new way forward.

Note: Not everyone will welcome your new boundaries. Some people may feel confused, resistant, or uncomfortable when you begin changing long-established patterns. This does not necessarily mean your boundaries are wrong. Healthy relationships can adapt to new boundaries, although doing so may take time, patience, and a commitment to practising new ways of communicating.

If this happens, continue practising the **Drop Your Shoulders® Methods**. Remember that change can be uncomfortable for everyone involved. Sometimes people are unwilling to change, and we will explore this further in the chapter.

## What happens when you communicate your boundaries and SAY IT, DO IT, and the other person keeps crossing them repeatedly?

You ask yourself, *"Do I stay or walk away?"* This is one of the most complex decisions to make because relationships are layered with emotional bonds, co-dependency, loyalty, history, hope, and the possibility of change.

Healthy relationships cannot be built by one person doing all the work. If you are the only one managing your nervous system, identifying your triggers, practising the techniques in this book, and holding space for the relationship, the dynamic can easily become unbalanced. You may find yourself in a parent–child relationship or taking on the role of a caretaker rather than an equal partner.

It is okay to love someone and still walk away, to see their pain and not take responsibility for it. You can be deeply compassionate and caring, and this same compassion and care should primarily be directed towards your own health and wellbeing. This is not selfish; it is self-love.

# Drop Your Shoulders® Method 25

## Changing The Way You Speak

This exercise focuses on communication in relationships and conflict, where statements beginning with "you" can trigger defensiveness and shut down connection. When used in this context, the word "you" often indicates that you are making assumptions or have created an expectation rather than seeking to understand the other person's experience.

- Start with the **Drop Your Shoulders® Method** to calm your nervous system and scribble if you feel tension, pain or emotions.

- Write down all the statements that start with ***"YOU"*** and that, when people say them to you. *"Does this type of communication trigger a negative, defensive response in you?"*

- Practise communicating each day differently. Never start a conversation or argument with the word "YOU"; replace it with a question to allow the other person to respond with their own truth.

For example:

*"Do you think I am...?"*
*"Do you feel angry?"*
*"Are you angry at me?"*
*"How do you feel?"*
*"Do you love me?"*
*"Would you like to...?"*
*"What do you need right now?"*
*"How can I help?"*

Activating the **Drop Your Shoulders® Method first** interrupts your stress response, calms your nervous system, and helps you return to a sense of emotional safety and presence. *"I am safe. Right now, I am..."*

This is especially important when your old patterns surface — when the urge to fix or please arises, or when you want to keep the peace.

Effective communication isn't about making yourself or others feel better. It is about understanding, not making assumptions or creating unrealistic expectations. It is about asking questions and empowering yourself and others to make their own decisions and respond clearly. It requires discernment about what is happening in the present moment.

When you do this, the entire energetic connection within the relationship begins to shift. Communication is not just an exchange of words; it is an exchange of energy. When your e**nergetic circle** is clear, your words can be truly heard and understood — and you can listen and truly hear what the other person is saying.

All healthy relationships are where both people's needs are met and honoured, not just one person's. It is where both individuals feel safe and loved in the relationship.

## Recognising Projection And Holding Space

Projection occurs when your partner, friend or family member cannot manage their own emotions, so they dump them onto you. It happens when their shame becomes your fault, their fear becomes your responsibility to keep them safe, and their anger becomes all-consuming, used to control their external environment and you. Many relationships go off track at this point; without emotional or energetic boundaries, you'll absorb these projections into your energetic circle and feel them as if they were your own emotions.

As you practise the **Drop Your Shoulders® Method** and calm your nervous system, you begin to recognise what energy is yours to process and what has been projected onto you.

When it is not your energy, you can activate your energetic boundaries and hold space for the other person. You recognise that they are activated into their emotional survival responses and choose not to react, instead becoming the adult in the room.

## Seeing The Inner Child In Others Without Taking It Personally

Everyone has an inner child that surfaces during conversations or arguments. They might become defensive, manipulative, withdraw, or become overly emotional. If you're unaware, you will end up responding to their inner child and triggering your own survival responses. When two adults communicate and both carry wounded inner children seeking love and safety, the conversation can immediately turn toxic. Both may shift into fight-or-flight mode, unable to listen to each other properly, with default responses like yelling or withdrawing. Now, you've got two children fighting for their lives.

When you are conscious and aware, and have learned to stay within your own energetic circle and communicate your boundaries clearly, you can remain present in your adult self.

You can drop your shoulders to interrupt your stress response by telling yourself, *"I am safe. This is not about me. This is not my energy."*

Now you can communicate in a way the other person can hear you. First and foremost, express empathy.

For example: *"I can see you're upset,"* or *"That must feel really difficult for you."*

Compassion is recognising the current situation without needing to fix or change it. It's also understanding that you don't need to feel or absorb another person's emotions to validate their experience.

As the other person feels heard, you can empower them to take responsibility for what is happening to them. At this point, you can ask a question: *"What do you need right now?"*

This is the most powerful question you can ask.

First, it empowers them to stop and reflect on what they truly need; then it encourages them to communicate that need to you. Usually, this will be one of the love languages, such as *"I need to be heard," "I need you to listen," "I need a hug," or "I need some time alone."* Once they identify what they need, they take responsibility for their situation, and their needs can be addressed.

You are also empowered in this communication; you can respond and offer what they have asked for, or, if that is not something you want to give, you can respond accordingly. *"I am unable to give that to you right now; what I can do is this..."* You have control over what you choose to give in these moments.

Remember, it is not your responsibility to meet their need for love and safety; it is an invitation and a gift if you choose to offer it.

# Healthy Relationship with Boundaries

## What Does A Healthy Relationship Look Like?

- Each individual takes responsibility for their own energetic circle, recognising what belongs to them and what belongs to others. They honour healthy emotional and energetic boundaries without enmeshment or projection.

- Communication is direct, kind, and honest. Example: *"What I need to feel safe and loved in this relationship is... What do you need to feel safe and loved?"*

- Everyone has the right to speak and express emotions without fear of threat, punishment, rejection, or emotional withdrawal.

- Emotional triggers are recognised and held with compassion. Reactions are not dismissed but witnessed and restored. Both people feel heard, and the inner child is given a voice and reassured.

- Needs, desires, and boundaries are expressed from an adult state of awareness — not from a reactive or wounded child state of awareness.

- No one is rescuing or being rescued. There are no roles of victim, perpetrator, or rescuer — just two people co-creating a conscious relationship.

- Each person remains centred within their own energetic circle, grounded in self-awareness, emotional regulation, and self-responsibility.

- Mutual accountability is present. Both individuals are open to growth and take ownership of their impact and patterns — without blame or avoidance.

- There is a shared commitment to repair and reconnect after conflict. Disagreements are seen as opportunities for deeper understanding, not as reasons to withdraw or punish.

- Boundaries are respected — not punished or perceived as rejection. A boundary is recognised as a form of clarity and self-care.

- The relationship is built on shared intentions, values, or vision, fostering emotional safety and aligned connection.

# Reflection

*Do you have the commitment and willingness to keep returning to your centre, even when it would be easier to revert to your emotional survival responses? Yes/No*

*Do you have the commitment and willingness to set healthy boundaries in your relationships? Yes/No*

When two people meet in this place, with clear communication, self-responsibility, and the adult self present, the relationship becomes a sacred experience of love and connection. It is a safe space to learn, grow, and evolve.

From here, you become available for deeply nourishing relationships where both people take ownership. Conversations are grounded in respect, and when you feel challenged or triggered, it is now an opportunity for healing and growth. An opportunity to practise **Drop Your Shoulders® Methods.**

This is the work not to be perfect or to get it right all the time, but to keep growing individually and together.

# Chapter Twenty-Five

# Significant Childhood Trauma

Are you navigating a relationship where significant childhood trauma is present — whether it is your trauma, your partner's trauma, or both? You are not alone. It is far more common than most people realise.

Global studies reveal some confronting truths:

Globally, an estimated one in five girls and one in seven boys experience sexual violence before the age of 18.

Emotional abuse, coercive control, neglect, and verbal degradation are even more widespread and often more difficult to identify, yet they can leave equally deep emotional and psychological imprints.

Physical abuse is reported in millions of homes worldwide, although many cases remain undisclosed or unrecorded, meaning the true prevalence is likely much higher.

Statistics sourced from UNICEF, Together for Girls, and the World Health Organization.

Beyond the statistics lies the unseen trauma — the repetitive, subtle experiences that often go unnamed. You, as a child, were never truly seen; you learned to perform for love, absorb your parents' grief, rage, addiction, mental illness, or emotional pain without ever being told, *"This is not your burden to carry."*

Using **Drop Your Shoulders® Methods** will be effective; however, you must be vigilant every day to manage your hyperactive emotional survival responses.

Healing from childhood trauma requires presence, boundaries, clear communication, and time. When one or both people in a relationship carry imprints of significant childhood trauma, such as physical, emotional, or sexual abuse, the space between you becomes charged not only with emotion but also with activated memories that continually trigger your emotional survival responses, keeping you on high alert.

It is no one's fault when this occurs. Childhood trauma is a lived experience of being emotionally hijacked by the past in the present moment. Your nervous system is often overactive, constantly scanning for danger and threats where there are none. Their responses may seem disproportionate, but they are not reactions to you or others around them; they are reactions to a memory of trauma they have endured, repeatedly triggered by the frozen energy of shock.

When you love someone with unresolved childhood trauma yourself, you may notice that the energy in the relationship feels hypervigilant. They can become triggered by almost everything you say or do, creating a cycle of constant reacting and feeling attacked.

If you have chosen to support someone with these survival patterns, or if both have similar patterns, you can heal from the past. It will take patience and time to work together with the **Drop Your Shoulders® Methods.**

Drop your shoulders now to calm your nervous system and reconnect with your body.

Now ask yourself;

*Are you intentionally choosing to support the other person, or are you slipping into the role of the rescuer from your own childhood trauma? Yes/No*

*Do you understand your role as the emotional caretaker and that the giving and receiving of love in this relationship can become unbalanced? Yes/No*

*Is your partner unable to hold space for you or support you emotionally? Yes/No*

It is crucial to understand that your needs must be met either by yourself or by inviting other to give your love and emotional support when needed.

Without conscious awareness and choice, this dynamic becomes a repeated pattern in which one person in emotional pain has all their needs met, while the other person's needs go unmet.

Some may call this a trauma bond; however, it is really a situation where no adult is in the room to offer love and compassion, and two inner children are continually fighting for love and safety. These bonds tend to be intense, magnetic, and often painful. They feel like a connection, but they are an enmeshment of the wounded child within, where two nervous systems wrap around each other, each seeking the love and safety they did not receive in childhood.

If you find yourself here, whether you are carrying trauma or supporting someone who is, drop your shoulders and return to yourself. Remember that love is not about rescuing another person or sacrificing your own needs. Boundaries are not rejection, and healing is not about abandoning yourself.

If you are the one who has deep trauma patterns, especially from childhood abuse, it is important to communicate the support you need. Not as a demand, but with honesty and awareness. Let the people closest to you know what helps you feel safe when your nervous system becomes overwhelmed. Share your love language, communicate your needs clearly, and invite support where appropriate.

At the same time, remember that your healing remains your responsibility. Support from others can be helpful, but no one else can do the work for you.

If you are supporting someone with trauma, your role is not to fix, rescue, or carry their pain. Your role is to hold space, maintain healthy emotional and energetic boundaries, and offer support without abandoning yourself. Be the adult in the room and invite their adult self back into the conversation with compassion, patience, and respect.

This is where boundaries and communication become acts of love. This is where the adult in the room, the adult in you, finally gets to take the lead. Supporting and loving yourself and those in your life who have experienced trauma looks like this. It won't be perfect, but if you remember to hold space or communicate clearly three out of five times, you're well on your way to a healthy adult relationship. There will be many uncomfortable moments; however, this is what it means to create a healthy relationship.

I saw this once and thought it was exactly what is needed when there has been childhood trauma: for someone to just say: *"I am not here to fix you. I will walk beside you while you fix yourself."*

The chances are high that either you or someone you love has experienced significant childhood trauma.

This does not make healthy relationships, love, or safety impossible, but it does mean that many relationships are influenced by past pain and childhood trauma. Unresolved anger, grief, shame, and guilt, combined with subconscious survival patterns still on high alert, create long-term fight-or-flight patterns and sustained adrenal stress.

You already understand the importance of emotional and energetic boundaries, as well as healthy communication; we are not just talking about tools for everyday stress. This is about learning how to be in a relationship without re-traumatising yourself or the other person.

*Have you been in a relationship that began with deep emotional intensity and a strong sense of connection, only to reveal itself over time as a tug-of-war between two people's emotional survival responses rather than love?*

In the beginning, it might feel as if you have found your soulmate, someone who truly sees you and with whom you can support and be supported. There is a magnetic pull and a sense of familiarity that draws you in.

As the layers unfold, you start to notice yourself slipping into roles you did not intend to play. You become the emotional caretaker, the one who softens, explains, fixes, and absorbs. Your nervous system scans for signs of safety before words are even spoken, and you constantly feel emotionally under attack. You begin adjusting your tone, your truth, and even your body language to avoid upsetting them.

What once felt like love has become a trauma bond, a connection built on mutual pain. These dynamics often resemble parent-child relationships, with one partner unconsciously assuming the role of protector while the other acts as the wounded child. The roles may shift over time or even reverse — if you've played the parent, you might find yourself shifting into the child, seeking the other person to take on the parental role. The core structure remains the same: one person feels responsible for the other's emotional wellbeing.

Your nervous system recognises familiar patterns and reaches for what it knows. What is missing is an embodied adult presence. Without conscious awareness, the relationship becomes a space of enmeshment rather than connection. There are no emotional or energetic boundaries; there is only entanglement.

When you become entangled in another person's emotional pain, fear, or unmet childhood needs, you start to lose your own clarity and sense of self. You might believe that your love and sacrifices can heal them, and you may feel responsible for their growth, carrying emotions that aren't yours. This often involves processing feelings they have been unwilling or unable to confront. The burden of supporting another person's physical and emotional wellbeing is draining. It becomes a one-way street, with no equal exchange of energy — you tend to over-give, and the other person takes without giving back, and vice versa.

This is where the turning point begins. Not in blame or judgement, but in truth. You already know the cost of staying in this dynamic, carrying the emotional load for both of you. Despite all your efforts, you cannot heal another person — only they can heal themselves, and only you can heal yourself. Love cannot replace personal responsibility.

**Drop Your Shoulders® Method Scribbling:** start to scribble as you feel the tension building. Keep scribbling while you read.

Now is the time to recognise what has been happening for months or years. You see yourself acting as the rescuer, the emotional parent, the peacekeeper, and you gently begin to let go of the belief that this is your responsibility.

You are reclaiming your personal power and choosing to stay connected to yourself first. You have already learnt many new tools and can begin to see that healthy love does not ask you to abandon or sacrifice your own needs. You are not responsible for parenting another adult, continuing patterns of enmeshment or co-dependency, or staying trapped in a trauma bond and calling it love.

True connection is one of shared responsibility. It asks both individuals to stay within their own energetic boundaries, witnessing each other's pain without taking it on, speaking truth without assigning blame, and listening without becoming defensive. When one person assumes the role of the adult in the space, a new dynamic becomes possible.

This shift can be painful and trigger a lot of fear. Your inner child will react, screaming to be heard and crying out for what he or she knows as love. This is the moment to go deeper into parenting your inner child. You can communicate clearly to your inner child with gentleness and love:

*"I am the adult. I will make the decisions now. I will keep you safe."*

## Healing From Childhood Abuse

When you carry the imprint of trauma, especially childhood abuse in its many forms, communication takes on a new meaning. It is no longer just about words; it is about feeling seen, heard, loved, and safe.

The emotional pain does not always announce itself loudly. It resides in your nervous system and manifests in constant hypervigilance, triggering emotional survival responses. You immediately shift into fear; your heart races when a voice's tone changes, and your muscles tighten even when there is no apparent danger. It involves reliving past trauma and often the initial shock when the energy becomes crystallised in your energetic field and body, then repeats in a circular pattern around key emotional trigger points.

*Have you experienced emotional, physical, or sexual abuse as a child? Yes/No*

You might find it almost impossible to ask for what you need right now. You weren't kept safe as a child, so you might not even know what you need to feel secure. Communicating this as an adult can be very challenging.

You have learnt many tools in this book, and with practice and awareness, you can begin to speak differently. You can now gradually begin speaking honestly, in alignment with your healing, and communicate in a way that allows others to support you.

You can communicate in a way that allows you to feel heard:

*Sometimes I get overwhelmed and do not know why. It is an old fear in my body from trauma in my childhood. I know it is not about this moment; however, the intensity in this moment is overwhelming for me. I need space to feel safe again.*

*I have experienced childhood abuse, and certain situations or tones of voice can make me shut down. I am learning to stay present and support myself. Would you like to help me in these moments when I am struggling? I will need you to....*

*When I seem distant or overly reactive, I'm not trying to push you away. This is my body recalling moments of feeling disempowered. I'm learning to take responsibility for my responses, but right now I need support. I need you to.*

*I do not need you to fix me. I need to be seen and heard. I need to be met where I am now, not where I was when I was abused. I need you to hold space and....*

If you are in a relationship with someone who carries this kind of trauma, it is crucial to understand that you are not the cause of their pain. This is pain that resides in their energetic circle, not yours.

The best thing you can do is first avoid being triggered by your own childhood pain and then make it about you. You can choose to be a safe presence in their life and in their healing, not by rescuing them or even trying to understand the complexity of their trauma and pain. You are not their therapist, and you do not need to be the dumping ground for unspoken emotional energy. You can stay grounded within your own energetic boundary while respecting theirs. Start by dropping your shoulders.

Ask the question.

*"What do you need right now?" (When you ask this, you empower the person to identify what they need to feel loved and safe.)*
*"How can I support you?"*

(You are not required to ask this, but if you do and the person tells you what they need, you can say yes, I can do this, or No, I cannot do this. You are empowered to choose, and they are empowered to own what they need. If you say No, I cannot do this, they then have the clarity to ask someone else for help or to help themselves in another way.)

*Alternatively, you can say, "You are safe right now. I am here for you. What do you need?"*

Once they have calmed down and returned to their adult selves with clarity, you can then expand the conversation.

*"I hear you and thank you for trusting me. I want to respect your pace. What can I do that would be helpful, or can we have a safe word to help me understand what's happening to you and how to respond?"*

*"You do not need to explain everything; I can just sit here with you."*

*"Is there anything I do that triggers you? I'd like to know, not to promise I will never do it again, because I can't do that, as it would create unrealistic expectations. However, I can use that information to understand how it affects you and do my best to support you."*

Note: these are just examples. Please express your needs in your own words.

## When Two People In A Relationship Are Healing From Childhood Trauma

When trauma exists, and both individuals are healing from childhood abuse and other trauma, it is easy to fall into enmeshment, child-parent dynamics, and codependency. With a little effort from both parties, healthy boundaries and relationships can be established, and the old patterns can be transformed.

Healthy communication, especially when both have experienced childhood trauma, relies on clear messaging and boundaries. Both individuals need to recognise their emotional triggers and communicate what they need to feel safe and loved. When no adult is present—meaning both people are triggered into emotional survival responses — each person is responsible for using the **Drop Your Shoulders® Methods** to calm their own nervous system and come back to the present moment. When the other person is willing and also doing their own work using these tools, the relationship can begin to hold both truths: the pain of the past and the hope for a different future. Together, you can build something grounded in mutual respect and love.

## When The Other Person Chooses Not To Work On Themselves

You are now in a position to choose: either continue to stay small, silence your voice, and mould yourself around someone else's emotional needs at your own expense — or affirm your identity.

OR

The realisation that you are now the only adult in the relationship can be heartbreaking; it can also be freeing. Because you are now awake, you can choose. It is not happening to you; you have a choice about how you want to move forward in the relationship and how you want to interact.

You have the choice to stay or leave. You can decide what you are willing to accept in your life. You can opt for acceptance and remain in the relationship, setting realistic expectations about the support you will or won't receive from your partner. You can choose to accept them as they are without expecting them to change.

OR

You can choose to honour your own truth, communicate your emotional and energetic boundaries out loud, and name what is true — not to control the other person, but to reclaim your clarity. From that clarity, you create space for both people to grow, whether together or apart.

Not everyone wants to learn and grow. Some people are comfortable where they are. Others are so deeply identified with their survival patterns that they cannot yet see another way.

This does not make either of you right or wrong. It simply means you are making different choices. At this point, the question is no longer how to change them. The question becomes:

*"What is true for you?"*

*Can you genuinely accept this person as they are today, without expecting them to change?*

If the answer is yes, you may choose to stay and adjust your expectations accordingly. If the answer is no, you may choose to create distance or leave the relationship.

Neither choice is wrong.

What matters is that you stop abandoning yourself while waiting for someone else to become who you need them to be.

Self-love begins when you stop trying to carry responsibility for another person's growth and return your attention to your own healing, boundaries, and wellbeing.

This is compassion for yourself, the beginning of self-love, and the foundation for healthy relationships with yourself, then with others.

There's a saying often attributed to Tony Robbins: *"You will only accept abuse of any kind to the extent that you are willing to abuse yourself."*

# Chapter Twenty-Six

# Survival-Based Imprints:

## Rewiring The Energetic Frequency Of Love And Safety

Accepting abuse of any kind is not a conscious choice or something you willingly agree to. However, the frequency of self-abandonment, self-rejection, or self-criticism can still linger in your energy field. That frequency attracts more of the same.

These patterns often lead you towards what feels familiar. This is not about what you consciously want; it is about what remains unresolved in your subconscious and what your nervous system has learned to recognise as normal and safe.

This invites you to look more closely at what you have been taught to believe is love, because you do not always move towards what you consciously desire. More often, you move towards what your subconscious expects and what your nervous system has learned to recognise as familiar.

When love has been associated with chaos, abuse, rejection, criticism, or abandonment, especially during early childhood, these experiences leave an energetic imprint on your cells. They create what I refer to as survival-based imprints.

While your conscious mind might say, "*I want a loving relationship,*" your body may still resonate with the imprint that love equals chaos, abuse, rejection, and betrayal. You have already learned how to identify your own love language, how to love yourself, and how to give and receive love through the five love languages. These practices are powerful; they have already begun to shift your nervous system and open you to healthier ways of connecting.

They have also transformed how you engage with your partner, family, and friends.

This next layer takes you deeper, beyond behaviours and languages, into the survival-based imprints themselves — the unseen frequency still residing within you that shapes what you attract and how safe love feels in your body.

You have completed the work, integrated the **Drop Your Shoulders® Methods** into your daily routine, and noticed the changes and results. You feel peace in your body, experience self-love as a way of being, and have improved your relationships. Yet a quiet voice inside still asks, "*Why am I still attracting people who are emotionally unavailable, disconnected, stuck in their own patterns, or unwilling to work on themselves?*"

This is not about effort or worth; the methods are working. You needed to learn to calm your nervous system and be present in your body before reaching this next layer — the part beneath the surface that hasn't yet been seen. The frequency still residing in your subconscious silently draws in the familiar. You are now ready to change your survival-based imprints.

When you enter a primary intimate relationship, it is not just personality or compatibility that draws you in; it is chemistry — not the kind from romantic movies. This chemistry is a vibrational frequency, a deep, unspoken energy that communicates between nervous systems before words are even spoken. You are drawn to what feels familiar. Even if that familiarity is chaos, emotional unavailability, or subtle forms of abandonment, your body recognises the frequency and still calls it love.

This is the part most people tend not to talk about.

If you have not experienced safe, steady love at any point in your life, your body does not have emotional-somatic reference points for it. The work you have already done is not lost; it is the foundation.

You cannot begin working on your survival-based imprints until you have committed to the process, practised the **Drop Your Shoulders® Methods**, and brought your nervous system into a calm state so you feel safe and loved within, through self-love and by loving your inner child.

This is not something you can shift through your mindset; it is a template for survival. It's an energy frequency that resides in your body, shaped by your earliest experiences and environment. Until your nervous system feels secure, you will struggle to access these deeper survival-based imprints because your body remains focused on staying safe rather than creating something new.

Your relationships do not arise solely from what you say you want. They are influenced by the patterns, expectations, and emotional reference points held within your subconscious and nervous system. That's why you might keep attracting emotionally unavailable partners or relationships that mirror your childhood trauma. Your subconscious mind and nervous system are not seeking the love you consciously desire; they operate at a survival-based love frequency. This imprint is embedded in your DNA and cellular structure. When the only love your inner child has known involved conditions, withdrawal, betrayal, or violence, that is the vibrational frequency that resonates — even if it causes pain.

You might find yourself in a relationship where you have made significant improvements, or where everything looks great on the surface. You practise the **Drop Your Shoulders® Methods**. You communicate, you hold space, and you are calm and centred. Yet you still feel anxious, shut down, unseen, or unsafe — especially in your primary relationships.

This does not happen to everyone; it occurs when there is no emotional or somatic reference point where love feels safe. It happens when there is significant childhood trauma; in this case, it's relevant to identify the survival-based imprints formed when emotional and physical safety were never present. You may not hold a subconscious or somatic reference point for safe, healthy love. Without that imprint, your nervous system will continue to attract and create the frequency it recognises, even if you are now consciously aware that chaos and abuse are not love.

This is why a significant part of your healing journey is not just about calling in love, but about establishing new emotional-somatic reference points for love.

In addition to the **Drop Your Shoulders® Methods,** you will now be able to anchor new emotional-somatic reference points with the vibration of love and safety.

The body must know it, your heart must feel it, and your nervous system must trust it.

This is how you begin creating new emotional reference points. As your nervous system learns that love can feel safe, kind, gentle, and nurturing, your choices, relationships, and experiences naturally begin to change. You start to carry and vibrate the frequency of love that is safe, kind, gentle and nurturing.

In the next section, I will guide you on how to intentionally establish emotional and somatic reference points for love and safety. These reference points help the subconscious and nervous system trust that love can feel safe, nurturing, consistent, and genuine.

You are now learning to create new patterns within your nervous system and subconscious mind.

# Drop Your Shoulders® Method 26

## Creating New Somatic Reference Points For Love and Safety

- Apply the **Drop Your Shoulders® Method.**
- Calm your nervous system and your body. This is about creating something new in your nervous system — a felt experience that becomes a living emotional-somatic reference point for love and safety.
- Begin by recognising the qualities you want to feel in your relationships. You now believe love means kindness, nurturing, desire, fun, laughter, care, respect, being chosen, and being wanted.
- Name them clearly: what you want to feel and what you want to attract into your life.

- Now ask yourself honestly;

*"Have I ever felt loved and safe in any of my relationships? "Yes/No*
*"Romantic?" Yes/No*
*"Friendships?" Yes/No?*
*"Family?" Yes/No?*
*"Colleagues?" Yes/No*

- If you have, close your eyes and allow yourself to return to a moment when you felt love as kind, gentle, caring, and nurturing. Find that memory. One precise moment is enough. Feel it in your body and notice the sensations of warmth in your chest, a drop in your shoulders, and a slowing of your breath. This is what your nervous system needs to anchor the somatic reference point. Let your body know by saying out loud:

*"This is what kindness feels like," or "This is what fun and laughter feel like."*

- If you have never experienced this and your body lacks an emotional somatic reference point, set the intention to receive it. This part may feel uncomfortable and may require stepping outside your comfort zone. You cannot give this to yourself, nor can you think what you have never felt and then manifest it. You need another person to assist because these reference points are typically given in childhood by a parent or caregiver, so you must allow them to come through another person.

That in itself can feel unsafe at first, especially if you have never known love without pain. Remember, you are not asking for a relationship; you are asking for one moment — a moment that becomes a new imprint, a new emotional-somatic reference point. One interaction where love and safety co-exist.

When you have the intention without attachment — letting go of your attachment styles — you are not seeking the love of a parent or a romantic relationship; you are intentionally seeking one moment to create a new emotional somatic reference point.

This is a moment of surrender and of opening your heart to receive without attaching meaning to the other person or making it their responsibility. Be open to accepting moments of kindness, nurturing, desire, fun, laughter, care, and respect. Start with one at first.

When the moment arrives, and it will, activate the **Drop Your Shoulders® Method.**

Feel into your body and receive this moment as a somatic reference.

If you later feel uncomfortable and your emotional survival responses attempt to overlay expectations and meaning onto the other person. Drop your shoulders, calm your nervous system, start to scribble and release all tension, resistance, discomfort, or fear that arises.

This is not about the other person; it's about you — your experience of love and safety, what you felt in that moment. Take responsibility for letting go of the idea that love equals chaos, abuse, and trauma, and replace that belief with love representing kindness, gentleness, nurturing, and caring. This is about overcoming your own fears and allowing love and safety to mean something different.

- Now breathe into your body and acknowledge what is happening. Let your cells register it.

- This moment, this new memory, is what kindness truly feels like. Acknowledge the new somatic reference point. Say to yourself or out loud:

*"This is what safe touch genuinely feels like."*
*"This is what being genuinely wanted feels like."*
*"This is what play and laughter feel like."*
*"This is what joy feels like."*
*"This is my new emotional somatic reference point for love and safety."*

- Feel the feeling of that moment in your body, stay calm and centred, and anchor it as a memory.

This is the new emotional somatic reference point you now carry. Change becomes possible not because you hope for it, but because your body has experienced it and your nervous system now recognises it as real.

You will not create all your new emotional somatic reference points at once. You can even name them as you go through your life and experiences. You can set an intention right now:

*"I am here to create new emotional somatic reference points of fun, joy, kindness, care, and safety."*

- Notice them as they come to you, especially when a person approaches you with kindness, care, fun, and laughter. Use the **Drop Your Shoulders ® Method** and embrace this one moment, anchoring it with intention and feeling.

- If you are courageous and prepared, you can invite someone else to join this space if they wish, and then be open to receiving. You might simply ask them, *"Can you hold me for a few minutes?"* Then allow yourself to soften, surrender, drop your shoulders, intentionally calm your nervous system and receive the feeling of safety in this one moment.

Remember, you are looking for moments in time to establish new emotional-somatic reference points. This person might not always be able to provide it, nor is it their responsibility to do so. You're not seeking a parent's love or a forever relationship; you simply need one moment when you're open to receiving that love — kind, gentle, nurturing, and caring. One moment when you can be open enough to anchor a new emotional-somatic reference point. This is about you; it's not about the other person. They will have their own experience, and it is not your responsibility to manage it at this time.

When you begin to create new emotional somatic reference points, you activate secure attachment within yourself.

It is one moment when you feel safe, one moment when you feel loved, or one moment when you allow someone to hold you. You use this one moment to create a new emotional somatic reference point within you. Anchor it into your body. *"This is what it feels like to ... "*. As you continue to create new emotional somatic reference points to start to attract more of the same into your life.

You have now started to create new emotional somatic reference points, this is where healing becomes embodied. It is the moment when your nervous system begins to recognise love, safety, connection, and new possibilities as familiar. This is where life starts to feel different and change becomes permanent.

For me, that shift occurred after I realised I was still carrying the frequency of love equals chaos, abuse, and trauma, and i began to use the **Drop Your Shoulders® Methods Creating New Somatic Reference Points for Love and Safety**. With the intention of stepping outside my comfort zone and unapologetically being myself, unexpected opportunities arrived — not by idealising a relationship or overlaying expectations onto another person, but by having the courage to be open and step into the unknown. With intention, in shared moments of laughter, tenderness, and curiosity, I found myself opening more fully in my body, without needing to contract or disappear.

There was space to be with myself while being met with truth and honesty. Something softened in my nervous system — a recalibration of what connection could feel like without my disorganised attachment style. It was about being present in the moment to receive what was offered, just as it was, without needing or wanting to change another person or control my external environment to feel safe.

With intention and by working with my nervous system, these moments became living imprints of joy, laughter, safety, and pleasure, allowing me to be myself without fear. This enabled me to anchor in new emotional somatic reference points, creating a new energetic frequency that now radiates within me — an unshakeable, secure attachment, both internally and externally.

Once you have created new emotional somatic reference points, you can explore manifestation processes and become clear about what you wish to attract into your life.

What changed most was not what was happening around me; it was what was happening within me.

For so much of my life, I had been responding to the world through survival-based imprints. My nervous system was constantly scanning for danger, rejection, abandonment, criticism, or betrayal. I did not realise how much energy was being used simply trying to stay safe.

As new emotional somatic reference points formed, something unexpected happened. Life began to feel different. I was no longer constantly preparing for what might go wrong. I was no longer waiting for love to disappear, for people to leave, or for situations to become unsafe.

Instead, I found myself becoming more present.

I naturally laughed more. I trusted myself and became curious about life. I stopped trying to control every outcome and started allowing myself to experience the moment in front of me. Now I live the majority of my time in joy, creativity, connection, and spontaneity. Using the **Drop Your Shoulders® Methods** daily to change how I feel in the moments when challenges arise.

I no longer feel trapped by my past. The greatest gift is the ability to attract something new: new experiences, people aligned with my life and future, and the ability to be present in each moment and enjoy this beautiful world we live in.

I realised that healing was never about becoming someone different. It was about removing the layers of fear, protection, and survival that had been covering who I truly was. Beneath those layers was a version of me that had always existed — calm, loving, playful, creative, connected, and a free spirit.

This is the greatest shift of all. When your body no longer believes it is in danger, your energy is no longer consumed by survival. You are now available to fully live your life.

You begin to create, connect, explore, love, and trust. You don't dream it is possible; you know it is possible.

And from that place, life naturally begins to unfold in ways that once felt impossible.

From this foundation, you can begin creating the life, relationships, and experiences you truly desire from a grounded, clear, embodied space where love feels kind, connection is safe, and intimacy supports your nervous system rather than destabilising it. All the work you have done throughout this book has brought you to this moment — a place where manifestation is no longer just a mental exercise or a vision board fantasy, but a deeply felt energetic truth that your body, heart, and field now recognise.

You naturally embody a different energy frequency and attract a new way of living, not from your words, affirmations, or longing. It responds to your emotional and energetic state.

Until now, that frequency was shaped by past trauma, unmet needs, and inherited patterns. Now, everything has shifted — your nervous system is calm, your body relaxed, and you have new reference points for love and safety. You know how to soothe your body, connect with your inner child, meet your needs in real time, speak your truth, and hold your boundaries without collapsing or withdrawing.

This is where you begin to attract relationships that meet you here. Where both people are self-aware, responsible for their own emotional wellbeing, and willing to walk side by side — not from co-dependence or fantasy, but from a grounded connection. You are no longer seeking someone to fill the void where the pain sits. You are inviting someone to walk beside you.

Manifesting now means creating clarity and making a choice from a new, grounded place, speaking and acting from a place of knowing. This is not about trying to get it right or forcing more effort. When you shift your energy frequency, it is already achieved. You can attract the love you desire because you have felt it in your body, anchoring somatic reference points for love and safety, and now you are a magnet for receiving it.

You are the creator of your life, and the people who enter your space now will sense the clarity and safety in your body. They will feel your boundaries, warmth, and depth. You no longer need to teach anyone how to love you. You only need to recognise when love is present — and when it is not.

At the beginning of this book, my aim was to provide practical tools you could use each day to change how you feel in the moment, empowering you to choose freedom from the past and move forward into your future. My hope is that by now, these practices feel less like techniques and more like a way of being — simple daily reminders that help you reconnect with your body, calm your nervous system, and return to the truth of who you are.

This is the foundation for building the life you have always wanted: the relationships you long for and intimacy that honours your heart, reflecting the truth of who you are. And it begins now.

# Drop Your Shoulders® Method 27

## Manifesting Your Future

- Activate the **Drop Your Shoulders® Method** to calm your nervous system.
- Now feel into your body and remember your new somatic reference points for love and safety.
- Feel it in your body.
- Create an image of what you would like to manifest.
- Imagine this image in your heart centre.
- Now move this image into a spiral in your solar plexus, near your navel.
- Expand this image into every cell in your body; expand it out as big as your energetic circle, now as big as the room you are in, the city, the country, the world.

- Now bring the image back through the spiral to your solar plexus and into your heart.

- Feel into your body; think of the image you are creating as if it has already happened. Feel the excitement in your body and the happiness and joy.

- Speak the truth of what you are ready to receive. This is your new frequency, and it is already here.

- Write your manifestation as though it has already happened, as if you are writing from the future and reflecting back. Begin with the words, "I am so grateful for..." Continue writing until you feel you have expressed everything you are grateful for.

- For example:

"I am so grateful it was such an easy process to purchase my new home."
"I am so grateful for the friend who introduced me to..."
"I love that I am in a healthy, loving, and caring relationship."

- You are now magnetic to receive your manifestation. You are creating from a place of self-love and safety.

- Now trust that what you have manifested is coming to you, and be open to the synchronicity of events that will bring it to you. Do not attach to or be defined by a specific way for it to arrive; just be open to it arriving. Notice the new opportunities as they present themselves in your life.

- Now drop your shoulders, feel the excitement building in your body as you start to feel a deep inner knowing that what you are creating is already coming to you. Enjoy your day.

# Chapter Twenty-Eight

# Integration — Living The Work

This book is more than a read. It is an energy frequency to feel and practise, helping you change how you feel each day and master your nervous system. It invites you to reconnect with your body, energy, and truth.

As you reach the end of this transmission, it marks the start of a new journey. Your life is no longer defined by what happened to you as a child; it is now a choice and a commitment to live with full awareness, grounded in the freedom of free will and choice in all facets of your life.

## What Will You Choose Now?

You can choose to adopt the daily and weekly practices in this book, allowing the changes to develop into a new way of living. Use this book as a resource and reference for continued growth.

Or you can choose to set this book aside, do nothing, and accept the path you have already been walking. This is the freedom of choice. You can choose to do nothing; this is still a choice.

This book is a living awareness, a journey of remembering your own personal power, with practical tools to connect with yourself and others on a deeper level. There is a sacred truth at the core of your human existence: you have free will and choice, always.

Regardless of what has happened in your life, no matter what pain has shaped your past, present, or future, you hold the power of choice. The power to return to yourself and honour the evolution of your emotional body. To choose what supports your healing instead of repeating what caused your harm.

# Daily Practices

Embrace the **Drop Your Shoulders® Methods**. Just like brushing your teeth in the morning, these practices only take a few minutes. Each morning, your body gives you signals. Each interaction reveals something about your energetic circle, your emotions, and your boundaries, and you are empowered to reclaim your power.

**Feeling Safe and Loved**. Start your day in your body. When you begin to wake up, before reaching for your phone, place one hand on your heart and one on your stomach. Relax your body, notice any areas of tension, and breathe in for 4 and out for 4. Repeat 4 times. Say: "*I am safe right now. I am lying in bed, relaxing.*"

If you want to grow: Ask yourself;

"*What do I need today to feel safe and loved?*" Let the answer come from within. Now ask yourself;

"*How can I love myself today?*" Remember your love language and make a list of self-love actions. Choose one each day.

To expand further:

"*How can I love someone else today?*" Consider their love languages and choose to give one person their love language today. This could be a hug, a kind word, a gift, or a thoughtful gesture.

**Energetic Boundary.** Picture your energetic circle surrounding you, your own protective boundary. Visualise a silver shield of protection, like a mirror reflecting outwards. I do this every morning in the shower. I let the water cleanse my body and energy field, then I bubble up for the day with a protective boundary about 1 metre from my body, with the intention that it remains intact all day.

**Boundaries In Action.** Every day, choose one boundary to honour as a sacred practice. Not to control your life, but to respect your field.

Some examples;

- Rest without judging your need for rest.
- Take a moment to drop your shoulders before replying to an emotional message.
- Turn your phone off and be fully present.
- Say "No" without guilt.
- What matters is that you show up for yourself. The power of boundaries grows through daily practice.
- Every time you follow through, you teach your nervous system that you are loved and you are safe.

**Interrupt the Stress Response** — at least five times a day, practise dropping your shoulders. Notice when your shoulders feel tense while driving, watching a movie, chatting with friends, or when your thoughts turn negative. Interrupt the stress response. Drop your shoulders, breathe deeply and relax the muscles. Say: "*I am safe right now. I am... present in this moment*" This will become natural over time, but initially, set a few phone alarms to remind you to drop your shoulders — 9 am, 11 am, 1 pm, 4 pm, 8 pm. Change the alarm times weekly to avoid subconsciously ignoring them.

## Emotional Triggers Throughout The Day

This is when you are emotionally triggered and in fight-or-flight mode. It is the moment you interrupt the stress response and release suppressed emotions and pain from your body. During this time, add **Drop Your Shoulders® Scribbling** to your daily routine. Scribbling only takes five minutes to clear energy from the body. Keep a scribbling pad in your bag, car, or at home. Whenever you feel triggered or uncomfortable in your body, ask the other person, *"Can you give me a moment?"* Please take five minutes to interrupt the stress response and scribble out the past pain that has been activated, whether physical, mental, or emotional.

While scribbling, ask yourself:

*"Is this my pain or someone else's?"*
*"Is this childhood pain, or have my boundaries been crossed?"*

No matter what it is, as you scribble with the intention of releasing it, focus on relaxing the muscles in your body.

## Evening Practices:

**Sleep Peacefully.** Before bed, take a moment to let go of the day. Say to yourself or aloud:

*"I release the day's events. I have done the best I can today, and that is enough. I allow my mind to rest. I sleep peacefully through the night."*

Your system will begin to trust that it is safe to rest.

## Weekly Practices:

Re-patterning the deeper layers of integration is not linear. It is layered, with some layers deep in the subconscious. Set aside one day each week for deeper work — a time to go inward.

**Visualisation and Inner Child Work:** Loving your inner child. Notice what your body reveals. Let your inner child speak. Offer comfort, set boundaries, and facilitate integration. When finished, bring that part of you back into your heart.

**Forgiveness of Self and Others.** True forgiveness is a release — a sacred choice to sever energetic cords that no longer support your healing. It is about freeing yourself from the emotional and energetic burden of the past. This week, choose one moment, one person, or even one version of yourself to forgive.

**Anger Management.** One of the most powerful, physically and energetically clearing practices you can do is the woodchopping exercise. This is not just an exercise; it is an act of energetic release. Note: This is not actually woodchopping with tools; it is a physical action that mimics woodchopping.

Integration is a new way forward.

Notice what is different, not what is the same.

And trust the changes that are already unfolding within you.

# Chapter Twenty-Nine

# Where To Next

This is not the end. This is the start of your journey back to your truth, energy, and voice. Consider this your invitation to keep choosing yourself, again and again, even when the world pulls you away. Even when old patterns whisper and even when others forget how to meet you, you are empowered to be free and true to yourself.

You now possess the Drop Your Shoulders® Methods, practices, awareness, and language that most people never access. You have somatic practices to regulate your nervous system, clear your energetic field, communicate your boundaries, and stay within your own energetic space. **You can honour your past without letting it define you.**

This is no small achievement; you have reclaimed your life.

You have journeyed through chapters of unravelling and remembrance. You have been challenged to go deeper than most, to feel what is truly yours and release what is not, and to stand in the frequency of love even when it feels unfamiliar.

You will forget; return to this book to remember. This book is alive, and the words on the pages are not a one-off read. **Drop Your Shoulders® How to Break Free from The Trauma Cycle** is a companion for the version of you that keeps evolving. Each time, you will find something new—not because the words changed, but because you are changing and evolving.

## When You Are Ready To Move To The Next Stage

- Purchase **Drop Your Shoulders® Methods** Practice Guide at www.dropyourshoulders.com.au
- Join the **Drop Your Shoulders® Methods Online Program,** where you will have access to book into the teachings in this book with daily integration, guided support, and more by visiting www.dropyourshoulders.com.au
- Attend one of our in-person retreats featuring **Drop Your Shoulders® Methods** to expand and grow, surrounded by others walking the same path. These retreats are not just events; they are 1, 2, or 3-day experiences of learning, growth, and transformation. Explore the Alchemy of Men Retreats specifically designed for men at www.alchemyofmen.com.au
- Alternatively, continue practising the **Drop Your Shoulders® Methods** and trust that you are already interrupting stress patterns. You do not need to know all the answers; this is a practice and a process. Change within you is already happening now.

# Revisit All Drop Your Shoulders® Methods

You are empowered with all the **Drop Your Shoulders® Methods** to grow and evolve.

1. **The Drop Your Shoulders® Method.** Interrupt your subconscious emotional survival patterns and calm your nervous system as naturally and effortlessly as brushing your teeth.

2. **Calm Your Nervous System.** Expanding to include feeling safe and loved in each moment.

3. **Releasing Tension and Pain.** Designed to help you let go, releasing pain and tension and further relaxing your body.

4. **Active Affirmations.** Go deeper to know what you need to feel emotionally safe and loved.

5. **Transform Subconscious Overthinking.** This process rewrites fractured statements that cause disharmony within you.

6. **Connecting With Your Inner Child.** Connect and start a reassuring dialogue with your inner child.

7. **Scribbling (Releasing physical, mental, and emotional pain).** The most profound emotional release to let go of the energy of pain.

8. **Recognising Emotions And Releasing Blocked Energy.** Effective for Anger, Grief, Shame, and Guilt.

9. **Identify Your Realistic And Unrealistic Expectations.** Anger is always the difference between your expectations and your reality.

10. **Woodchopping For Anger Release.** To release suppressed anger from your body and reclaim your personal power.

11. **How To Release Anger In The Car**. Another version for anger release that can be done in the car for convenience.

12. **Releasing Suppressed Emotions From The Past.** Releasing this energy to feel lighter.

13. **Grief And Loss.** Acknowledging and releasing grief.

14. **Loving Your Inner Child.** Giving your inner child the love you never received as a child.

15. **Forgiveness, Dissolving Contracts, And Cutting Cords.** Letting go of energy that has been projected onto you.

16. **Giving Love To Self.** Give yourself your own Love Language.

17. **Giving Love To Others.** Knowing how to give love to others in a way they can receive it.

18. **Secure Attachment.** Developing secure attachment in relationships.

19. **Self-Forgiveness**. You do the best you can at any given time, forgiving yourself for the past.

20. **Activating Your Energetic Circle and Boundaries.** Energetic boundaries are equally as important as your physical body.

21. **Clearing Your Energetic Circle.** Knowing what your energy is and what another person's energy.

22. **Cutting Energetic Cords With Your Parents — Womb Healing**

23. **Cutting Energetic Cords With Your Parents — Inner Child By The Fire**

24. **Cutting Energetic Cords With People From The Past.** Working with conflicts between you and others.

25. **Changing The Way You Speak.** Practice not to start any communication with the word "YOU" and replace it with a question.

26. **Creating New Somatic Reference Points For Love and Safety.** Manifesting your future from the vibrational frequency of love and safety.

27. **Manifesting Your Future.** Using your new somatic reference points to manifest your future.

# Reviews

## Individual Sessions using Drop Your Shoulders® Methods

"*Thank you for helping me heal past wounds that were still affecting my life. I feel like a weight has lifted from my shoulders, and I now understand my triggers and how to move forward.*" M.Y.

"*I cut ties with false beliefs that had been shaping my life. The session was profound and deeply transformational.*" B.P.

"*I left feeling lighter, calmer, and more grounded. I will always remember to drop my shoulders.*" N.M.

"*I worked through unresolved past experiences and felt a deep sense of clarity. What was beneath the surface finally made sense; I feel free from the constant overthinking.*" H.H.

"*I felt safe and supported from the beginning. My confidence has grown, and I now feel clearer, more equipped, and able to move forward without the constant stress.*" A.H.

## Alchemy of Men Retreat using Drop Your Shoulders® Methods

*"I arrived overwhelmed and without direction. I left with clarity, practical tools, and a sense of purpose I didn't have before. This experience was life-changing."* B.V.

*"I learned how to understand and manage my emotions (anger). The tools are simple, practical, and I now use them every day."* R.S.

*"Understanding love languages, boundaries, and not taking on other people's energy were key takeaways for me; these tools have saved my marriage."* D.C.

*"I healed deep childhood wounds I had ignored for years. I now feel free from the past and able to show up for myself and my relationships, as a father and as a MAN."* G.F.

*"A powerful weekend of self-discovery. Real practical tools, real support, and change in a safe, non-judgemental environment. I highly recommend it to any Man at whatever stage you are at; don't wait until a traumatic event compels you, just do it."* J.J.

## Empowering Women Retreat using Drop Your Shoulders® Methods

*"A safe and supportive space where I reconnected with myself and learned practical tools to support my emotional wellbeing. My key takeaway was communication in relationships and creating healthy boundaries."* J.N.

*"This program brings you face to face with your struggles and supports you to move through them and reconnect with yourself. I realised how much I hang onto my emotions and learnt how to clear them."* A.S.

*"I was able to understand the effects of my upbringing and how this contributes to my current behaviour. My biggest takeaway is how to calm my body before I react."* E.R.

# GLOSSARY OF METHODS

**Adrenal Stress** Prolonged state of stress caused by repeated survival response activation.

**Conscious Mind** The analytical, thinking part of the mind responsible for awareness and decision-making.

**Drop Your Shoulders® Method** A somatic technique to interrupt stress and create safety in the body.

**Emotional Imprint** Stored emotional experiences influencing present reactions.

**Emotional Safety** The internal sense of feeling safe to experience and express emotions.

**Embodiment** Fully integrating awareness, emotions, and physical experience in the body.

**Energetic Field** The non-physical layer where emotional and trauma imprints are stored.

**Fight, Flight, Freeze Response** The body's automatic survival reactions to perceived danger.

**Generational Trauma** Inherited emotional and behavioural patterns passed through family lines.

**Inner Peace** A regulated, calm state free from survival-driven reactions.

**Neural Pathways** Brain connections formed through repeated experiences and responses.

**Nervous System** The body's system that regulates stress, safety, and emotional responses.

**Reference Points (Subconscious)** Internal cues identified subconsciously to determine safety or threat.

**Reprogramming (Subconscious)** The process of creating new mental and emotional patterns.

**Shock (Initial Shock)** The first moment of trauma activation when the body cannot process an experience.

**Somatic Practice** A body-based method for regulating emotions and releasing tension.

**Somatic Shift** A physical change in the body that alters emotional state.

**Subconscious Mind** The part of the mind storing beliefs, memories, and automatic responses.

**Survival Patterns** Automatic responses developed to protect against perceived danger.

**Trauma** An emotional and physiological response stored in the body and nervous system.

**Trigger** A stimulus that activates a stored emotional or trauma response.

# DISCLAIMER

This book is intended for educational and informational purposes only. It is not a substitute for medical, psychological, or therapeutic care, diagnosis, or treatment.

The practices and perspectives shared in this book are offered to support self-awareness, reflection, and personal insight. Readers are encouraged to take responsibility for their own physical and emotional wellbeing and to seek appropriate professional support for physical, mental, or emotional health concerns as needed.

The author does not make medical or therapeutic claims and encourages readers to engage with the material in ways that feel safe and supportive for them.

# ACKNOWLEDGEMENT

Thank you to my friends who helped bring this book to light — for believing in my work. I am deeply grateful for your support, your encouragement, and your help in bringing my life's work into the world. Together, we build a better future for the next generation.

I acknowledge that sharing my personal life experiences in this book stems from past events and is intended to provide real-life context for my work. I have a deep love and gratitude for my parents and family members, and I trust they will always know how much I appreciate the good times we have shared, and that I love them dearly.

While the practices shared in this book are my own, they have been shaped by years of study, lived experience, and extensive work with individuals and groups.

I honour the teachers, frameworks, and lineages that have contributed to my understanding of trauma, nervous system regulation, communication, and relational dynamics. This includes the foundational training that supported my Diploma in Holistic Kinesiology and Energy Healing Certification with Cyndi Dale, as well as broader influences from attachment theory, nonviolent communication, and relational psychology.

These bodies of work have informed my perspective; however, the **Drop Your Shoulders® Methods** represent an integrated and original application developed through practice, refinement, and real-world experience.

# ABOUT THE AUTHOR

## Geraldine Zadkiel

Geraldine is a qualified Kinesiologist and the founder of Heart Connection, a self-empowered approach to health, and the creator of the Drop Your Shoulders® Methods, an embodied framework for working with generational and childhood trauma through practical somatic methods that interrupt automatic survival patterns and create lasting change through the nervous system.

With over two decades of experience specialising in anxiety, depression, and childhood trauma, Geraldine developed the **Drop Your Shoulders® Methods** through her work with individuals and in group settings. She recognised that while many traditional approaches could explain trauma, they did not always offer clear, practical guidance for what to do when survival patterns take over in everyday life.

In **Drop Your Shoulders®: How to Break Free from the Trauma Cycle**, Geraldine weaves together professional expertise and lived experience, demonstrating how these somatic tools work beyond theory — in relationships, parenting, communication, and the real moments when childhood trauma and learned patterns impact daily life.

Her work bridges knowledge and embodiment, translating nervous system principles into accessible practices that create measurable change in everyday experience.

Through live programs, retreats, and community spaces, Geraldine continues to guide individuals out of survival patterns and into embodied safety, connection, and emotional steadiness.

Geraldine is known for communicating truth with both clarity and compassion.

# Copyright



For licensing or permissions, contact:

Email: info@heartconnection.com.au

Made in the USA
Monee, IL
04 November 2026

67386646R00223